Letters from
England, 1895

Letters from England, 1895

Eleanor Marx & Edward Aveling

Edited by

Stephen Williams and Tony Chandler

Translated by Francis King

Lawrence Wishart
London 2020

Lawrence and Wishart Limited
Central Books Building
Freshwater Road
Chadwell Heath
RM8 1RX

Typesetting: e-type
Cover design: River Design
Cover artwork/photo credit: Edward image: Joseph Heller, 1886. Eleanor
image: International Institute of Social History, Amsterdam.
Printing: Imprint Digital

First published 2020
Edition and introduction © Stephen Williams and Tony Chandler 2020
Translation © Francis King

British Library Cataloguing in Publication Data.
A catalogue record for this book is available from the British Library

ISBN 978-1-912064-43-4

Contents

Acknowledgements

As editors we would like to express our thanks to the Barry Amiel and Norman Melburn Trust for the Nina Fishman Translation Award which made this publication possible. The objectives of the Amiel and Melburn Trust are to advance public education, learning and knowledge in all aspects of the philosophy of Marxism, the history of socialism, and the working-class movement. Nina Fishman was a long-term trustee. She was an important political thinker, activist and historian. The award commemorates her legacy by enabling the publication of significant works on topics that would have interested her.

We owe special thanks to Francis King for his expert and meticulous translation of the letters from Russian to English. We are also indebted to Francis for his guidance in correcting and sharpening our review of Eleanor Marx's and Edward Aveling's involvement with the many radical Russian political writers living in London and abroad in 1895.

Thanks are due to John Attfield for his tireless assistance in translating articles and correspondence written in German. Steve Grindlay kindly let us have access to the original lease for Moraston Lodge (later The Den) to which Eleanor Marx and Edward Aveling moved in December 1895.

We acknowledge the International Institute of Social History in Amsterdam for permission to reproduce the image of Eleanor Marx and the British Library for permission to reproduce the illustration on the back cover.

Special thanks are due to the staff of the following institutions where archives were consulted: Bodleian Library, Oxford; International Institute of Social History, Amsterdam; British Library; British Library of Political and Economic Science; Bishopsgate Institute; National Art Library; Hoover Institution, Stanford University.

Stephen Williams and Tony Chandler

Translator's note

The *Letters from England* were written by Eleanor Marx and Edward Aveling in English, but the originals are no longer extant. We do not have any information about how these letters were submitted to *Russkoye bogatstvo*, who, specifically, translated them into Russian, or what editorial changes may have been introduced by the journal for the benefit of its readers or the tsarist censor. The published Russian versions are all we had to work on. These translations are therefore best regarded as *reconstructions* of the authors' texts, rather than *restorations* of the originals. Occasionally we noticed evident typographical slips in the published Russian version – especially with proper names – as well as places where the Russian version made no sense, but it was obvious from the context what the authors were saying. These have been corrected without comment. Where published English sources have been cited, we have endeavoured to locate them and use the original wording, rather than retranslate them.

Francis King

Introduction

Stephen Williams and Tony Chandler

When Eleanor Marx (1855-1898) and Edward Aveling (1849-1898) were writing their series of seven 'letters' for publication in the socialist Russian journal *Russkoye bogatstvo* ('The wealth of Russia') in 1895, the pair were among the best-known socialists in Britain.

Both attracted large audiences to hear them speak, and their work was widely read and influential. Along with her record of intense political activity from 1883 onwards, Eleanor was known as the daughter of Karl Marx, the founder of what was then propounded as 'scientific socialism'. For his part, Edward, a scientist by training with a doctorate from University College, London, had made waves as a prominent secularist before joining the socialists in 1883, among whom he established a track record as a lecturer and organiser, albeit with a reputation as an inveterate borrower of money and a womaniser. The couple lived together in a 'free union' relationship from the summer of 1884 – she adopted the name Eleanor Marx Aveling – because Edward had an existing marriage that had ended in separation but not divorce.[1]

The Marx-Avelings' life together in politics was hectic and productive, and their little-known co-authored letters (really articles) to a Russian political journal, written with lively candour and plenty of opinion on the state of Victorian England, represent a curiosity in the story of socialism in both Russia and England, as at first sight the pair, so closely associated with the 'scientific socialism' of Eleanor's father and his collaborator Frederick Engels, were not obvious candidates for publication in *Russkoye bogatstvo*, the flag-ship journal of the Narodnik party in Russia, which espoused a rather different kind of socialism.

Russkoye bogatstvo, founded in 1876, was transformed when Nikolai Mikhailovsky became its editor in 1892.[2] Mikhailovsky, a sociologist, was a towering figure in the Narodniks ('Friends of the people'), a key socialist movement in Russia founded in the 1860s. Mikhailovsky used the journal as a vehicle for developing *narodnichestvo*; the Narodnik philosophy and political programme, also known as 'populism', which soon became the preeminent Russian political movement in opposition to tsarist absolutism.

An intriguing element in the story of Eleanor Marx and Edward Aveling's 1895 letters to *Russkoye bogatstvo* is the journal's growing opposition to Marxism. Initially sympathetic to Marx in the 1870s, whom he had defended against his detractors, by 1894, Mikhailovsky was hostile to what he saw as the inhuman indifference of the Russian Marxists to the suffering wrought by the famine of 1891-92; the determinism of 'scientific' Marxist philosophy apparently denying individual freedom of choice, and the Marxists' overt support for the growth of capitalism in Russia, to which the Narodniks were opposed.

The Narodniks had maintained ideological hegemony within the Russian socialist movement for decades, until challenged in the 1880s and 1890s by the growing influence of Marxism over the radical intelligentsia. Leading Marxists writers involved included Georgii Plekhanov, known to many as the 'father of Russian Marxism', Vera Zasulich, Pavel Axelrod, and the young Lenin. In response to the Marxist challenge, Mikhailovsky launched a polemical debate against the 'spreading epidemic'[3] of Marxism in the pages of *Russkoye bogatstvo* in 1894. Lenin offered a forensic rebuttal with his 1894 pamphlet 'What the friends of the people are, and how they fight the social democrats'.[4] Plekhanov joined the fray in early 1895, responding to Mikhailovsky's critique of historical materialism with his pamphlet 'In defence of materialism'.

Nikolai Danielson, who had translated and published Marx's *Capital* in Russia in March 1872, joined the debate on the side of Mikhailovsky, contributing a number of articles critical of the Russian Marxists in 1895, just as Eleanor and Edward's 'Letters from England' were also being published in *Russkoye bogatstvo*. The polemical battle raged, with a series of articles contributed by both sides until 1898, and the publication of Plekhanov's 'The role of the individual in history',[5] to which there was no further riposte from Mikhailovsky or any other Narodnik. In the struggle for theoretical leadership of the Russian revolutionary movement, Plekhanov had profoundly strengthened the position of Marxism.

Eleanor and Edward in 1890s socialist London

Eleanor and Edward's political and romantic partnership went back many years before their publication together in this site of socialist theoretical struggle in a distant country. They were deeply involved in the fissiparous world of London socialist politics, having in 1883 joined the Westminster branch of the Democratic Federation, which had been set up under the leadership of Henry Mayers Hyndman in 1881. At first a radical organisation proposing land nationalisation, abolition of the House of Lords, adult suffrage and Irish independence, the Federation was pushed towards a specifically socialist programme by new recruits, a position characterised by commitment to common ownership of the means of production. These recruits moved the adoption of nationalisation of the means of production at the Federation's conference in August 1884, when it also changed its name to the Social Democratic Federation (SDF). Election to the executive of the Federation at this conference brought Eleanor and Edward to the heart of decision-making in one Britain's first major socialist organisations, where they observed close up Hyndman's autocratic style that Engels, with whom they were closely associated, had warned them of. Hyndman's domineering personality, his fondness for intrigues, and his latent jingoism all figured in the decision taken at the end of December 1884 by ten members of the executive, including Eleanor, Edward and William Morris, to leave the Federation with a cohort of supporters and form the Socialist League. Within weeks the League had its own newspaper, *Commonweal,* jointly edited by Morris and Edward.

For a time the League proved to be a more congenial home for Eleanor and Edward, with each undertaking their share of lecturing, journalism and organising. However, by 1887 the League's insistence that it would not contest parliamentary or municipal elections began to jar with the evolving view supported by the couple – and bearing the imprimatur of Engels – that in Britain it was possible for socialists to advance the political power of the working class through representation on elected assemblies. This was anathema to Morris and the influential anarchist tendencies in the League, who characterised those demanding political action as 'parliamentarians'. The issue came to a head at the 1888 annual conference, where the group supported by Eleanor and Edward were defeated on key votes on electoral strategy, prompting them to decide it was time to leave.

Since the death of her father, Eleanor had lived in or near the Bloomsbury district of London, first in Great Coram Street (1883-4), then Fitzroy Street – the first home she shared with Edward – (1884), Great Russell Street (1884-7), and then Chancery Lane (1887-1892), all addresses close to family friends and, significantly, the Reading Room of the British Museum, where she had been a regular since 1877. Bloomsbury also provided the locus for the next phase in the couple's political affiliation. The Bloomsbury branch of the Socialist League had more than a hundred members, the majority of whom supported the decision taken in the summer of 1888 to secede and establish an independent Bloomsbury Socialist Society (BSS). As well as providing continuity of political activity in the district, which was now extended to contesting municipal elections, this new Society gave members credentials to other bodies where they could act as delegates and not be accused of 'freelancing', a common charge levelled by activists keen to portray their opponents as representing nobody but themselves. In this way members of the Bloomsbury Society demonstrated their solidarity with the Bryant and May ('matchgirl') strikers in 1888, London dock workers and Silvertown rubber workers in 1889, industrial disputes that helped propel forward 'new unionism', an emerging form of trade unionism that sought to represent all workers – not just the skilled – and which had a socialist outlook.

The Silvertown dispute brought Eleanor into closer contact with the Gas Workers' and General Labourers' Union led by Will Thorne, whom she had befriended and assisted with the administration of the new union since 1888.[6] Because of Eleanor's direct role in the strike she was elected to the union executive, a position she retained until 1895, topping the polls in the annual elections.[7] Contemporaries remembered Eleanor being cheered when speaking from the platform by gas workers with the cry of 'Good old stoker!'[8] Though Edward's commitment to the Gas Workers' Union did not match the depth of Eleanor's solidarity, he too was elected to its executive, somewhat incongruously – given his own notorious problems with money – as auditor.

The agency of the Bloomsbury Socialist Society was also decisive in establishing the first Labour Day demonstration in London, in May 1890, which was brought about in part by Eleanor, Edward and the Society's secretary, William Bartlett, working in association with Thorne and the Gas Workers' Union.[9] The idea for a demonstration had originated in a decision of the Paris International Socialist Congress of 1889 to hold a series of unified transcontinental events on 1 May to demand an eight-hour working day enforced by legislation. The feat of organisation that compelled the previously reluctant London Trades Council to get behind the Labour Day and mobilised hundreds of thousands of trade unionists, members of radical clubs, and political associations to take part on 4 May 1890 was in large part down to the skilful work of the BSS, which demonstrated an influence disproportionate to its tiny size.[10]

The demonstration's signal success lay in linking an industrial demand for a reduction in working hours with a political campaign for legislation to support its implementation. The scale of this achievement was not lost on Eleanor and Edward or on their mentor Engels, who was present on the platform on the day and later recounted his feelings of optimism:

The demonstration here on May fourth was nothing short of *overwhelming*, and even the entire bourgeois press actually had to admit [it]. I was on platform four (a heavy goods wagon) and could only see part – a fifth or an eighth – of the crowd, but it was one vast sea of faces. Between 250,000 and 300,000 people, about three quarters of them demonstrating workers ... the *real socialist movement mass movement began on the fourth of May* ...

When for the first time in forty years, the voice of the English proletariat rang out. I carried my head a couple of inches higher as I climbed down from the old goods wagon.[11]

Given this success it came as no surprise when the ad hoc committee responsible for it was in a matter of weeks transformed into what was conceived as a permanent body: the Legal Eight Hours and International Labour League, with Edward as chairman and strategist. Successive demonstrations continued the triumph of 1890, and for a short time it seemed as if the newly formed League might be able to bring together the forces capable of forming a united labour party, as envisaged by Engels and articulated by Edward at early meetings of the executive.[12] That this did not happen had much to do with the tailing off of militant 'new unionist' activity in the early nineties; the concurrent emergence of the Independent Labour Party (ILP) with its distinct brand of ethical socialism making it, in the minds of 'scientific socialists' such as Eleanor and Edward, suspect and lacking in rigour; the relentless sectarian squabbling of London socialists making any notion of common cause very difficult to achieve; and not unreasonable misgivings about Edward as a leader.

Edward's decision in March 1895 to stand down as chairman of the Legal Eight Hours Demonstration Committee, by this time a joint organisation with the London Trades Council, because of the refusal of the Trades Council to accept 1 May, and not the first Sunday in May, as the designated day for the labour demonstration – a preference based on the greater challenge presented to employers by workers taking a day from the working week to demonstrate – marked the end of any ambition he had for this body, and henceforth he turned back to the SDF, which he and Eleanor had left a decade earlier.

The pair's readmission to the SDF in March 1896 prompted Keir Hardie's *Labour Leader* to comment acidly: 'Dr Aveling has joined the SDF. The ILP having expelled him, and the Eight Hours League being defunct, he had to get a footing somewhere for the coming International.'[13] Edward had indeed spent time in the ILP following its establishment at Bradford in January 1893, where he attended as delegate of the Bloomsbury Socialist Society and the Legal Eight

Hours League. Eleanor was also there, in a journalistic capacity. Elected at the Bradford conference to the ILP's ruling National Administrative Council as London representative, Edward served only one term before losing the seat at the 1894 conference at Manchester. His defeat likely reflected a growing animosity towards 'continental socialism', and the differences between himself and Hardie, whose status, already high in the party as its only sitting MP, was elevated once he was elected president in 1895.[14] Hardie accused Edward of having marginalised the ILP in preparations for the 1894 labour demonstration, which Edward believed was the principal reason for his expulsion by the ILP's London district later in the year.[15] Hardie had similar suspicions in the following year when he asked if Edward was responsible for excluding the ILP from a list of organisations contributing to the forthcoming International Socialist Congress, something Edward denied.[16]

One critical observer of the socialist scene in the 1890s summed it up with the words, 'Brotherly love! Talk rather of brotherly jealousy and all uncharitableness'.[17] The SDF, first on the scene, resented the arrival of the ILP and belittled it for lack of theoretical rigour; the ILP viewed the SDF as 'the vehicle of a dry, dogmatic Marxism, wholly out of touch with working-class experience';[18] both mistrusted the Fabian Society. SDF leader Hyndman conducted a campaign against Engels – 'the Grand Lama of Regent's Park Road' – for 'vilifying any social democratic organisation not under his direct control';[19] Engels considered Hyndman an autocrat incapable of the strategic thinking necessary to build a mass socialist workers' party.

The 'Engels clique' and opposition to the ILP

These divisions and animosities feature in *Letters from England* particularly where the authors discuss unemployment and socialist electoral work from their perspective as members of the small but significant group – Hyndman described them as a 'clique' – close to Engels. Engels's group were critical of Hardie, both for his presentation of the problem of unemployment to the House of Commons in 1895, and for the ILP's election strategy and performance in the same year. Eleanor and Edward's correspondence and essays written for continental journals show glimpses of this perspective, but it is in their 'letters' to *Russkoye bogatstvo* that their views are most explicit. Influence within this group around Engels was by no means one way: Edward's perspective in particular may be detected in some of Engels's pronouncements.

One way that the letters reflect a perspective shared with Engels is their vituperation of Keir Hardie and the ILP. Soon after Hardie was elected for the West Ham South constituency in the summer of 1892 he made it clear he would use his position in Parliament to raise the question of unemployment and the plight of the four million of the working population and their families living without means of subsistence. Hardie's early efforts to get the issue discussed ended in failure, which Engels put down to his 'blunders' in the use of parliamentary procedure, remarking that if this continued, he would 'soon be laid low'.[20] By the spring of 1894, Engels was claiming that Tory money was subsidising *Labour Leader* and that Hardie's appearances in Parliament were reserved for 'demagogic occasions to make himself important by speeches about the unemployed without achieving anything'.[21] Whilst it is easy to detect Edward's influence in shaping Engels's assessment of Hardie, particularly the intrigue about Tory funds supporting *Labour Leader*, Engels also took seriously the views of John Burns, the member for Battersea, who also did not see eye to eye with Hardie.[22] Engels had a high opinion of Burns, and respected his diligent work in the House of Commons and the London County Council.

Hardie's determined efforts to get the unemployed question properly discussed were eventually successful in February 1895 when the government, facing defeat on an amendment he submitted, agreed to establish a Select Committee on 'Distress through want of work'. While this was viewed initially as progress, with Hardie getting the credit, the committee soon revealed it would not be proposing practical measures to alleviate the suffering of those in need. Burns, a member of the committee along with Hardie, was dismissive of proposals submitted by Hardie for Treasury-funded schemes to create work and relieve distress. Burns's line of questioning to Hardie was noticeably hostile, leading some to conclude that the member for Battersea resented the publicity Hardie and the ILP were receiving on the issue.[23] He continued to deprecate Hardie's efforts, it being reported months later that he had criticised Hardie's attendance record on the committee, suggesting that he preferred instead to travel 'all over England delivering lectures on [Robert] Burns and Ruskin at five guineas a time'.[24]

A similar critique of Hardie was made in the *Letter* for April and by Edward alone in an article for the French socialist journal (edited by Eleanor's brother-in-law Paul Lafargue), *Le devenir social*. Scathing about what he believed to be Hardie's inability to master the statistics on unemployment and his admission before the committee that he had never served on any body dealing with distress, Edward launched a broadside against the member for West Ham for 'proclaiming throughout the country that he had a ready solution and that if only the government listened to him and followed his advice, the question would not be difficult to resolve'. He went on:

> What appears to me personally almost as dangerous is that he went on to say the same thing to the unemployed poor. Instead of telling them, as any frank and honest socialist must do, that there is absolutely no cure for unemployment in the present conditions of society, he has deceived them with false hope, saying we could do something for them without recourse to the only possible remedy, the nationalisation of the means of production and distribution.[25]

Such criticism was not only wide of the mark but seriously disingenuous, because Edward would have been aware of Hardie's repeated statements that any relief of distress, while essential, could only be palliative. Hardie told the House of Commons on 7 February 1895 that 'nothing short of the entire reorganisation of our industrial system on a socialistic basis would meet the difficulty permanently; but the people out of work could not wait for this'.[26] Some months later, when word of Edward's *Le devenir social* article reached Hardie, he commented that 'It is statements and conduct such as ... [this] ... which [have] cost Dr Aveling so many friends'.[27]

In their letters to *Russkoye bogatstvo*, Eleanor and Edward were scathing about the ILP's electoral strategy; damning the policy of abstention where no ILPer was standing as 'stupid and damaging', and 'tantamount to suicide'. The application of this policy in the 1895 general election 'suited completely the interests of the Tories and was to a certain extent one reason why we now have such an enormous Tory majority in the House of Commons'. The authors were at pains to argue that the aggregate vote of the ILP was enhanced by 'plumper' votes – that is, by votes in constituencies that returned two members instead of one – and should be 'almost halved' to arrive at the correct level of support. In fact, ILP candidates only stood in seven two-member constituencies where a 'plumper' vote could be cast. Special mention was reserved for Hardie in his defeat at West Ham, which the authors attributed to the desertion of Irish voters who 'can hardly be blamed for that, since Hardie had broken, most blatantly, all the promises made in 1892, on the strength of which he was elected'. Hardie had come under pressure from Catholic priests in West Ham during the 1895 campaign over the ILP's decision to stand against Home Ruler John Morley in Newcastle. In response he made clear that it was Morley's longstanding opposition to the legal eight-hour working day that his party sought to expose. Hardie was able to demonstrate support for Home Rule dating back to 1879, which he had stated would most likely be achieved by English and Irish workers uniting to fight the interests of those who owned capital and land. But he was not ashamed to declare at a public meeting 'Do you say it is Home Rule first? I can understand an Irishman in Connemara saying that, but here in West Ham it is labour first.'[28]

Eleanor partly shared Edward and Engels's antipathy to Hardie, telling her sister Laura in February 1893 that he had a '*very strong hankering after the Conservative fleshpots* – which oddly enough he tries to mix up with the support of the non-conformist conscience'.[29]

Just weeks earlier Engels had reported to German social democratic leader August Bebel that:

Aveling's verbal accounts have reinforced the previous suspicion previously entertained by me, namely that Keir Hardie nurtures the secret wish to lead the new party in the same dictatorial fashion as Parnell led the Irish and that his sympathies incline more towards the Conservatives than to the Liberal opposition party. He said openly that, come the next elections, there should be a repetition of Parnell's experiment whereby he forced Gladstone to toe the line and that where no Labour candidate can be put up, people should vote Conservative by way of giving the Liberals a taste of their power.[30]

Concurring with the verdict of the group closely connected to Engels was the considerable intellect of the German social democrat Eduard Bernstein, who had made himself familiar with British politics since arriving in the late 1880s. Domiciled in Kentish Town in north London less than two miles from Engels's Regent's Park Road home, Bernstein was a frequent and esteemed visitor. With a generally low opinion of British socialists, Bernstein commented on a meeting he had with the 'bigwigs' of the socialist parties in 1895: 'The vanity of the leaders is limitless, and of the others some are sectarians and place hunters'.[31] Bernstein increasingly saw merit in the work of the Fabian Society and its leaders, especially Sidney Webb, who 'didn't get hung up on phrases but rather go to the bottom of the matter. Thus they approach much closer to the Marxist praxis.'[32] And it was no coincidence that the Fabians trumpeted their efforts shaping Progressive policy on the London County Council on wages, slum clearance, and public health, work that Engels saw real value in, and which he urged the ILP and SDF to support, and which is cited in Eleanor and Edward's letters as an example of worthwhile social improvements.[33] In a letter to Laura in March 1895 soon after the London County Council elections, Engels rounded on what he believed to be the mistaken policy of both the SDF and the ILP:

> Their latest exploit was at the County Council election where both of these organisations put up candidates, and only against 'Progressives'; the result was 1,300 votes in all out of 486,000 and the election of four Moderates (Conservatives) for seats held formerly by Progressives and the cry in both *Justice* and *Labour Leader* that *they* had beaten the Progressives. ... But – to support the Progressives would have been to acknowledge that John Burns had behaved well in the County Council, and to endorse

the policy of Sidney Webb and his Fabians who, muffs though they be as *socialists*, are really doing very good municipally, and fighting energetically and cleverly for an autonomous London. And so the 'socialists' prefer to support the party which refuses to allow London its self-government and fights hard to keep the County Council powerless. Now the County Council is the next and best and easiest to-be-conquered piece of government machinery – the working class could have it tomorrow if they were united. And what would Parliament be with a socialist autonomous Council for London![34]

Discussions with Engels helped inform Bernstein's view, expressed in *Vorwarts*, the newspaper of the German social democrats, that the ILP's decision to contest a significant number of seats in the general election and advise its members to abstain where the party was not in the field was wrong. He made his initial comments as the polling was still concluding, but there was already certainty about a Conservative victory, a victory that Bernstein argued had been assisted by the ILP. He was 'unable to understand the rejoicing of the ILP at the defeat of the Liberals and could not share in its gratification'.[35] These arguments were snapped up by the Berlin correspondent of the Liberal-supporting *Daily Chronicle,* and repeated as confirmation of its own editorial position that the ILP had damaged Liberals in some constituencies.[36] Two days later, Bernstein reiterated his view that the ILP had been partly responsible for the size of the Conservative majority and the loss of a number of Lib-Lab MPs.[37] In private communication with Hardie's *Labour Leader,* Bernstein made assertions about sources of ILP election funding, the suggestion being that Tory money had been accepted, an innuendo that also features in Eleanor and Edward's letter for August. Hardie's challenge that Bernstein produce evidence ended the matter when he was unable or unwilling to substantiate the allegation.[38]

Through the correspondence of Engels, Eleanor and Edward on the subject of Hardie and the machinations following Edward's expulsion from the ILP in 1894, it is possible to identify the genesis of what came to form the bitter attitude of the authors when they wrote their *Letters from England.* Unspoken, but almost certainly present in the mix, was Edward's personal ambition to lead the movement which, although there was no official leader as such, was understood by most to be Hardie's.

In contrast to Engels and some others in his group, Eleanor and Edward, at the time seeking readmission to the SDF, were barely critical of the SDF's performance at the 1895 general election. Unlike the ILP, they argued, the SDF had 'both a programme and policy. Its programme is well defined and clear, and corresponds to the programmes of similar parties on the continent', while its performance in the general election's four contests 'showed fairly significant progress since the last election' (August letter). There was not a word on the voting behaviour of SDF members where no socialist was standing, despite the fact that it was likely that many followed the ILP's abstention policy, nor mention of the fact that in two of the Federation's contests, its candidates' votes – including that of one senior trade union official – appeared to be decisive in the Liberals' defeat.[39]

For Engels the result of the general election – in which the Conservative and Unionist parties secured a large majority – was not a surprise. He reported to Laura that the Liberals had been soundly beaten and were in 'full dissolution', while 'The brag of the ILP and SDF [came] face to face with the reality of some 82,000 votes for Labour Candidates ... and the loss of K. Hardie's seat. Still that was more than they had a right to expect.'[40]

This letter, written on 23 July 1895, from Eastbourne, his favourite resort, was the last Engels would write, as he was in the final stages of cancer of the oesophagus and larynx. His friend Samuel Moore, who knew Engels didn't have long to live, travelled to Eleanor and Edward's home in Green Street Green to tell Eleanor 'as gently as he could of Engels's revelation' that the long-held suspicion of the Marx daughters that Engels was the father of the child, known as Freddy, born in 1851 to Helen Demuth, the family housekeeper, was unfounded, and that instead Marx was the father. Eleanor, 'shattered but disbelieving', and 'determined to hear it from Engels's own lips', visited the Regent's Park Road home but the old man was 'beyond the power of speech'.[41] In one account of this visit it is said that when asked by Eleanor to give the name of Freddy's father, Engels wrote on a slate 'Mohr', the name by which Marx was known in the family.[42]

Following Engels's death on 5 August 1895, Eleanor spent several months resolving complex matters of the will: the sale of securities and wine; transferring her father's manuscripts and correspondence from Regent's Park Road to a safe depository in Chancery Lane, where a sorting process was started; settling terms with publishers over the copyrights of Marx's published works; ensuring that Dr Ludwig and Louise Freyberger, a couple who had lived with Engels since 1894, took no more of his estate than they were entitled to under the terms of the will; and making sure that the amount willed to the children of Jenny Longuet, Eleanor's sister who had died in 1883, was invested well. These duties weighed heavily on Eleanor's shoulders, especially those relating to her father's work that she felt must be brought to publication.

Edward was quick into print in September with a two-part article on 'Frederick Engels at home', offering anecdotes about those who attended the Sunday gatherings Engels held at his home in Regent's Park Road. Always anxious to place himself in the company of 'great' men, Edward mentioned Engels in the list of 'the most impressive personalities I have ever met', the others being Marx, Charles Darwin and 'in quite another direction of life, [the actor] Henry Irving'.[43]

Internationalism and the Russian connection

Eleanor and Edward shared with Karl Marx and Engels the firm conviction that internationalism was central to the socialist cause. This conviction was apparent in their writings and activities in 1895. In early September Edward wrote for *Justice* and *Le devenir social* from the Trades Union Congress in Cardiff, noting approvingly that the majority in favour of the previous year's motion to restrict 'pauper immigration' was much diminished at the 1895 Congress. He also welcomed the emergence of a truly internationalist perspective exemplified by Congress support for German workers and socialists, who were facing repressive measures imposed by the Kaiser. Edward believed, as did Eleanor, that this internationalism could be instrumental in making the Socialist Workers' and Trade Union Congress to be held in London in the summer of 1896 a success, and provide a springboard for the next stage of socialist advance.[44]

This belief in the centrality of internationalism also underpinned the close interest they all took in the politics and economic development of Russia. Marx had been deeply interested in the economic development of Russia since the 1870s, corresponding about it at length with Nikolai Danielson, the translator of the first volume of *Capital* in Russia, until his death in 1883. Engels then maintained this correspondence with Danielson until his own death in 1895. Engels and Eleanor shared a tightly knit friendship group of radical Russian exiles living in London and elsewhere in Europe.

Since the early 1880s Eleanor had been interested in and had written about revolutionary movements in Russia.[45] She knew Plekhanov well and translated his *Anarchism and Socialism* in 1895, the same year as the *Letters*. However, the suggestion of one of her biographers that Plekhanov was partly responsible for the letters' publication in *Russkoye bogatstvo* cannot be substantiated and is unlikely, given Plekhanov's hostility to the journal's editorial stance.[46]

In the second volume of her seminal biography of Eleanor, Yvonne Kapp speculates that it was the Russian Marxist activist Vera Zasulich who introduced her and Edward to *Russkoye bogatstvo*.[47] Expelled from Switzerland in 1889 along with fellow Marxists Plekhanov and Pavel Axelrod, Zasulich moved to France and stayed there for five years until 1894, when she was again expelled, along with other foreign political exiles, as part of a government response to a wave of anarchist terrorist acts across France. That expulsion brought her to London, where she stayed until 1897. In London, she became a close confidante of Eleanor's and they were both friends with Ukrainian-born radical Stepniak (Sergei Kravchinsky) and his wife Fanny. Edward described the extraordinary life of Zasulich in a long and detailed piece in the *Clarion* newspaper in February 1895, as a means of introducing her to the British labour movement. *Russkoye bogatstvo* editor and Narodnik opponent of Marxism Mikhailovsky had reportedly been greatly impressed by Zasulich's attempted assassination of the brutal Colonel Fyodor Trepov, governor of St Petersburg, whom she shot with a revolver and nearly killed in January 1878. Extraordinarily, she was acquitted at the end of her trial but immediately went into hiding and escaped to Geneva to avoid being arrested again and undergoing a second trial, which was clearly on the cards. She was at the time a Narodnik and member of the revolutionary organisation Zemlya i Volya ('Land and freedom'), and knew the leading Narodniks, including Mikhailovsky.

Once in Geneva, however, she had rapidly become a Marxist, and in 1883 co-founded the first avowedly Russian Marxist organisation, the Emancipation of Labour group, with Plekhanov and Axelrod. They had become convinced that social revolution could only be led by class-conscious industrial workers, who were increasing in numbers in Russia as the growth of industrialisation and capitalism gathered pace. By contrast, the Narodniks argued that the revolution would be made by the peasantry. Narodnaya Volya, the Narodnik revolutionary party established in 1879, also had a current which held that terrorist acts targeting the tsar and officials of tsarist absolutism were an effective way of bringing about political reform. Ironically, the terrorist wing of the Narodniks had been inspired by Zasulich's assassination attempt, which left her distraught, since the new Marxist group was completely opposed to such terrorist tactics. Instead, these first Russian Marxists focused on translating the works of Marx and Engels into Russian throughout the 1880s and having them smuggled into Russia, with the clear intention of drawing the radical intelligentsia to Marxism. This proved to be a successful strategy, with the influence of Marxism slowly growing throughout the 1880s, eventually provoking the assault from Mikhailovsky and Danielson in the 1890s, as they attempted to tackle the threat that Marxist ideology now posed to their erstwhile Narodnik hegemony.

By 1894, with a working class growing apace in industrialising Russia, the Marxist exiles in Geneva set up a political organisation of emigrant Russian socialists, the Union of Russian Social Democrats Abroad. It had its own printing press for issuing revolutionary literature, and published the newspapers *Rabotnik* ('The worker') and *Listok rabotnika* ('The workers' paper'). It was this group, involving Lenin, Plekhanov, Axelrod and Zasulich, that went on to establish the powerful political journal *Iskra* ('Spark'), to carry forward socialist agitation in Russia.

Politically, therefore, it seems unlikely that Zasulich, or indeed her comrade Plekhanov, would have encouraged and enabled her close friend Eleanor to write for the leading Narodnik organ, when the Marxists were engaged in a historic struggle for ideological leadership of the revolution. Furthermore, the timing of Zasulich's arrival in London, probably February 1895,[48] makes it unlikely that she could have acted as the intermediary, since the first letter was published in the January 1895 issue and would have been written in December 1894.

Another possible intermediary between Eleanor and Edward and *Russkoye bogatstvo* was Danielson, the translator of *Capital*. Despite his admiration for *Capital* and his closeness to Marx and Engels, Danielson had remained a Narodnik in his outlook. His voluminous correspondence with Marx, running to some sixty letters, provides fascinating insights into Marx's developing analysis of the political and economic prospects for capitalism vis-à-vis socialism in Russia. Marx's opinion of how Russia might develop was of growing interest to the radical Russian intelligentsia from the 1880s onwards. The crucial question for the socialist Narodniks was posed in 1881 by Zasulich in a famous letter to Marx. She asked Marx to clarify his views about whether the devastating consequences of capitalism for the English working class as described in *Capital* Volume 1 could be avoided via a short-circuit – specifically Russian – path to socialism. Or did he anticipate that Russia would need to traverse all the stages of capitalist development before being able to progress to socialism?

A central tenet of the Narodnik stance on a Russian path to socialism was that the communal peasant system, known as *mir*, or *obschtschina*, might somehow avoid being destroyed under capitalist social relations and instead form the basis of a collective socialist organisation of agrarian production.[49] Under the *obschtschina* system, the peasant did not inherit his land via the family, but rather from the commune (*mir*), which distributed, and periodically redistributed, land between community members. Danielson had further argued, citing Marx,[50] that capitalism would be unable to develop in Russia, because foreign markets were already dominated by Western capitalist countries, thus choking off Russian capitalist expansion, and furthermore, there was no significant internal Russian market to fuel the growth of capital from within. The Narodnik hope was that Russia could avoid both the catastrophic impact of capital on workers, with its harsh and alienating division of labour and exploitation, and the destruction of peasant social structures on which, they believed, an agrarian socialism in Russia could be built.

Both Danielson and Mikhailovsky accepted Marx's analysis in *Capital*, but argued that it only applied to the conditions out of which 'Western' capitalism had grown and which did not, and indeed could not, apply in Russia. The Russian Marxists, on the other hand, applauded the growth of capitalism as the necessary precondition for the creation of an industrial proletariat, which in their view was the only class capable of overthrowing the capitalist order and building socialism. The Narodniks were appalled by Marxists seemingly supping with the capitalist devil and, just as bad, welcoming the dissolution of the agrarian commune system central to the socialist Narodnik vision.

Marx sent Zasulich a deeply thought-out response in his letter, which went through three drafts.[51] Somewhat surprisingly, he gave support and credibility to the Narodnik argument. On top of that, both Marx and Engels expressed their support and admiration for the Narodnaya Volya terrorist wing of Russian populism, with Marx scathingly dismissive of the emerging Russian Marxists, including Plekhanov himself, who in 1879 had set up the Chernyi Peredel [usually translated as 'Black Repartition'] anti-terrorist group after splitting from Narodnaya Volya.[52] This outlook perhaps helps to explain how both Danielson and Mikhailovsky were able to maintain cordial and productive relations with Marx and Engels in London, whilst at the same time attacking the Marxists at home.[53]

After Marx's death in 1883, Engels explored this question of a specifically Russian path to socialism in correspondence with Danielson for another twelve years. This correspondence went on in parallel with Danielson's attacks on Marxism, and Plekhanov in particular, in the pages of *Russkoye bogatstvo*. Despite Engels finally losing patience with Danielson, as he wrote in a letter to Plekhanov in February 1895,[54] he never did publicly criticise Danielson's clearly Narodnik position, as Plekhanov was urging him to do.

In 1896, there was a very cordial exchange of letters between Eleanor and Danielson about the translation of Volume 3 of *Capital* into Russian, with no mention of the raging debate underway. Eleanor opens her reply to Danielson with: 'My dear Sir, I cannot tell you with what pleasure I received your letter: I remember how glad my dear father always was to hear from you.' And ends: 'With sincere greetings and all good wishes to yourself.'[55]

It seems highly unlikely that with so many close Russian friends involved in the struggle with the Narodniks, and with Engels's 1895 criticism of Danielson, Eleanor was unaware of the dispute. Could it be that despite this, she chose to extend the same warmth and loyalty to Danielson and the Narodniks that her father and Engels had maintained for years, and which was so steadfastly reciprocated by Danielson himself? Perhaps both she and Danielson were able to put the sectarian polemics characterising the Russian revolutionaries to one side, both for the sake of past loyalties, and in the name of open non-sectarian discussion and thought across political boundaries. It was, after all, Marx himself who famously said he was not a 'Marxist'. From this perspective, Eleanor and Edward would have seen nothing wrong with working with Narodniks such as Danielson, and writing for *Russkoye bogatstvo*, in spite of the argument going on in its pages.

On this reading, Danielson emerges as the more likely go-between between *Russkoye bogatstvo* and Eleanor and Edward. Yet there is no mention of the journal in the correspondence between him and Eleanor, which is odd, given that it was so fresh. With no other correspondence available from the 1890s, Danielson's probability as the link between the journal and Eleanor recedes.

Another longstanding friend of Eleanor's was Sergei Kravchinsky, better known by his pseudonym Stepniak, who tragically died in December 1895 when he walked into the path of a train at a level crossing in west London. Stepniak had escaped from Russia following his assassination of General Nikolai Mezentsov, head of the Russian secret police, with a dagger in the streets of St Petersburg in 1878. He was at that time a believer in the doctrine that terrorist acts could bring about political reform. Remaining in Russia in hiding for a while, he eventually had to flee, initially to Switzerland, before moving with his wife Fanny to live in London from 1880 to his untimely death. During his time in London, Stepniak became an energetic agitator within the incipient socialist movement, very quickly earning the high esteem and friendship of its leading actors, with George Bernard Shaw, William Morris, Keir Hardie and Eleanor herself being some of the socialist and anarchist leaders to speak at his funeral. He was also exceptionally good at networking with Liberals. He had a talent for bringing people of different political persuasions together in the common cause of opposing the Russian autocracy. He published his book *Underground Russia* in London, which was hugely popular, with three print runs in 1883, its year of publication, and about which Eleanor wrote an appreciative review.

Stepniak was an effective campaigner, raising awareness of the realities of tsarist tyranny and shifting English public opinion towards opposing the tsarist government. He cofounded the Society of Friends of Russian Freedom in 1890, and published the journal *Free Russia*, which was pivotal in bringing the atrocities of the tsarist police and the cruelties of the Russian penal and exile system to the attention of the English public. Stepniak rapidly established himself as the central figure of the Russian radical émigré community in London and Europe, gathering information on developments in Russia, and attracting letters and articles from Russian revolutionaries in exile elsewhere in Europe, including from Plekhanov in Geneva, which he published in *Free Russia* and drew on for influential articles published in *The Times*. He spoke alongside George Bernard Shaw, William Morris, John Burns and Prince Kropotkin, the leading Russian anarchist, at a major demonstration against the violence of the tsarist regime held in Hyde Park on 9 March 1890, with an attendance of 5,000 despite driving snow and freezing temperatures.[56] Both Edward and Eleanor addressed the gathering.

In June 1891 Stepniak, together with other émigrés, established the Russian Free Press Fund as the Russian-language vehicle for their publications. The purpose of the Fund was to bring awareness of what was going on in Russia to the attention of Russians themselves, who because of censorship were often unaware of developments inside their own country. They did this via the publication of a bulletin, *Letuchie listki* ('Flying leaflets'), and by smuggling copies of banned books into Russia.[57] Just before Stepniak's death, he was laying plans for a new journal, *Zemskii sobor*,[58] which translates roughly as 'Constituent assembly'. This project was welcomed by I.V. Shklovskii, who wrote under the pseudonym Dioneo, and was the London correspondent of *Russkoye bogatstvo* in 1896. While Shklovskii did not arrive in London until 1896, and so could not himself have been the mediator between the journal and Eleanor and Edward, his existence in this role makes it possible that Stepniak could have introduced the pair to a previous London correspondent. Stepniak, or someone from his circle, therefore, seems the most likely candidate for making the connection. He was avowedly non-partisan and broad in his approach, and his Society of Friends of Russian Freedom brought together Marxists, other socialists, and liberals.

Edward Aveling: A scoundrel and worse

This world of revolutionary émigrés formed the populous and lively background to Eleanor and Edward's publication in a Russian journal with a complex relationship to their own international socialist politics. The letters themselves, which very much reflected the disputes churning within British socialism if not those of the Russian radicals, were the product of an intellectual and emotional partnership between Eleanor and Edward that became increasingly troubled and troubling. A key element in this was Edward's unusually rebarbative personality.

Although it is possible that Eleanor and Edward had their first encounter during the 1870s, it wasn't until 1882, when they met on regular basis in the Reading Room of the British Museum, that they established a close relationship. Even then, she probably kept it quiet until after her father's death in March 1883, because of Marx's hostility to the secularists with whom Edward had been aligned since 1879.[59]

The Avelings' partnership, which lasted until Eleanor's death by suicide in 1898, was for her at first deeply emotional, as she later revealed to her friend Aaron Rosebury, telling him, 'It was Edward who really brought out the feminine in me. I was irresistibly drawn to him'.[60] However, fairly quickly, Eleanor became increasingly aware of transgressions on his part such that, Eleanor's biographer Kapp notes, a mere two years in, their relationship 'found its level', that is: 'She could not rely on him; she did not honour him; but she did love him and nothing could shake her loyalty once given'.[61] The couple's shared passion for literature, the theatre, and above all the cause of international socialism, acted to bind Eleanor to Edward. By the mid nineties, anxiety about Edward's declining health ruled out any question of Eleanor leaving the relationship.

Edward's close associate Eduard Bernstein stated many years later that the real reason for Edward's expulsion from the ILP in 1894 was more serious than a dispute about the labour demonstration, and if made public 'would have sufficed to land him in prison'.[62] Bernstein's suggestion of a serious misdeed by Edward would not have come as a surprise to those close to the centre of socialist activity in London in the 1880s and 1890s. Edward's arrival in the socialist movement in 1884 had occurred as his conduct in the National Secular Society (NSS), with which he had been heavily involved since the late 1870s, was coming under close inspection – in particular his propensity for getting into debt.

The NSS's president, Charles Bradlaugh, had been fully aware of Edward's weakness for debt when he sponsored the promising young man's progress in the Society, including awarding him the vice presidency in 1880. Bradlaugh was seemingly relaxed about a substantial loan of £480 he made to Edward in that year until early 1883,[63] when a London stationer took Edward to the City of London Court to secure payment of debt of thirty-five shillings for goods supplied.[64] Edward, who failed to appear in court, was given a ten-day prison sentence for contempt, which he started in Holloway Prison before being rescued by Bradlaugh.[65] Now at least aware of the potential spread of Edward's debts, Bradlaugh asked him in May 1883 about his loan, which he was told would be repaid when able.[66] The issue did not surface again until July 1884, when Edward informed Bradlaugh that he was living as 'man and wife' with Miss Eleanor Marx.[67] At this point Bradlaugh, perhaps spurred on by his colleague in the NSS, Annie Besant, who was probably involved romantically with Edward, pressed for repayment of the remainder of the loan, which stood at approximately £125, and moved against him in the Society on the grounds of 'repeated and increasing complaints of borrowing of moneys', it becoming clear by this time that other members had made loans, including one of £100 from a member in Manchester.[68] After some negotiation, Edward agreed to resign from the Society and made regular repayments to Bradlaugh, the legal status of this settlement being guaranteed by a judgement in the High Court in October 1884.[69] With a number of delays in making monthly repayments, accompanied by pleas of extenuating circumstances, over the next seven years Edward repaid something close to the original loan from Bradlaugh, who died in 1891.

Edward's shift away from the secularists and towards the socialists in the early 1880s was the occasion for bad-spirited exchanges between leading lights of the two groups, demonstrating the personal bitterness and rancour that tended to gather around Edward and his associations.

At the end of 1883, Annie Besant had launched a public attack on Eleanor to the effect that she was working to undermine the secularists, an accusation Eleanor rebuffed but took as evidence of Besant's resentment that Edward had joined the socialists and established a relationship with her.[70] As Eleanor told John Mahon, a young engineer working for the socialist movement, in the spring of 1884:

> In calumniating me – & Mrs Besant is doing this systematically – Mrs Besant is only trying to imitate Mr Bradlaugh, who has tried for years to calumniate my father. The reason for this 'Lady's' animosity is not far to seek. The one clear thinker and scientific student whose popularity in the Secularist Party almost equals Mr Bradlaugh's – Dr Edward Aveling – has joined the ranks of the socialists, and Mrs Besant does me the honour to make me responsible for this. I am very proud of Dr Aveling's friendship for myself, but I hope I need not tell you that this conversion to socialism is due to the study of my father's book and not me.[71]

The mutual antipathy between Eleanor and Annie Besant festered over the decade and reached its apotheosis with Besant's bizarre conversion to theosophy in 1889, which Eleanor and Edward were able to characterise in the April number of their letters as the latest instalment in a career of jumping from one cause to another. Edward had a major part in drafting the assessment of Besant, not least the suggestion that her tendency to throw in her lot with the latest fad was connected to the influence of significant men with whom she was familiar at the time. He was characteristically unabashed in identifying himself in the pantheon, reminding readers that in the recent past he had been regarded as the third part of a triumvirate, with Bradlaugh and Besant, leading the NSS. His enforced resignation from the Society on charges of misconduct and unpaid debt were brought forward by Bradlaugh and Besant in September 1884, but this did not prevent him writing to Besant, who was in Scotland, only weeks after setting up home with Eleanor, expressing anxiety at his position and declaring: 'How I miss and ache for you! When you come back may I come sometimes and just get what I called, and now more than ever call, the rest of your presence?'[72]

Bernard Shaw, who had known Edward since the early 1880s, was well aware of his habit of running up debts and there seems little doubt that the character of Louis Dubedat in his play *The Doctor's Dilemma* drew heavily on him. When asked by the actress Ellen Terry in 1898 whether she should lend money to Edward, Shaw gave typically amusing advice:

> Shut up your purse, tight, or else give me all your money to keep from you ... His exploits as a borrower have grown into Homeric legend. He has good points... for instance, he does not deny his faiths, and will nail his atheism and socialism to the masthead incorruptibly enough. But he is incorrigible when women or money or the fulfilment of his engagements (especially prepaid ones) are in question. Better write to him as follows: 'Dear Dr Aveling: You must excuse me; but I know a great many people, among them some of your old friends from the National Secularist Society and the Socialist League, and some of your pupils. Don't ask me for any money. Yours sincerely, Ellen Terry'. If the application takes the form of a post-dated cheque, don't cash it.[73]

Edward tried on the post-dated cheque routine with long-term acquaintance Henry Irving, the leading Shakespearian actor of the day, in a letter of January 1891 that brings to mind not only Shaw's warning to Ellen Terry, but also the modus operandi of the 'swindler' George Brooks so sharply exposed, without any sense of self-awareness, in the December letter.[74] And then, following the success of his production of *Judith Shakespeare* at Stratford in June 1895, Edward offered the play to Irving as a way of settling past debts: 'To tell you the truth, I don't know how much I owe you. But I should be more than content to sell you the play, represented by wiping off the arrears and say another £10.' Heartbreakingly referring now to Eleanor, he added that he needed the £10 'badly tomorrow to settle the landlord and to redeem my wife's typewriter. She has a lot of work to be done tomorrow and to be paid for if we can manage this fairly early in the day'.[75]

Not that Edward confined his requests for loans to the wealthy and relatively well off. He would also borrow money from comrades in the socialist movement; William Morris lent him at least £50, probably more.[76] Most reprehensible was his willingness to approach working-class socialists for money. One example of this came from Aaron Rosebury, a Russian émigré in London who worked in an East End factory and came to know Eleanor and Edward in the early 1890s. Many years later Rosebury remembered an occasion when after a socialist meeting at which Eleanor and Edward both spoke, the group went to the pub:

He [Aveling] ushered us in through the 'Gentlemen's' door and then ordered the cheapest drink, ale, which I had not learned to enjoy. Although he was a good platform speaker his private conversation tended to be banal. When he thought he would not be overheard he asked me gruffly to lend him a sovereign – a goodly sum at the time. Eleanor was visibly distressed; but, before her eyes could warn me, I handed over the gold coin, remarking that it was part of my club's funds. He promised to repay it in a week and added that if he didn't 'Tussy' would. I had not heard that nickname before. Aveling grinned oddly as he pronounced it – somewhat maliciously, I thought; and

Eleanor, flushed and trying to smile, explained that it was the name her parents used for her. There ensued some strained banter between them, with a feeble effort to pass the thing off as humorous. Eleanor had evidently been hurt, but Aveling did not seem disconcerted.[77]

Rosebury's recollection discloses a good deal about the relationship between Eleanor and Edward. Edward's shabby call for money from a worker comrade filled Eleanor with embarrassment and humiliation, feelings she had undoubtedly experienced many times since they started their relationship. Whereas it would seem that Eleanor felt these emotions profoundly, Edward thought nothing of them, having, to use her words about him to her friend Olive Schreiner, 'an absolute incapacity to feel anything – unless he is personally incommoded by it'. In the same letter to Schreiner, which was written less than twelve months after the couple set up together, Eleanor revealed a deep melancholy and loneliness, conditions she was predisposed to suffer from, but which Edward did nothing to assuage. She wrote: 'Edward is dining with Quilter and went off in the highest of spirits because several ladies are to be there ... and I am alone, and while in some senses I am relieved to be alone, it is also very terrible ... the solitude is more than I can bear.'[78]

It is probable that Eleanor suspected Edward's fidelity when he socialised in London. If we accept as true the content of Schreiner's seething letter to Dollie Radford written three months after Eleanor's suicide in March 1898, then we can be certain she did. Schreiner wrote: 'I don't know if you know the life she had with him. She has come to me nearly half mad having found him in her own bedroom with two prostitutes.'[79] Schreiner left London to return to South Africa in 1889, so this incident would have occurred between 1884 and then.

Eduard Bernstein's cryptic remark that the real reason for Edward's expulsion from the ILP if revealed would have led him to prison should be considered in the context of reports of his sexual behaviour, which surfaced soon after Eleanor's death. While it was undoubtedly the case that the febrile atmosphere immediately following her death threw up accusations about Edward's role in the suicide that may not all have been carefully evidenced, two comments by individuals close to Eleanor are surely of significance, especially as they are corroborating.

In a letter to Victor Adler, a leading Austrian social democrat, in the week following Eleanor's death, Bernstein reported that a good deal of Engels's bequest to Eleanor had already been spent, and went on: 'I don't know how much of it was spent on hush money to cloak his infamies with women and children, but it must have been very much'.[80] Mention was also made of Edward's alleged predilection for sex with young girls by Maria Mendelson, a close friend of Eleanor's since her arrival in London in the early 1890s. Mendelson, a prominent Polish socialist and wife of Stanislaw Mendelson, himself a leading figure in the revolutionary movement, wrote to Vera Zasulich recounting how those at Eleanor's cremation spoke of how Edward had 'impregnat[ed]' the sixteen-year-old daughter of a socialist family he was staying with and then raped her nine-year-old sister. When the parents of the girls approached Eleanor, she agreed to give them money to prevent it being taken to the police. Mendelson went on to say that Edward was known to have told people that towards the end, Eleanor 'was so repelled by him ... that he used *chloroform* to have relations with her. It is easy to understand why she took her own life'.[81]

It is possible that Eleanor was indeed fully aware of Edward's actions and was party to covering up the worst of them with payments to those affected. Mendelson told Zasulich that two days before her death, Eleanor had instructed her solicitor, Arthur Crosse, 'don't pay anymore – I am sick of it'.[82] She certainly believed Edward to be 'morally diseased', as she told Freddy Demuth in February 1898, continuing that she had 'learnt this through long suffering – suffering in ways I would not tell even you'.[83]

On the face of it a far less troubling aspect of Eleanor and Edward's lives together was their shared love of the theatre, which prompted both frequent visits to London's playhouses and appearances, sometimes together on stage, in small-scale productions. Interest in the theatre for both predated their association with each other, with Eleanor at one point thinking she might be able to earn a living from the stage. There is little doubt that Edward made use of his position in the theatrical world – objectively on the margin of the margins, but talked up by himself – to facilitate his access to young women. One example was his relationship with aspiring actress Eva Frye. The first reported public connection between Edward and Eva Frye took place when she appeared under the stage name of Lilian Richardson, in a 'dramatic entertainment' he organised at the SDF Hall in the Strand on 15 June 1895. Such social events were common in the socialist movement in these formative years, usually taking the form of a 'variety' of entertainments – song, comedy, recitation, drama – a format Edward was experienced in putting on. For this occasion, Edward brought out the one-act play *In the Train*, first adapted from the French in 1888 by his acquaintance Ernest Radford, and performed in April of that year with Edward and Eleanor playing the lead roles at the Athenaeum Hall, Tottenham Court Road, in aid of the Law and Liberty League.[84] The couple revived their performance three years later at a benefit for the Legal Eight Hours League at the Central Reform Club in November 1891, but when *In the Train* was next performed, at the 'dramatic entertainment' in June 1895, Eleanor's role was taken by Eva Frye/Lilian Richardson.[85] The production had been advertised to include a contribution by Eleanor, but the fact that her name was not mentioned in reviews suggests she did not take the stage.

The production was well reviewed in the theatrical press and *Justice*, where its critic made the apparently knowing comment that 'Miss Lilian Richardson made a charming widow with whom any travelling companion might certainly be pardoned for falling in love. The travelling companion, the Deputy Governor of Portsmouth Prison, was played on this occasion by Dr Aveling.'[86] Unknown to Eleanor, the relationship developed, and on 8 June 1897 Edward, using his stage name Alec Nelson, married Eva Frye at Chelsea Registry Office. He was able to remarry because Isabel, his first wife, had died in 1892. As if nothing had changed, he returned to the family home he shared with Eleanor in Sydenham before setting off ten days later to St Margaret's Bay in Kent, supposedly alone, pleading his illness (he had renal cancer). There seems no doubt that the 'convalescence' in Kent was subterfuge for Edward and Eva's honeymoon.

The theatrical context for this latest betrayal may have been a particularly bitter context for it, as Eleanor took great pleasure in both performing in and writing for the theatre. She had published her highly regarded translation of Flaubert's *Madame Bovary* in 1886, before going on to learn Norwegian so that she could translate two Ibsen plays into English for the first time.[87] Her version of *An Enemy of Society*, subsequently retitled *An Enemy of the People*, was published in 1888, and her translation of *The Lady from the Sea* followed in 1890.

Eleanor: activist and writer

Eleanor had taken up the typewriter as a means of production in the late 1880s to supplement her existing income from editing, translating and 'hack writing', none of which was regular work, and certainly not well paid. Hours spent at the typewriter, first in the Chancery Lane apartment and then in the Gray's Inn Square rooms, reinforced Eleanor's isolation, a condition she mentioned in correspondence with sister Laura, usually rounding off with a heartfelt plea for her sister to visit. Edward's hobnobbing in the West End – 'He is out supping with some theatrical friends ... and it is nearly one and the fire is out ...' – meant many evenings alone with her thoughts, which often turned to happier times – 'I think I live more in the past memories of my dear ones than in present things'.[88]

The profound sense of duty Eleanor felt to honour the socialist movement – through which she believed she would also honour her father – helped drive her on even when exhausted. At its best, the socialist movement engendered a spirit of comradeship much needed by her. Public meetings were often emotional experiences in which enthusiasm for the 'cause' was palpable and lifted by communal singing from a canon of favourite socialist songs.[89] Eleanor never shirked her speaking responsibilities, and during 1895, the tumultuous years of her and Edward's letters to *Russkoye bogatstvo*, she appeared on dozens of platforms: in the East End of London for the mantle makers, gas workers, and Jewish trade unions; in support of George Lansbury's candidacy in the Walworth by-election of May; and for the SDF and ILP in Lancashire and Scotland on week-long tours with Edward. She was delighted by the presence of so many children with their parents at the 1 May labour demonstration of 1895, of which she was one of the organisers, wearing red and white clothing and caps of liberty as they processed from the Embankment to Hyde Park. The Canning Town contingent, many of whom she would have known personally, drove their van, decorated with 'fresh green boughs and spring flowers', through the West End streets and attracted much attention and many cheers with its inscription 'If the old 'uns can't, THE YOUNG 'UNS WILL'.[90] These children were connected to the fledgling branches of the Socialist Sunday School movement pioneered by Eleanor's friend, Mary Gray, first set up in Battersea in the early nineties and by 1895 establishing a presence across London.

In the last months of 1895, Eleanor and Edward's speaking engagements intensified, with gruelling tours of Scotland in October and Lancashire in November. Edward's main subject in these months was the political situation following the general election of the summer, which he predicted would see an offensive against organised labour and a shift within the Liberal Party towards the more radical policies advanced by the 'younger party' of Herbert Asquith and Arthur Acland. This, Edward argued, would be designed to 'ensnare' the working class back into liberalism and so set back the socialist cause. Any progressive measures offered by the radical Liberals must, however, be grabbed by the socialists, he argued, 'and used as a weapon against them to sooner attain the inevitable end of socialism'.[91] At Glasgow in October he returned to a favourite subject, 'Karl Marx and Charles Darwin', giving him the stage to expound on the greatness of both figures, about whom it was announced in the advance publicity that 'the lecturer has the unique experience of having enjoyed the personal acquaintance of both men'.[92] Edward was regarded as one of the best speakers on the socialist circuit – one reporter said his style was characterised by 'hammer-like tones of strong conviction'.[93] Will Thorne, who knew him well, thought him to be 'one of the greatest orators this country has ever heard'.[94]

In contrast – and in the gendered language of the time – Eleanor's public speaking voice was described as having a 'musical quality', but yet powerful enough to make her words audible to the whole audience.[95] According to her sister Jenny, Eleanor had 'perfect elocution', which she had mastered in her theatrical training in the early eighties.[96] Usually speaking without notes, her expressiveness was often remarked upon and admired. Fluent in German and French as well as her native English, she could intersperse her speeches to great effect with references from those languages, as she did on one of her favourite subjects, the Paris Commune. Writing in his autobiography, Henry Hyndman, erstwhile chair of the SDF and an on-and-off political adversary, describes Eleanor speaking at a meeting to commemorate the Paris Commune. Her speech was

> One of the finest speeches I ever heard. The woman seemed inspired by some of the eloquence of the old prophets of her race; as she spoke of the eternal life gained by those who fought and fell in the great course of the uplifting of humanity: an eternal life in the material and intellectual improvement of countless generations of mankind. It was bitter outside, but in the hall the warmth of comradeship exceeded that of any Commune celebration I have attended. We were one on that night. The day after, the antagonism recommenced.[97]

When not on the speaking circuit, Eleanor was house hunting, having received the proceeds of Engels's will. After much searching she found Moraston Lodge, a mid-century house in Jews Walk in leafy Sydenham, then on the borders of London and Kent. The property was advertised to rent, but on the advice of the Marx family solicitor Eleanor purchased a ninety-six-year lease for £525.[98] By the second week of December the couple were in their new home, renamed 'The Den', and Eleanor was able to tell Laura that she was 'Jewishly proud of my house in Jews Walk'. For the first time in a comfortable home with space for her own study, Eleanor joyfully described the layout to Laura and encouraged her to visit, adding, lest her sister think the expense was all one-sided, that Edward was to furnish the property. This was to be paid for with money from a mortgage raised against a property he part-owned in the City of London.[99]

The move to Sydenham coincided with the publication of the concluding letter in *Russkoye bogatstvo* in December 1895. It was in this new home that Eleanor was to die, by her own hand, three years later, in a context of marital misery and distress.

The letters

The series began with the somewhat ambitious claim that it would cover 'events in English life' that would be of interest to Russian readers, and include discussion of the 'political parties, the evolution of social life of the people, new tendencies in literature, science and theatre'.

This desire to range so widely makes the letters appear disjointed in places, and there is the suspicion that as they progressed, the authors became less interested in their preparation. It is possible that receipt of the Engels bequest in the autumn of 1895 relieved pressure on the couple to earn their livings through writing, with a negative effect on the quality of the final letters. Published under the by-line 'Av.', it is our contention that the letters were, as Chushichi Tsuzuki states, a joint enterprise – contrary to the verdicts of Eleanor's other biographers Yvonne Kapp and Rachel Holmes, who attribute them to Eleanor alone.[100]

It is evident to us from reading the letters that they are the work of two authors, with very distinct voices. The contrast can be seen both in subject matter and in tone. Those passages marked by declamation, didacticism and haughtiness bear, to our mind, the unmistakeable stamp of Edward Aveling. The more measured and nuanced assessments are likely to have been crafted by Eleanor. We may surmise that Edward was responsible for the opening paragraph of the first letter, with its metaphorical use of stereoscopic vision to describe the bringing together of two authorial perspectives, one male the other female, on the basis that 'men and women look at things from different points of view'. In spite of this claim, very soon it becomes clear that it was Edward's lens that dominated.

Edward seems to have taken the leading part in the first letter, with a discussion of events at the London School Board taking up more than half of the essay. He had been a member of the Board for a short time in the early 1880s, after which he kept a close secularist eye on the emerging controversy over religious education, which reached a high point in the Board elections of November 1894. The remainder of the essay concerned itself with a variety of recent and forthcoming municipal elections and a review of Thomas Hardy's recent volume of short stories, *Life's Little Ironies*, where Eleanor's voice is recognisable.

Something like this pattern was repeated in two of the remaining letters, where book reviews were included, but political and industrial matters continued to have top billing. The final two letters included nothing on literature, which, in the case of the August number, we can put down to the priority of covering the general election and the period immediately following the opening of the new Parliament. The same cannot be said of the December letter, in which one senses a certain fatigue or loss of interest, as disparate items were assembled without the coherence of the earlier contributions.

It is likely that Edward took the lead in writing on political issues, which included comment on the dying days of Lord Rosebery's Liberal government, its replacement by a temporary Conservative and Liberal Unionist administration led by Lord Salisbury, the subsequent general election, and the installation of Lord Salisbury as prime minister of a Unionist government with a substantial majority over the ravaged Liberal Party.

Interwoven within this narrative the letters offered a well-informed commentary on wages, trade unions, labour legislation and industrial disputes, which almost certainly came from Eleanor's pen, specialising as she had in these matters since the 1880s. Like her father, Eleanor was familiar with government 'blue books' and was adept at extracting official information and statistics that could be turned against the employer class. She was particularly concerned to overcome hostility to destitute foreign workers who had recently arrived in England. She worked with Jewish trade unions in the East End of London to organise and persuade others that 'these men are brethren with the English worker and ought to be welcomed as such. No man or woman is an alien who was willing to work on equal terms with English trade unionists. The demands of the workers were identical all over the world.'[101] Unhappy at the recent decision of the TUC Congress to call on the government to prevent pauper immigration, Eleanor rebuffed the myth, which lay behind much of the prejudice against them, that these workers would not join trade unions, with evidence that of the 18,000 Jewish (mostly Eastern European) workers in London, 3,000 were trade unionists – a larger ratio than English workers.[102]

Eleanor's most significant literary review was included in the letter for July, where she considered the work of three 'New Woman' novelists, Ménie Muriel Dowie, George Egerton and Pearl Mary Craigie. She did not accept the view then being widely discussed, that there was a 'woman question' distinct from the questions of all humanity. This was a corollary of her general view, held at least since the mid 1880s, that the problem of 'sex rule' – her preferred nomenclature for relations between men and women – was entirely subordinated to the abolition of class rule. This view was offered by her and Edward in their co-authored pamphlet of 1886 on *The Woman Question*, which insisted on understanding the position of women in capitalist society by beginning at the 'bed-rock of the economic basis' and the relation between classes.[103]

This position informed Eleanor's relations with women involved in a variety of campaigns for women's suffrage, opposition to the Contagious Diseases Act, and for higher education of women – campaigns that she and Edward deemed 'good as far as [they go]', but which did not fundamentally challenge capitalism and propose a new society without which 'women will never be free'.[104] In dialogue with Ernest Belfort Bax, a leading SDF theoretician and opponent of women's suffrage, Eleanor criticised him for referring to her as a supporter of 'women's rights'. She told Bax that as a socialist she viewed the 'women's rights' question as a bourgeois idea, whereas her approach started from the view of the working class and the class struggle.[105]

The unambiguity of this stance led Eleanor's preeminent biographer, Yvonne Kapp, to write in 1976 that 'she went her own way without fuss, feminism or false constraint', a verdict that has been challenged by feminist historians, who have seen her as a pioneer of socialist feminism.[106] Most recently, Rachel Holmes has gone further, suggesting that Eleanor and Edward's 'landmark essay', *The Woman Question*, 'makes it absolutely clear that the struggle for women's emancipation and equality of the sexes is a prerequisite for any effective form of progressive social revolution'.[107]

A good deal of the content of the *Letters from England* is simple lively description; the authors conveying to radical Russian readers what was happening in England, particularly in the political arena. There is mention of events and personalities which may perplex those not familiar with Britain in the 1890s. To assist readers, we have included with each letter introductory passages and extensive annotations, to explain who and what is under discussion, and sometimes recommending further reading.

In spite of the authors' opening statement that the letters would include discussion of 'literature, science and theatre', it is clear that their primary passion is politics. Treatments of literature and theatre in the letters are often superficial and tacked on to the end of essentially political essays. There are glimpses of real cultural insights, such as the comments in the May letter on Oscar Wilde's aestheticism, but they are brief and quickly cut off. With the exception of a mention of Alfred Russel Wallace's support for a land scheme to tackle unemployment, Thomas Huxley's death and Darwin's son's parliamentary contest, the world of science is ignored.

It will not go unnoticed that the letters include numerous references to conflicts over religious teaching in state schools, to unemployment, poverty, inhuman working conditions, inequality, and hostility towards immigrants, all issues sadly still with us today. Speaking to Blackburn SDF members at the end of 1895, Eleanor assured her audience that such problems would be swept away with the coming of socialism. She believed this transformation to be inevitable because of the tendencies within capitalism towards labour becoming 'more and more socialised whilst the results of that collective production were being concentrated into fewer hands'. This process, she argued, to loud applause, meant that they were already 'living in the midst of a revolution, and they desired to shorten the struggle and reduce the suffering, but even if tomorrow there remained not a person to preach socialism, economic conditions were bound to bring it about'.[108]

A hundred and twenty-five years later, it goes without saying that this element of her father's theory has been found wanting. Nevertheless, many remain convinced of the validity of the elder

Marx's critique of capitalism, and believe that the creative application of his ideas can help bring to an end the system that Eleanor Marx
and Edward Aveling were dedicated to replacing with socialism.

Notes

1. For detailed accounts of the lives of Eleanor Marx Aveling and
   Edward Aveling see the two best and most original published
   biographies: Yvonne Kapp, *Eleanor Marx: Volume One, Family Life
   (1855-1883)*, Lawrence and Wishart: London, 1972; *Eleanor Marx:
   Volume Two, The Crowded Years (1884-1898)*, Lawrence and Wishart:
   London, 1976; Chushichi Tsuzuki, *The Life of Eleanor Marx: 1855-
   1898, A Socialist Tragedy*, Clarendon: Oxford, 1967.

2. James H. Billington, *Mikhailovsky and Russian Populism*, Clarendon:
   Oxford, 1958, p157.

3. *Ibid.*, p174.

4. The pamphlet is available here: https://www.marxists.org/archive/
   lenin/works/1894

5. The article is available here: https://www.marxists.org/archive/ple-
   khanov/1898/xx/individual.html

6. Will Thorne, *My Life's Battles*, George Newnes: London, n.d., 1925.

7. John Tully, *Silvertown*, Monthly Review Press: New York, 2014.

8. Kapp 1976, p475.

9. Stephen Williams 'William Walter Bartlett, (1861-1950), socialist', in
   Dictionary of Labour Biography, Vol. 14, eds. Keith Gildart and David
   Howell, Palgrave Macmillan: London, 2018, pp20-35.

10. *The Legal Eight Hours Demonstration in London: A Brief History of the
    Movement*, Workman's Times: London, 1891.

11. Frederick Engels to August Bebel, 9 May 1890, *Karl Marx and Frederick
    Engels Collected Works* (hereafter *MECW*), *Vol. 48, Letters, 1887-1890*,
    Lawrence and Wishart: London, pp 493-5.

12. *People's Press*, 17 May 1890, p12.

13. *Labour Leader*, 16 May 1896, p6.

14. Tsuzuki 1967, p239.

15. *Justice*, 8 August 1896, p2.

16. *Labour Leader*, 2 December 1895, p2; 4 January 1896, p3.

17. William Hill, *Socialism and Sense: A Radical Review*, Walter Scott:
    London, 1895, p49.

18. David Howell, *British Workers and the Independent Labour Party, 1888-
    1906*, Manchester University Press: Manchester, 1983, p284.

19. *Justice,* 21 February 1891, p1; Hyndman wrote of Engels: 'Why is it

that he carefully secludes himself, Grand-Lama-like, in the Thibetan fastnesses of Regent's Park Road, as if he were qualifying for the first socialist Mahatma?', *Justice*, 1 April 1893, p1.

20. Frederick Engels to August Bebel, 9 February 1893, in *MECW, Vol. 50, Engels, 1892-1895*, Lawrence and Wishart: London, 2004, p103.

21. Frederick Engels to Frederick Sorge, 10 April 1894, quoted in Kenneth O. Morgan, *Keir Hardie: Radical and Socialist*, Orion: London, 1997, p71.

22. Engels repeated his comments about Hardie, including the accusation about Tory money, in a letter to Victor Adler, 25 January 1895, *MECW, Vol. 50, Engels, 1892-1895*, p434.

23. See Joseph Burgess' comments on this in *Manchester Courier*, 19 February 1895, p10.

24. *Labour Leader*, 14 September 1895, p7.

25. Edward Aveling, 'Les sans-travail en Angleterre', *Le devenir social*, April 1895, p64.

26. House of Commons Debates, 7 February 1895, Vol. 30, cc 244-248.

27. *Labour Leader*, 6 July 1895, p2.

28. *Labour Leader*, 20 July 1895, p2.

29. Eleanor Marx Aveling to Laura Lafargue, 7 February 1893, *The Daughters of Karl Marx: Family correspondence 1866-1898*, Commentary and notes by Olga Meier, Penguin: Harmondsworth, p244.

30. Frederick Engels to August Bebel, 24 January 1893, *MECW, Vol. 50, Engels, 1892-1895*, p87.

31. H. Hendall Rogers, *Before the Revisionist Controversy: Kautsky, Bernstein and the Meaning of Marxism, 1895-1898*, Garland: New York and London, 1992, p144.

32. *Ibid.*, pp 156-7.

33. For an assessment of Fabian Society influence on the LCC, see Alan M. McBriar, *Fabian Socialism and English Politics, 1884-1918*, Cambridge University Press: Cambridge, 1966, pp187-233. For Bernstein and the Fabians see Manfred B. Steger, *The Quest for Evolutionary Socialism: Edward Bernstein and Social Democracy*, Cambridge University Press: Cambridge, 1977.

34. Frederick Engels to Laura Lafarge, 28 March 1895, *Frederick Engels, Paul and Laura Lafargue Correspondence, Vol 3, 1891-1895*, Foreign Languages Publishing House: Moscow, 1959, pp367-8.

35. *Vorwarts*, 23 July 1895, p2.

36. *Daily Chronicle*, 24 July 1895, p7.

37. *Daily Chronicle*, 26 July 1895, 7.

38. *Labour Leader*, 17 August 1895, p6; 24 August 1895, p6.

39. In South Salford, a Conservative majority over the Liberals was

seventy-four votes. Henry Hobart, the SDF candidate, polled 813 votes. In Northampton, a two-member constituency, where one Liberal and one Conservative was elected, the second official Liberal candidate, Edward Harford, an official of the Amalgamated Society of Railway Servants, finished third, 117 votes behind the successful Conservative candidate. Fred Jones of the SDF polled 1,216 votes.

40. Frederick Engels to Laura Lafargue, 23 July 1895, *MECW, Vol. 50, Engels, 1892-1895*, p526.

41. Kapp 1976, p597.

42. It is now widely accepted that Marx was Freddy Demuth's father. The most recent biography of Marx by Gareth Stedman Jones provides a useful summary of the evidence; Gareth Stedman Jones, *Karl Marx: Greatness and Illusion*, Allen Lane: London, 2016, pp 373-75. This view is challenged by Terrell Carver in his *Friedrich Engels: His Life and Thought*, Macmillan: Basingstoke, 1989, pp162-9 and https://www.marxists.org/subject/marxmyths/terrell-carver/article.htm. Another doubter is Paul Thomas, *Karl Marx*, Reaktion Books: London, 2012, pp120-2.

43. Edward Aveling, 'Frederick Engels at home', *Labour Prophet*, September 1895, p140. Edward concluded the article in the October issue, p149. He made much of his association with Darwin, beginning in 1882 with two articles about his visit with Dr Ludwig Bucher, a German populariser of Darwin, to Darwin's home in Kent in the autumn of 1881. Edward Aveling, 'A visit to Charles Darwin', *National Reformer*, 22 October 1882, pp273-4; 29 October 1882, pp291-3. He revisited this encounter in 1897 in his 'Charles Darwin and Karl Marx: A comparison', *New Century Review*, April 1897, p232. (Part One of this article appeared in the March number, pp232-243). On the basis of his own discussion with Darwin, he published *The Religious Views of Charles Darwin* in 1881 and in the same year his primer, *The Student's Darwin*, appeared, incorporating much of what he had published in the *National Reformer* since 1879. *The Student's Darwin* was widely read in the secularist movement, where it was required reading for those lecturing on behalf of the National Secular Society. Prior to its publication, Edward had written to Darwin asking for his approval to dedicate the volume to him. This letter surfaced many years after a letter from Darwin to an unnamed individual ('Dear Sir') refusing permission to dedicate a volume to him, which it had been assumed was Marx in respect of his English translation of *Capital*. Margaret A. Fay, 'Marx and Darwin: A literary detective story', *Monthly Review*, March 1980, Vol. 31, No. 10, pp40-57. On Aveling and Darwin see Evelleen Richards, *Darwin and the Meaning of Natural Selection*,

University of Chicago Press: Chicago and London, 2017, pp493-9. For Edward's pamphlet on *Darwinism and Small Families* published in 1882, see William Greenslade, 'Revisiting Edward Aveling' in *Eleanor Marx (1855-1898): Life, Work, Contacts*, John Stokes (ed.), Ashgate: Aldershot, 2000, pp47-9.

44. *Justice*, 7 September 1895, pp4-5; 14 September 1895, pp4-5; 21 September 1895, p4. Edward Aveling, 'Le congress des Trades Union de Cardiff, *Le devenir social*, October 1895, pp605-22; *Blackburn Standard*, 3 November 1895, p6. In a letter to Laura dated 4 September 1895, Eleanor wrote: 'Things at the TUC are bringing about a more definite split than there yet has been between the "old" and "new" unionists, and as Sam writes, it "looks like a grand scrimmage". Burns is playing a somewhat sorry part, and although I have always believed our General's faith in him would be justified, his present action makes one feel doubtful.' Meier 1982, p274. 'Sam' was Samuel Moore, lawyer, friend of the Marx family and Engels, and translator of *Capital* into English. 'General' was the name given to Engels by members of the Marx family.

45. Eleanor Marx contributed a series of articles on Russia to the London newspaper *St James's Gazette* during 1880. Tsuzuki 1967, p47n. She also wrote two articles on 'Underground Russia' in 1883 making use of Sergei Stepniak's (see pp19-21 of Introduction) book of that name, *Progress: A Paper for the People*, August 1883, pp106-10; September 1883, pp172-6.

46. Rachel Holmes claims that Plekhanov and Vera Zasulich invited Eleanor to become the British correspondent for *Russkoye bogatstvo*, but provides no source for this. Rachel Holmes, *Eleanor Marx: A Life*, Bloomsbury: London, 2014, p386.

47. Kapp 1976, p636.

48. Jay Bergman in his biography of Zasulich has her coming to London some nine months before the death of Stepniak (see note 45 above), that is, in February or March 1895. February seems more likely, if Edward Aveling's *Clarion* article about her, printed in February, was timed to coincide with her arrival. Jay Bergman, *Vera Zasulich: A Biography*, Stanford University Press: Redwood City, 1983, p136.

49. Nikolai Danielson, 'Sketches of the Russian economy after the peasant emancipation', cited in Kurt Mandelbaum, 'Introduction to the correspondence of Marx and Engels and Danielson', in *Development and Change*, Vol 10, 1979 [1928], 519.

50. Cited in Mandelbaum 1979, p530.

51. Marx's letter to Zasulich can be found via this link: https://www.marxists.org/archive/marx/works/1881/zasulich/reply.htm.

52. For an excellent discussion of the role of Plekhanov, see Samuel H. Baron, 'Plekhanov and the origins of Russian Marxism', in *Russian Review*, Vol. 13, No. 1, January 1954, pp38-51.

53. For an incisive examination of this fundamental question of Russian socialist history, see Mandelbaum 1979.

54. *Ibid.*, p533.

55. Kapp 1976, p644.

56. Robert Henderson, 'The Hyde Park Rally of 9 March 1890: A British response to Russian atrocities', *European Review of History*: Vol. 21, No. 4, 2014, pp457-8.

57. For an in-depth discussion of Stepniak's work in London, see Donald Senese, *S.M Stepniak-Kravinskii: The London Years*, Oriental Research Partners, 1987.

58. *Ibid.*, p84.

59. Deborah Lavin, *Bradlaugh contra Marx: Radicalism versus Socialism*, Socialist History Society, 2011.

60. Aaron Rosebury, 'Eleanor, daughter of Karl Marx: Personal reminiscences', *Monthly Review*, January 1973, p45.

61. Kapp 1976, p123.

62. Eduard Bernstein, *My Years in Exile: Reminiscences of a Socialist*, Leonard Parsons: London, 1921, p203.

63. Edward Aveling to Charles Bradlaugh, 28 April 1880, Bradlaugh Papers 585, Bishopsgate Institute. The sum of £480 would have been four times the annual average wage of a skilled worker.

64. *St James's Gazette*, 22 February 1883, p11.

65. Note prepared by Bradlaugh for a speech, Bradlaugh Papers, 1156.

66. Edward Aveling to Charles Bradlaugh, 23 May 1883, Bradlaugh Papers 1035.

67. Edward Aveling to Charles Bradlaugh, 29 July 1884, Bradlaugh Papers 1127.

68. William Robinson to Charles Bradlaugh, 11 February 1885, Bradlaugh Papers 1199.

69. Bradlaugh Papers 1171.

70. *National Reformer*, 23 December 1883, p422.

71. Eleanor Marx to John L. Mahon, 8 May 1884, included in E.P. Thompson, *William Morris: Romantic to Revolutionary*, Lawrence and Wishart: London, 1955, pp858-9.

72. Edward Aveling to Annie Besant, 22 September 1884, Bradlaugh Papers 1158.

73. Bernard Shaw to Ellen Terry, 5 January 1898, in *Bernard Shaw, Collected Letters, 1898-1910*, Dan H. Laurence (ed.), Max Reinhardt: London, 1972, pp7-8.

74. Edward Aveling to Henry Irving, 23 January 1891, National Art Library, Victoria and Albert Museum, THM/37/1/31. In October 1890, Irving had sent the couple a gift of his recently completed eight-volume set of *The Works of Shakespeare,* acknowledged by Eleanor with great thanks. She wrote: 'It is very generous of a man in your position to send to two lovers of your art, younger than yourself, and so much less known. And we don't forget that to Mrs Grundy, who after all forms the larger part even of the Lyceum audience, we are rather a disreputable couple.' ('Mrs Grundy', a common figure of speech in the nineteenth century, denotes one who is priggish and conventional). Eleanor Marx Aveling to Henry Irving, 26 October, 1890, National Art Library, THM/37/1/31. It is likely that it was this set of Irving's *Shakespeare* that was advertised by 'Impecunious' in *Clarion* in the summer of 1895. The advertisement appeared several times but was withdrawn, we can assume not coincidentally, after Engels's death in the first week of August. *Clarion,* 6 July, 1895, p3; 10 August 1895, p3.

75. Edward Aveling to Henry Irving, 5 May 1895, National Art Library, THM/37/1/35.

76. Edward Aveling to William Morris, 27 August 1895, British Library, Add Ms 45345, f. 259; Edward Aveling to Sydney Cockerell (Morris's executor), 1 December 1896, Add Ms 45346, f. 96.

77. Rosebury, 'Eleanor, daughter of Karl Marx: Personal reminiscences', *Monthly Review,* January 1973, pp36-7.

78. Eleanor Marx Aveling to Olive Schreiner, 16 June 1885, included in Havelock Ellis's 'Eleanor Marx', *The Adelphi,* September 1935, pp349-50. Harry Quilter was an art critic and writer.

79. Schreiner to Dollie Radford, June 1898, British Library Add Ms 89029/1/26.

80. E. Bernstein to V. Adler, 5 April 1898, *Victor Adler, Briefwechsel mit August Bebel und Karl Kautsky,* Verlung der Wienel, Volksbuchhandlung: Vienna, 1954, p244.

81. M. Mendelson to V. Zasulich, 18 April 1898, B.I. Nicolaevsky Archive, Series 16, Box 40/4, Hoover Institution, Stanford University. See Stephen Williams and Tony Chandler, 'Tussy's great delusion: Eleanor Marx's death revisited', *Socialist History,* 58, 2020.

82. *Ibid.*

83. E. Marx Aveling to Freddy Demuth, 5 February 1898, *Labour Leader,* 30 July 1898, p 251.

84. *The Stage,* 20 April 1888, p10.

85. *Workman's Times,* 7 November 1891, p5.

86. *Justice,* 22 June 1895, p7.

87. Kapp 1976, p. 99.

88. Eleanor Marx Aveling to Laura Lafargue, 11 November 1893, in Meier 1982, p246; Eleanor Marx to Wilhelm Liebknecht, 12 March 1896, Karl Marx/Friedrich Engels Papers, International Institute of Social History, Amsterdam, Section G. G38-74.

89. Stephen Yeo, 'A new life: The religion of socialism in Britain', *History Workshop Journal,* Spring 1977, Vol. 4, No. 1, pp5-56; James Leatham's *Songs for Socialists,* Aberdeen: 1890, was a favourite songbook for many years going through numerous editions.

90. *Reynolds's Newspaper,* 5 May 1895, 3.

91. *Blackburn Standard,* 30 November 1895, p5.

92. *Glasgow Evening Post,* 26 October 1895, p5; *Labour Leader,* 2 November 1895, p10.

93. *Sunday Times,* 27 March 1892, p6.

94. Thorne 1925, p47.

95. *Burnley Express,* 4 December 1895, p4.

96. Kapp 1976, p105.

97. Henry M. Hyndman, *The Record of an Adventurous Life,* Macmillan: London, 1911, pp346-7.

98. *Norwood News,* 16 November 1895, p2. We are indebted to Steve Grindley, who found the lease and then donated it to the Marx Memorial Library, for this information.

99. Eleanor Marx to Laura Lafargue, 10 December 1895, in Meier 1982, p285. Edward mentioned the Austin Friars property to Bradlaugh in 1887 as a source of possible capital to repay his debts because the family were considering selling it. Edward Aveling to Charles Bradlaugh, 24 April 1887, Bradlaugh Papers, 1355. There has been some doubt about the house which Edward professed owning a share in, with one author suggesting that 'It is hard to imagine that Aveling had owned a property'. Mary Gabriel, *Love and Capital: Karl and Jenny Marx and the Birth of a Revolution,* Black Boy Books: New York/Boston/London, 2012, p577. Rachel Holmes states with certainty, but no evidence, that with money inherited from his first wife after her death in 1892, Aveling 'invested in a residential property in Austin Friars'. Holmes 2014, p420. Yvonne Kapp's suggestion that the property was 'possibly left him by his father or even, it may be, an investment of a legacy from old Miss Elizabeth Bibbins, after whom he was named', comes closest to the truth. In fact, Edward and his siblings had inherited from his father a part share in No. 1 Austin Friars on the latter's death in 1884. Will of Thomas William Baxter Aveling, died 3 July 1884, Probate Office. The property, off Old Broad Street in the City of London, was ideally placed for letting to

companies involved in finance and stockbroking, and accordingly a variety of named businesses gave No. 1 Austin Friars as their registered address during the 1880s and 90s. Supervised by a couple who acted as live-in caretakers and housekeepers, the property had an estimated rental value of £310 per annum in 1896.

100. Kapp 1976, p636; Holmes 2014, p386-7. Tsuzuki 1967, p271, in our view correctly identifies the letters' joint authorship.

101. *Tower Hamlets Independent* 23 February 1895, p3.

102. *Reynolds's Newspaper,* 8 December 1895, p4.

103. Eleanor Marx Aveling and Edward Aveling, 'The Woman Question – From a socialist point of view', *Westminster Review,* January 1886, Vol. 125, No. 249, p210.

104. *Ibid.*

105. *Justice,* 23 November 1895, p8.

106. Kapp 1976, p89; see for example Lyn Pykett, '"The daughter of today": The socialist feminist intellectual as a woman of letters', in Stokes 2000, pp13-22; Sally Alexander, 'Eleanor Marx's political legacy – self-sacrifice or self-realisation?', *Women's History Review,* September 2007, Vol. 16, No.4, pp595-616; and Alexander's preface to the Verso edition of Kapp's study, brought together in a single volume and retitled *Eleanor Marx: A B*iography, Verso: London, 2018, pp ix-xx.

107. Holmes 2014, p262. This view is challenged in a critical review of Holmes' book by Ludmila Melchior-Yahill, 'Eleanor Marx viewed through the lens of a twenty-first century feminist', *Socialism and Democracy,* July 2017, Vol. 31, No. 2, pp145-63.

108. *Blackburn Standard,* 30 November 1895, p3.

Chronology

Eleanor and Edward in 1895

Preceding months

Eleanor and Edward had lived in a flat on the top floor of 7 Gray's Inn Square, Holborn, since March 1893. The accommodation was let to the couple by a Master of Gray's Inn, who was permitted this privilege as a way of earning income.

Edward, in recent years in delicate health, in particular with kidney disease, had travelled to the Scilly Isles at the end of September 1894 on the recommendation of his doctor. While there he penned two seemingly fictitious articles for socialist newpaper *Clarion* under his nom de plume, Alec Nelson, in which he described incidents of his travel to and stay in the Scillies.

Edward returned to Gray's Inn Square, unusually sporting a beard, on 16 November, complaining of a pain in his side, which Eleanor said was caused by a large abscess, presumably a renal abscess. Surgery was followed by a further period of rest for Edward, with Eleanor as his nurse. In the days before Christmas, Eleanor undertook a lecture tour of the Manchester area speaking on 'The International Socialist Movement', 'Socialism: Scientific and Otherwise', and 'Women and the Socialist Movement'.

During 1894 Eleanor had become increasingly anxious about the influence on Engels of Dr Ludwig and Louise Freyberger. The couple had married in February – Louise had formerly been married to Karl Kautsky, a leading German social democrat – and lived in Engels's Regent's Park Road house in north London. Eleanor suspected the Freybergers of working to orders of the German Social Democratic Party (SPD) to capture the manuscripts and correspondence of Karl Marx held in trust by Engels. Eleanor's fears reached fever pitch towards the end of the year, when she urged her sister Laura to visit London and, with her, have the issue out with Engels. Laura wrote a letter to Eleanor expressing her anxieties about the Marx manuscripts, with permission for its contents to be shared with Engels. Engels was at first angry at what he believed to be a lack of trust in him, but over Christmas confirmed that Marx's papers would pass to Eleanor and Laura on his death. In March 1895 this was confirmed by Engels in a codicil to his will.

1895

January

Eleanor's translation of Georgii Plekhanov's *Anarchism and Socialism* appeared in serial form in the *Weekly Times and Echo* from 6 January until 24 February. Later in the year it was published as a pamphlet by Twentieth Century Press.

Eleanor celebrated her fortieth birthday on 16 January.

February

Edward's recovery continued as he began to undertake activity as a leading member of the committees planning the International Socialist Workers' and Trade Unions Congress to be held in London during the summer of 1896, and the forthcoming labour demonstration held annually in May. On the latter, a decision had been made by some socialists to persuade the organising committee, which also included the London Trades Council, individual trade union branches and radical clubs, to hold the 1895 demonstration on Wednesday 1 May, and not wait until the first Sunday, as had been the practice in the previous four years. This would have brought the London demonstration in line with European counterparts.

Edward took responsibility for the international section of the *Clarion* edition published in the week before the labour demonstration, putting him in contact with Wilhelm Liebknecht, Karl Kautsky, Georgii Plekhanov, Pierre Lavrov, Emile Vandervelde and Emile Millerand – all leading figures in their respective countries and confidantes of Engels and those in his circle.

Edward published a short biographical study of Russian Marxist Vera Zasulich in *Clarion* of 23 February.

Eleanor told Natalie Liebknecht that 'Edward's long and serious illness has kept my hands full – not to speak of the housework, the literary work, business correspondence and lectures, committee meetings and so forth that seem to take up every moment of the twenty-four hours'.

March

On 3 March Eleanor chaired a meeting of the 1st May Celebration Committee at the Social Democratic Federation (SDF) hall in the Strand, which, following a decision of the London Trades Council and others to continue with the first Sunday in May as the date for their demonstration, decided to go ahead with plans for a separate event on Wednesday 1st. Unable to persuade the broader committee of trade unionists and radical clubs to support the new date, Edward resigned from the committee, with the intention of putting all efforts into the 1 May event.

Soon after, the couple departed for a holiday in Hastings to aid Edward's slow recovery. Eleanor told Liebknecht, 'though it is bitterly cold ... the few hours of fresh air have done him good. Still he is not strong yet.' Eleanor broke her Hastings holiday to travel to Burnley to speak at meetings of the local SDF branch on 10 March on the subjects of 'The International Working Class Movement' and 'The Materialist Conception of History'.

At the end of the month the couple spoke from the platform of the National Union of Gas Workers and General Labourers' sixth anniversary celebration at Victoria Park, Hackney.

April

On 7 April Eleanor again chaired a meeting of the 1st May Celebration Committee, at which Edward's adversary Ferdinand Gilles attempted to move what she believed was a deliberately disruptive amendment to the resolution to be read on the day. After a long debate, in which Eleanor took a leading part, the amendment was defeated.

Edward published an article on 'Unemployment in England' in the first issue of *Le devenir social*, a journal co-edited by Paul Lafargue (Eleanor's brother-in-law) from Paris.

Edward travelled to Stratford-upon-Avon for the production of his play *Judith Shakespeare* at the Shakespeare Memorial Theatre on 27 April. The play was well received, following which Edward offered exclusive rights to actor Henry Irving in settlement of debts. At some point Eleanor joined Edward in Warwickshire because both appeared on the platform of a meeting of agricultural workers at Bidford on 26 April. The couple knew Bidford well, and had contacts with agricultural workers' trade unions there, having rented a cottage at nearby Dodwell in the late 1880s.

May

The 1 May demonstration assembled on the Embankment and marched to Hyde Park. Arrival in the park coincided with a heavy downpour of rain curtailing the speeches, including those given by Eleanor and Edward. In the evening, Eleanor spoke at an SDF rally at the South Place Institute alongside H.M. Hyndman, George Lansbury, Andreas Scheu and J. Hunter Watts.

The couple returned to Hyde Park on Sunday 5 May to speak at the demonstration organised by the Legal Eight Hours League and the London Trades Council. Edward urged all to support the 1 May demonstration in 1896, and Eleanor stressed the importance of winning universal suffrage, 'and in that they must remember to include the women'.

Eleanor supported the candidature of George Lansbury for the SDF in the Walworth by-election at a meeting at Browning Hall on 13 May. She was joined on the platform by William Morris, Keir Hardie and Frank Smith.

June

Edward, as 'Alec Nelson', organised and directed a benefit evening of entertainment at the SDF on 15 June, with receipts going to the forthcoming International Socialist Workers' and Trade Unions Congress. A series of readings, comedy and popular songs was followed by the production of the one-act drama *In the Train*, featuring Edward, H.W. Lee, the SDF secretary, and Lilian Richardson, who was almost certainly the same person as Eva Frye, who would in June 1897 marry Edward at Chelsea Registry Office. Eleanor was also billed to perform on the evening, but there is no report that she did so.

At the end of the month the couple travelled to Eastbourne to join the ailing Engels at his favourite seaside resort. Laura was also there.

July

In the first week of July the couple moved to Green Street Green, a small village near Orpington in Kent, connected to London by Orpington and Chelsfield railway stations. It is likely the move out of London was prompted by a desire to provide healthy surroundings for Edward. A local estate agent advertised: 'Comfortable apartment with board or without: good air, pleasantly situated in Green Street Green', making it a likely candidate for the couple's accommodation, details of which they did not reveal.

Edward was approached by the Glasgow central branch of the Independent Labour Party (ILP) to be its candidate in the forthcoming general election. Edward told the ILP that while he was honoured by their offer, he had to decline on health grounds. He went on to add that he 'was not in a financial position to contest or, if successful, to make time and labour available'.

Engels told Eleanor that he believed the ILP invitation might be a 'trap' set by Keir Hardie and directed her to the *Labour Leader* of 6 July, in which Edward was taken to task for caricaturing Hardie's position on unemployment in an article originally published in *Le devenir social* and then summarised in *La jeunesse socialiste,* a French youth monthly. In full conspiracy mode, possibly brought on by declining health, Engels wrote to Eleanor: 'Now the noble nature of K.H. [Keir Hardie] shines out brilliantly. While E.A. [Edward] attacks him, K.H generously finds him a candidature, which if E.A. accepted K.H. could on general grounds get cancelled by the Executive Council'. For his part, Hardie believed Edward's statements and conduct in this case were typical, and sadly 'cost Dr Aveling so many friends'.

Edward was re-elected as auditor of the Gas Workers' Union. Eleanor spoke at a meeting of the Nottingham ILP on 28 July.

August

Engels died on 5 August of cancer of the oesophagus and larynx. Edward and Eleanor attended the gathering at Waterloo railway station on 10 August, from which Engels's body was taken to Woking for cremation.

Probate of the Engels will was granted on 28 August, in which Eleanor and Laura each received £7,842. Each would give a third of the sum they received to the children of their sister Jenny, who had died in 1883.

Eleanor liaised with Laura, Samuel Moore, Engels' executor, and the solicitor Arthur Crosse about the sale of securities and wine. She expressed anxieties about these responsibilities and the task of ensuring publication of her father's outstanding work, especially the fourth volume of *Capital*.

Eleanor's article on Engels, originally published in 1890 to mark his seventieth birthday, was reproduced in the August issue of *Le devenir social*.

Edward published an article about the Scilly Isles, 'A strange island people', in *Die Neue Zeit*.

September

Edward attended the Congress of the TUC at Cardiff in the first week of September as reporter for *Justice, Reynolds's Newspaper* and *Le devenir social*. The first of Edward's two articles on 'Frederick Engels at home', was published in the *Labour Prophet*.

Eleanor was forced to contend with irritating demands from the Freybergers for the return of borrowed money, in spite of the codicil to Engels' will that stated that the sums be treated as free gifts. A transfer of her father's manuscripts to a deposit in Chancery Lane was organised by Eleanor, and a provisional search of the papers revealed a series of articles on Germany in 1848 that excited her very much. These articles were later attributed to Engels.

Eleanor's historical study of the 'The English working-class movement' was published in *Volks-lexikon*, a German encyclopaedia edited by Emanuel Wurm, and later in the year as a Twentieth Century Press pamphlet.

On 27 September Eleanor, Edward, Eduard Bernstein and Frederick Lessner disposed of Engels' ashes six miles out at sea from Beachy Head, near Eastbourne.

October

The couple undertook a lecture tour of Scotland between 7 and 14 October, speaking at Edinburgh, Dundee, Glasgow, and Blantyre. On her return to Green Street Green, Eleanor wrote to Kautsky that the tour for the SDF and ILP had been a great success.

Eleanor continued to be irritated by the Freybergers, who, now sole occupants of the Regent's Park Road house, insisted that Eleanor and Edward remove all their possessions from the house. Eleanor told Laura that Dr Freyberger, 'that unmitigated cad ... was ill-bred enough to add ... [that the removal should be]..."at our own expense"'. In a similar vein, Eleanor wrote to Laura objecting to the announcement by August Bebel and Paul Singer of the SPD acknowledging the bequest of books by Engels without mentioning Marx: 'I thought it would be decent to say that a good half of the twenty-seven cases contained the admirable library of Marx, presented to the German party ... by Marx's children'.

Eleanor and Laura issued a public appeal for those with correspondence from Marx to send them for copying with a view to publication.

Eleanor and Edward began house hunting but without any initial success. Eleanor told Laura that: 'We find all the nice houses are either let or too dear. And the "noble residences" we go to see are more often than not in some unspeakable slum. Rents are really fearful. If, however, we can find a really nice place, Crosse strongly advises buying instead of paying rent'.

Edward got into a spat with David Lowe, assistant editor at the *Labour Leader,* over the accuracy of a translation from an original in *Die Neue Zeit.* Lowe defended the translation, which he said conveyed the same ideas as that given in Edward's alternative, but 'if anything the Dr's is worse English. Hypercriticism, nought else, could incline one's knuckle to pen such a note.'

Le devenir social carried Edward's extensive analysis of the recent TUC Congress. Edward published an appreciation of 'Thomas Henry Huxley: The friend and expositor of Darwin', in *Die Neue Zeit.*

Edward, as Alec Nelson, organised an evening concert and theatrical performance on 24 October in the village hall, Orpington. The dramatic element was provided by two of Edward's plays, *For Her Sake* and *In the Train*, in which Lilian Richardson made a return performance following her debut at the SDF Hall in June.

Eleanor spoke at a meeting of the Bermondsey Socialist Club on 27 October on 'Socialism: Scientific and Otherwise'.

Eleanor made a will on 16 October, leaving the interest in royalties from her father's work accruing to her to Jenny's children, and the balance of her estate to Edward. A year later, doubtless persuaded by Edward to amend the will, Eleanor made a codicil leaving the royalties of her father's publications to him.

Edward returned to Scotland to lecture on 27 October at the Albion Hall, Glasgow on 'Karl Marx and Charles Darwin'.

November

Edward performed at a social event for the Crays and Orpington Cricket Club on 7 November. A renowned cricket enthusiast, Edward had in 1891, as Alec Nelson, published *Comic Cricket*, a series of amusing sketches on the game. At the Orpington social Edward gave a recitation of Edgar Alan Poe's 'The Bells', a favourite of his which he often performed. At the end of the month Edward put on his comedietta *The Landlady* at Morley Hall, Hackney.

Eleanor objected to the views on women of Ernest Belfort Bax, the leading SDF theoretician, and challenged him to a public debate, insisting that it be framed as the 'The sex question and its economic basis', and that 'the so-called "women's rights" question ... is a bourgeois idea'. Bax rejected the challenge of a public debate and instead proposed written exchanges. Eleanor and

Edward undertook an eight-day tour of Lancashire for the SDF with appearances at Blackburn, Clitheroe, Darwen, Nelson, Colne, Rochdale, Barrowford, Padiham, Great Harwood and Burnley. While in Lancashire Edward celebrated his forty-sixth birthday on 29 November.

Eleanor finalised the purchase of Moraston Lodge, a four-bedroomed detached house in Jews Walk, Sydenham, on her return to London following the Lancashire tour.

December

Eleanor told Laura that she was 'Jewishly proud of my house in Jew's Walk', which she immediately renamed 'The Den'. In the same letter, Eleanor stressed that Edward would furnish the house from receipts of a mortgaged property he owned in the City of London: 'I want you to know this as it would not be fair to think *I* was paying it all'. The couple moved in on 16 December.

Edward chaired a protest meeting at the Mile End Assembly Hall on 7 December of Jewish trade unionists against the decision of the recent Congress of the TUC to exclude 'alien paupers'. An estimated three thousand people were present. Edward justified his presence on the platform 'by being an Irishman, he was an alien in this country, and one of those whom a certain class of Englishmen had dealt with much in the same way as they proposed to deal with aliens coming from the continent'. He went on: 'The passing of anti-alien resolutions was doing the work of the capitalists', and he appealed to 'British workmen at large to say whether they would side with the masters or whether they would give their sympathies to the workers.' When Edward had to leave the meeting to go elsewhere, Eleanor took over in the chair.

Two of Edward's plays, *The Landlady* and *For Her Sake,* were put on at the Athenaeum Hall on 14 December in benefit of the forthcoming International Socialist Workers' and Trade Unions Congress.

Keir Hardie asked Edward if he was responsible for the exclusion of the ILP from a list of organisations given in the *Westminster Gazette* as contributors to the International Congress. Edward denied writing the piece.

Eleanor spoke at a meeting of the Battersea Labour League on 22 December on 'Education of our Children'.

On 28 December Eleanor was present at the gathering at Waterloo railway station as the body of Sergei Stepniak, killed in a railway accident five days earlier, was taken to Woking for cremation.

LETTER ONE

January 1895

This letter was written in early December 1894, soon after the results of the election to the London School Board had been declared.

Established in 1870 to provide schooling for all children in London between the ages of five and thirteen, the London School Board was directed by a Board of members elected on a triennial basis. Edward had himself been elected in November 1882 for the Westminster division, having declared himself in favour of 'free, secular, compulsory education'. Despite his resignation from the Board in October 1884, Edward maintained a keen interest in its work, especially when it became embroiled in religious controversy in the early 1890s, the background and detail of which form a significant part of this first letter. There seems little doubt that he composed these sections.

In common with others in the socialist movement, Eleanor and Edward were critical of Gladstone's Liberal government, which had been elected in 1892, for its failure to deliver on radical promises. Aside from some hope that the introduction of parish and district councils would establish elements of democracy in rural areas, the letter is scathing of the government's performance and pessimistic about prospects for the administration which, since March 1894, had been led by Lord Rosebery.

The letter concludes with an extended favourable review of Thomas Hardy's volume of short stories, Life's Little Ironies, *likely to be from the pen of Eleanor, who admired his writing.*

The letters presented here will deal with events in English life which, we believe, will also be of interest to Russian readers. The position of the political parties, the evolution of the social life of the people, new tendencies in literature, science, theatre – these are the subjects we intend to discuss in our letters. These letters will be produced jointly by writers of both sexes. Men and women look at things from different points of view. It may be that, in order to get the broadest possible perspective on human society, it would not go amiss to look at it from two different, although certainly not opposing, points of view – male and female. This method of joint investigation brings to mind what in physics is known as stereo-scopic vision. If you look at an object with one eye open and the other closed, and then do it again the other way around, you get two quite distinct, but live impressions of that thing. But if you look at it with both eyes, you get an impression of it which is the result of combining two separate impressions, and it is precisely that combination which is needed to get the most accurate impression of the object. In a stereoscope the axes of vision of both eyes are separated by an opaque barrier. Each eye looks from one side at an image, adapted for the angle of vision of that eye. If you close one eye and look with the other down a stereoscope, the image looks completely flat. Perspective disappears and the front of the image looks to be on the same plane as the back. But if you look at the image with both eyes, everything changes instantly, and you get a fully realistic impression of the object.

In England, and particularly in London, we are currently in the full throes of elections. The excitement caused by the elections to the school boards still has not died down. At the very beginning of December 1894 the first elections in rural constituencies to parish and district councils were to take place. We shall discuss those elections in more detail below. But first we shall say a few words about the intense struggle around the elections to the London School Board.[1]

Not once since 1871 has there been such excitement as that caused by the elections of this year. The London School Board consists of fifty-five members and is in charge of the 327 London schools known as 'board schools', or, rather, government schools as distinct from the others, which are private enterprises. There are 2,392 school boards across England and Wales in charge of various schools. However, here we shall consider only the question of the London school system. Before 1871, all schools in London were private concerns. Anybody who so wished could open a school, wherever he liked, and consequently many who had failed in other

fields tried their luck in education. The organisation of the afore-
mentioned board schools was intended to achieve a higher ideal
in rational education. Parents, of course, want to send their children to the schools which provide the best education. Up to now,
especially among adherents of the Church of England, there has
been a very firmly entrenched bias in favour of private schools run
by the clergy of that church. Moreover, many were biased against
schools with a broader educational curriculum. For example, one
concerned mother wrote to a teacher at one of the government
schools which taught a very small amount of physiology to the
senior classes: 'Don't teach my daughter physiology, it won't do
her any good and it's a rude science.' Moreover, before the establishment of the school boards in 1871, in many private schools
one could encounter not only poor teaching but also many cases
of physical neglect and mistreatment of children which are hard
to imagine. Unfortunately the dreadful depiction of one such
school in Yorkshire given by Charles Dickens in his story 'Nicholas
Nickleby' is far from exaggerated.

The Act of Parliament which established the London School
Board was passed by the House of Commons in 1870 after long and
impassioned discussion. The Conservatives fought with all their
might against creating any kind of school boards. But once there
was no longer any doubt that they had lost that battle, a new fight
broke out around the very question which was to arise twenty-three
years later and cause new sharp clashes. That question concerns
religious instruction in schools. In 1870 the great majority of the
most serious defenders of the establishment of government schools
hotly objected to any religious instruction in these schools. The
opponents of religious instruction argued that given the multi-
plicity of religious denominations of various types in England, it
would be best if the government schools were to teach the children
only those subjects around which there was common agreement.
However, the Liberal government then in power resisted this. In
the end the Bill passed, but it included a paragraph granting each
school the right to teach the rudiments of religion in whatever form
it sees fit. This was a kind of parliamentary, or rather national,
compromise. The English people, as we know, loves any kind of
compromise. There were two provisos to this paragraph: the first

forbade the teaching of any kind of special catechism in school, and the second, known as the 'conscience clause', gave parents the right to remove their children from Scripture lessons. However, parents have rarely availed themselves of the right they are granted by that clause. Many parents suppose that if their children do not take part in Scripture classes they will lose many rights. In view of such considerations and out of concern for their children, parents oblige them to attend Scripture classes and learn things about which they often have completely opposite views. It is said, not without foundation, that the behaviour of the Liberal government on this question played a part in the defeat of Gladstone and the Liberal Party at the 1874 general elections.[2]

The law of 1870 laid down that all children between the ages of five and thirteen must attend one or another school, either a government one or a private one which had satisfied the not-too-stringent demands of the government inspectors. Education was thereby made compulsory, and twenty years later, in 1891, an Act of Parliament abolished school fees. Unfortunately, thanks to the inventiveness of the opponents of this system in the School Board and the local school boards this freeing of education from all taxes remained more or less a dead letter. The collaboration between the forces of reaction is best illustrated by the fact that as soon as free education was confirmed by the 1891 Act, the landlords in the workers' quarters immediately raised leases and rents for workers. In this way, the few pennies that mothers had hoped to save and spend on increasing their families' meagre resources found their way into the landlords' pockets.

The same 1870 Act of Parliament which established the schools also set up the London School Board. At the time the board was created, interest in questions of education was reflected in the election of its members. This is not to say that they were all well-known teachers or people renowned for their remarkable minds. But at any rate they were people with, as they say, status, and in one case the board included people with very high positions in the worlds of science and education. Lord Lawrence, former Viceroy of India, was elected as the first chair of the board, and the vice-chair was Charles Reed, later Sir Charles Reed, an extremely rich City broker with a very high position among the Dissenting party.[3] The following tale is told of Charles Reed: there was a ceremony to renew one of the cemeteries in London. Almost all the people buried there are Dissenters, including all the leaders of the Dissenting movement from 1662, a period when there was a split in the established church, up to the present day. Charles Reed was selected to chair it. In his speech he mentioned Daniel Defoe who, he informed his listeners, was the author of two works: *Robinson Crusoe* and *The Pilgrim's Progress*.[4] In the election of Lord Lawrence, an adherent of the Anglican Church, as chair of the first London School Board, and Mr Reed, a Dissenter, as vice-chair, it is impossible not to see the spirit of compromise between the representatives of the two main religious parties who decided to work together in this instance. Other figures elected to the board included two bishops, Dr Angus, who had a literary reputation, and Samuel Morley, a very rich City broker with authority among the Dissenters. Then there was Mr Smith who subsequently rose, or, rather, was elevated by the cynicism of Disraeli, to lead the Tory aristocracy and be made leader of the Tories in the House of Commons. The Board also contains such a figure as Professor Huxley, whose scientific authority is recognised around the world.[5]

Parliament agreed to the compromise and a little later that compromise was accepted by the board that Parliament had established. However, it was the resolution adopted on that matter by the board which became the cause of the recent heated struggle during the elections to the board. The resolution states that in the schools set up by the board there should be Bible classes, with explanations and homilies in the areas of morality and religion appropriate to the capabilities and comprehension of children. Following the good old English principle of always resorting to a compromise, the adherent of the Anglican Church Mr Smith proposed the resolution and the Liberal Dissenter Samuel Morley supported it. A very tiny courageous minority on the board nonetheless fought doggedly against this resolution, demanding the complete exclusion of religious teaching in schools established and maintained at the expense of the people whose religious views are so divergent. In a word, this minority on the board, as in Parliament, stood for what is known as secular education. This includes teaching the usual subjects in all branches of knowledge, but completely excludes any teaching which favours or disfavours established religious beliefs. Overall, they regarded the teaching of religion as a private matter which is not the concern of the public authorities. But in this respect the school board went even further than Parliament, and in the very first days of its existence it issued a programme, which is still in use, obliging all schoolteachers to read and explain the Bible, regardless of the fact that many sects in England interpret that book in their own way. In 1878, there was one factory owner who had accumulated enormous wealth through exploiting his workers and, presumably, reckoned that he needed to do something to justify himself to his celestial judges. He dreamed up the following scheme: rather than give money to the church, he gifted it to establish annual prizes for the school pupils who did best in Scripture lessons. As a reward for their diligence the children were given Bibles. Thanks to this innovation, the school board eventually resolved that all schools should devote three quarters of an hour each day to Scripture lessons, usually in the morning when the children arrive at school fresh and alert, not yet fatigued by their day's study.[6]

Let us now return to these recent elections. In order to make sense of these elections, we should add that the two contending parties are called the 'Moderates' – the conservative and church party, and the 'Progressives' – the Dissenting and Liberal party.[7] Besides the candidates put forward by these two parties there were also candidates who, strictly speaking, did not belong to either party but who offered the electors their own programme for secular education. Not one of these 'secularists' was elected, but we cannot but consider the voting in certain divisions as highly portentous for the future.[8] The previous board consisted of twenty-eight Moderates, twenty-two Progressives and five so-called 'Independents' who should essentially be lumped together with the Moderates. The new board, elected in November, is now comprised of twenty-six Moderates, twenty-six Progressives and three Independents.[9] Despite the fact that the reactionaries still retain a very small majority, the elections themselves were very notable in view of the significant increase in the numbers voting in London. Overall, the total number of votes given to the Progressives rose massively in comparison with the previous election, and significantly exceeded the number of votes cast for the Moderates. The Moderates in 1894 received 671,134 votes while the Progressives got 807,632. Nonetheless the Moderates still have a majority, albeit a highly insignificant one. This contradiction can be explained by the abysmal way the elections are organised, and inadequate thoroughness in the counting which meant that the Progressives lost hundreds and thousands of votes. It should not be forgotten that here in England there are no second rounds in elections. Therefore, most workers who cast their votes for the Progressives in order to keep out a party openly opposed to the system of government schools would probably, if there had been a second ballot, have cast their votes differently. In order to finish with dry figures once and for all, we should also mention that the last four elections have been marked by a continual rise in the vote for the Progressives, while the number cast for their opponents has remained almost static. But even more notable is the massive rise in the numbers casting votes this year. This, without a doubt, shows a growing interest among the London working classes in elections which are of great importance for their children today and in the future. Previously workers had been largely indifferent to these elections. The following figures for the four previous elections show how the numbers voting has gradually increased and how the number cast for the Progressives has grown:

1885:
Moderates – 468,579
Progressives – 261,195

1888:
Moderates – 471,815
Progressives – 381,475

1891:
Moderates – 470,915
Progressives – 391,726

1894:
Moderates – 671,134
Progressives – 807,632

What, in reality, should be the outcome of the heated, lively struggle around the elections to the London School Board? The main question, around which all others were clustered, concerned religious instruction in schools. Long ago, about fifty years before the 1870 Act, the two main and most powerful religious groupings in England were contesting over control of the schools. There was an ongoing struggle between the established Church of England and the dissenting Nonconformists, who were themselves divided into numerous sects of various denominations and connected only in their antagonism towards the Anglican Church. The Nonconformists were prepared to accept the compromise discussed above because they feared that otherwise the laws governing schools would be framed in a way even more favourable to the Anglican Church. Over the last three years of the School board's existence, its Moderate majority has displayed a fairly clear intention to get religious instruction in schools more definitely in line with the views of the Church of England.[10] The Moderate members of the board have attempted, by passing resolutions, to interpret this notorious compromise the way they want. In line with this, teachers were instructed that the ideas of the Moderate members of the board were the ones they were to inculcate into their pupils' minds. The circular issued on this question stated that those teachers 'who cannot, in conscience, teach the Bible in the spirit of the Moderate majority on the board, are exempted from this duty, and this should not adversely affect their position with the board'. In this way a particular standard was set in religious instruction, against which the Dissenters have continually protested. That said, the Progressives were not against introducing religious instruction in schools. Like the Moderates, they supported religious instruction. The only difference was that the Progressives wanted to circumscribe it as far as possible, so that no children would be taught any religious doctrines not in accord with the doctrines of the Progressives, while the Moderates, who always had the upper hand, strove to compel teachers to instruct children in their own special doctrines. The only logical way out of that situation would be to exclude religious instruction from schools altogether and keep it within the family. That will probably happen eventually.[11]

In truth, this whole religious dispute is strongly hampering progress in the field of education and is delaying the resolution of other practical matters pertaining to the setting up of new schools, the very ones in which children would get completely normal education. The Moderates stand for retaining private schools; the Progressives, to their credit of course, want to support state schools. The Moderates tried in every way they could to delay the implementation of the Act of Parliament, while the Progressives of course did everything within their power to ensure that the Act was duly implemented. It is therefore in the interests of the Moderates to drag out and sustain this unfortunate religious dispute as much as possible. By making the school board put the real business on the back burner, it threatens to scupper the work of the new board as well. A few more words about the shameful insouciance with which the reactionaries regard the vital, sacred task which has been entrusted to them – it turns out that they do not even pay due attention to the private schools under their supervision, and completely fail to oversee them. There has been a lot of attention recently to the question of how many cubic feet of air are needed per head, and physiologists have now established that the appropriate amount is at least ten cubic feet. In constructing public buildings and schools in particular this calculation should be taken into account, and architects are guided by it when building state schools. In private schools, however, this rule is not observed, and in them each child has no more than eight cubic feet.

Now let us relate what has been done, or rather, not done with regard to the so-called 'extra schools'. This refers to night schools and schools of further education. The night schools were founded by some of the Progressives, in particular, board teachers. Their original purpose was to give boys and girls who were too old to start at a normal state school the chance to acquire the essential knowledge taught at those schools. Undoubtedly, when the state schools were established, there were hundreds and thousands of children of artisans and workers who were too old to start at these schools. It was for them that the night schools were set up. Subsequently these schools branched out in all directions, thanks to Mr Acland, the Minister of Education in the present Liberal government. It would be no exaggeration to state that Mr Acland is the only member of the present cabinet who has in a certain sense fully justified the high hopes of the Radical supporters of the present government.[12] Some children who had completed their ordinary schooling also attended night school. Unfortunately, again thanks to the obstructionist tactics of the Moderates, only a very small percentage of children get to night school. The sad fact is that for the great majority of London children education finishes when they reach thirteen years of age. There is a sharp contrast here, because thirteen is the very age at which the children of the middle and upper classes enter the 'public schools' – Eton, Harrow, Rugby, etc. The earliest age at which the children of the privileged classes enter the public schools is the very one at which the children of the workers leave school for good. The shameful neglect of the night schools in London is best illustrated by the following percentages of children attending night schools: Bradford – 5.9, Nottingham – 3.9, Manchester – 3.3, Leeds - 2.6, Birmingham - 1.8, London – 0.4. Moreover, in London, compared with other large cities, at least 100,000 children should have been attending night schools when in fact in 1892-93 only 11,000 attended them. In this and everything else to do with education, London lags far behind the provinces, just as England as a whole lags behind Scotland and even Ireland in this respect. As for fees for night schools, one of the previous boards, with a better composition than its predecessors, passed a resolution in July 1891 establishing free tuition in these schools. The new board, elected in November that year, quickly reversed that decision.

The high schools, as their name suggests, exist to give the cleverest and most able children, who have completed their ordinary schooling, the chance to continue their education. In this area too, London lags behind provincial cities. There are only three of them in London, when there should be at least forty. An interesting fact, incidentally, is that among the students who achieved a first-class mark in higher mathematics in Cambridge was one Miss Johnson, who received her elementary education in a state school.[13]

But the opponents of any broader system of education are guilty of many other, no less serious, sins. For example, they did not even make sure that there were enough school places for the children. The school board's own figures show a shortfall of 17,000 places.

The reactionaries' response to this is that concentrations of schools in one area makes up for a shortage of places in another area. But in a city like London with its chaotic omnibus traffic and dizzying whirlpool of all manner of goods traffic, with its enormous distances which are daunting even for adults, children cannot go to a school in another district. A more accurate calculation shows that London needs at least a few thousand more schools to meet the needs of the population. Additionally, these calculations reveal a fact studiously ignored by the reactionaries, that the school-age population of London is increasing by 11,000 annually.

The schools, moreover, are not adequately equipped. The number of teachers is quite insufficient for the number of pupils. The calculation is that for teaching to go well, there should be no more than forty pupils per teacher. Experienced teachers, however, find that figure excessive. In the high schools, the schools of the best sort, for the children of the middle classes, fifteen is considered the maximum number of pupils per teacher. But even on the most modest calculation, there is a shortfall of 400 teachers in London schools. We should remember that the great majority of children turn up at school in a state of extreme exhaustion as a result of poor nutrition. Moreover, conditions at home for most of these children are such as to develop many undesirable facets of their characters. Consequently, such children need a lot of attention in school, attention which cannot be given to them. In a class where the number of children can reach 100 or more, teachers have to spend their time not so much on teaching as on maintaining order. In addition, there is the almost unbelievable fact that in London schools there are not enough schoolbooks for all children. And this is why in 1894, in schools run by a board consisting of fifty-five esteemed citizens, we can encounter the same conditions Dickens described in Yorkshire schools fifty years ago.

The London School Board is also guilty of disregarding many essential sanitary rules and regulations. For example, ventilation in many schools is extremely poor. In the winter the board did not bother to heat the schools, despite the cold and the fact that many children turn up at school in thin clothes which do not protect against the cold, with holes in their shoes, and then cannot warm up at school. During the previous board's term of office it was constantly receiving reports from various schools that the premises were dirty and damp. All this was ignored, and, having successfully completed its term of office this year, shortly before the elections the board refused to approve the payment of a small sum spent by teachers on cutting and washing their pupils' hair. One board member, who had particularly insisted on the introduction of religious instruction, also supported a resolution which justified the refusal to reimburse the teachers' expenses on sorting out their pupils, on the grounds that such behaviour on the teachers' part reflected socialist theories.

This same board prevented the introduction of musical instruments into schools. A piano, of course, would be very useful in large schools, both for gymnastics and singing, especially in small classes. But the wise board decided otherwise. Its members, fretting over every penny, showed that a musical instrument is a luxury which cannot be permitted in a free school. There were great difficulties in getting the board to consider setting up swimming baths and swimming lessons. Besides the importance of swimming baths for hygienic reasons, there is another consideration – the great majority of London schoolchildren will then go on to work at the docks or on vessels, and it is therefore very important that they should be able to swim. In the end, the board agreed to constructing these baths and setting up swimming schools, but only in four districts.[14]

The board has taken a very hostile attitude to the working classes, even though the board itself is one of the major employers and needs lots of labour for building and repairing schools. However, throughout its term the board has sought to hinder trade unions. Board members have not wanted to recognise any agreement between building workers and their masters on wages and working hours. The board took on subcontractors and allowed them to conclude secondary contracts to perform work. Often a subcontractor, who had ostensibly undertaken to carry out construction works, subcontracted them again to a third party, who in turn subcontracted to a fourth. Such a system led both to the most shameless exploitation of the workers and to shoddy workmanship, with school buildings poorly built and unfit for purpose in sanitary terms.[15] Consequently there have been frequent outbreaks of epidemic illness in schools, which the sanitary inspectors have directly blamed on poor sanitary conditions. If there were no other charges to lay against the board, its dismal attitude towards maintaining schools and their sanitary arrangements would be enough to condemn it. We shall see what the new board does and whether, despite public opinion, it follows the old path, disregarding the children's most vital interests, taking a hostile stance to them and wasting time and energy on futile squabbles about irrelevant questions.

Besides the elections to the school board, all England has been excited recently by the first elections to the parish and district councils.[16] In accordance with the new Act of Parliament, these councils are to administer all the local affairs of the parish or district. The district council has the right to appoint officials and the obligation to take care of street cleaning, the state of repair of the roads, the fire engines etc. In addition, it is concerned with acquiring spaces for public games and recreation, setting up libraries, laundries, water supply and the observance of sanitary regulations in buildings and villages. Every parish with 300 or more inhabitants is to have its own council. A parish of between 100 and 300 inhabitants has the right to elect its own separate council only if a general meeting of parish members pass a resolution to do so. There was a case a short time ago in which a parish had recently become deserted as a mass of workers who had been living there constructing the Manchester Ship Canal left the village when their work was done. Only one resident remained, but as a member of the parish he could use his right to call a meeting and elect himself, thereby becoming the entire parish council.[17]

One of the most notable facts revealed by the parish council elections was the general defeat of the clerical element.[18] The elections took place at meetings, without ballots, by a show of hands. But where this method of election raised objections from even one person present, they decided to resort to secret ballot. In this way, none of the leading people in the rural areas – neither the employers, nor the farmers, nor the squires, nor the clergy, could know who was being voted for. Recently a vicar declared to his parishioners that he was prepared to serve on the parish council, but only on condition that his two chief assistants were also elected. The important thing was that there be no Nonconformists on the council. In many districts smallholders make up the bulk of the council. The ruling classes of rural society, the employers, farmers, squires and clergy are of course trying everything to prevent the population from deriving the full benefit from the new Act of Parliament. They are using all sorts of methods and tricks, and where possible the above-mentioned people are being helped by various institutions and large companies. One of the largest railway companies, Great Northern, has banned its employees from standing for district councils on pain of dismissal.[19]

The opening of Parliament is scheduled to take place soon, and consequently ministers have recently been frequently gathering for discussions. They have to devise their programmes for the coming session. But at present the position of the ministers in the Liberal cabinet seems hopeless.[20] There is widespread dissatisfaction within the Liberal Party itself over the fact that the cabinet has done so little and its promises have been so poorly fulfilled. Nobody has any idea what legislative measures will be presented to Parliament in the coming session. One of the newspapers which is fairly well informed about what is going on behind the scenes of politics has declared that the three main questions on which legislation will be brought before Parliament are as follows: payment of MPs, a long-promised new Factory Act, and a reform of London's local government. The so-called 'City of London' covers a very small part of London's total area. Six days a week all manner of business takes place in the City, mainly trading transactions. On Sundays the City is completely deserted. All around this small area, in every direction, there are the large local authorities of the real London, but the City, representing the London of antiquity, is run by a special jurisdiction, the Corporation, comprised of the richest and most reactionary of the City traders. The other local authorities are mainly under the jurisdiction of the London County Council, the members of which are elected by the citizens, including some women. Up to now this council has always been characterised by a progressive spirit in the best sense of the term. In the outermost London boroughs, so-called 'outer London', as distinct from the 'inner London' we have been discussing hitherto, there are suburbs which have their own separate local government. So now the question has been raised of unifying London, of uniting all the boroughs of outer London, inner London and the City under the jurisdiction of one single corporation, elected by all the citizens. Another newspaper, also considered well-informed on the intentions of the Liberal Party, has reported the 'worrying rumour' that the government intends in the next session to concern itself solely with the matter of the separation of church and state in the Principality of Wales, the land question in Ireland, and the question of controlling the sale of spirits. The uncertainty of the situation is reflected in the fact that this newspaper is demanding strict measures with regard to the House of Lords, which has been delaying the progress of Liberal legislation. However, there are huge differences within the Liberal Party itself regarding the ultimate aim of the agitation against the House of Lords. And it should be said that Lord Rosebery, the leader of the Liberal Party, gives no instructions on any of these questions which interest it. He either says nothing at all, or says something which does not please the Liberal Party. Nonetheless, to give him his due, whatever he does say, he says well. He is a genuinely fine speaker; with his clean-shaven face, his facility with gestures and facial expressions, his fine voice which he uses with great artistry, and his knowledge of all the oratorical tricks, he greatly resembles Coquelin the Elder.[21] He also has another statesmanlike quality, one which Disraeli had also perfected – the ability to speak a lot while saying nothing at all.[22]

The Tory Party is enthusiastically gearing up for the coming struggle, while the new workers' party, for all its diversity, its lack of discipline and the indistinctness of its aims and objectives, will doubtless play a notable role on the political scene in future. The main principle of this party, expressed by its best leaders, is its antagonism to both traditional political parties.[23] We shall discuss this new movement in greater detail on another occasion.

The London County Council, whose progressive direction we have already mentioned, recently took a very important decision for the social life of London. The council intends to consider the expediency and practicality of organising municipal pawnshops in London on the same basis as the Mont de Piété in France.[24] Up to now, moneylenders and pawnshops in England have been private enterprises aiming for individual profit. And the profit has always been very great, since the rates levied on loans from these institutions has been four times the rate charged on the continent. The resolution of the London County Council will of course meet with sharp opposition from all the moneylenders and pawnbrokers, of which there are many in England. The moneylenders have influence and, above all, money. For that reason, any measure which damages their interests will not get through without a stubborn fight. But if the various practical considerations which the London County Council will probably advance in this case can sway the English people, then the moneylenders and pawnbrokers will certainly lose this fight.

In case English political events are not of all-consuming interest, we propose to supplement our political commentary with some remarks on new English books which we think might be of interest to Russian readers.

Life's Little Ironies by Thomas Hardy (Osgood McIlvaine and Co., London, 4/6d) is the latest work by this writer, whom we consider to be one of the most remarkable contemporary English novelists.[25] The book consists of eight short stories, all under the above general title, and nine further even shorter ones under the general heading 'A few crusted characters' or 'Some colloquial sketches'. The title of the first eight longer stories completely corresponds to their content. Each of them is full of life, each deals with some event or other which serves to illustrate the author's main idea and confirm the eternal truth that we are all the playthings of fate. In this case the events which illustrate the author's idea do not concern large masses of people, but just individuals of no particular prominence. However, the events depicted by the author are quite vivid, even though they are confined to a narrow circle, and therefore they nonetheless make an impression. It is very difficult to convey the content of these short stories even in general terms, but we shall try to present the contents of one of them, although of course such a summary will necessarily suffer from sketchiness and will not give an impression of the subtlety and artistry of Hardy's work. The story we want to present is called 'The Melancholy Hussar', and is set in the first decade of this century, when George III was on the throne. At that time there was a German legion in the Royal Hanoverian Army, which was the main part of the division which accompanied the king to the coastal town of Weymouth in the south of England. Five miles from the soldiers' camp lived a doctor with his daughter, Phyllis. She is betrothed to the rich Englishman Gould, to whom she had given her word partly against her will. The fiancé had gone away to Bath, from where he writes to her regularly throughout the winter. His letters, however, have been completely dry and formal. Finally, Phyllis hears a rumour that her groom has cheated on her. Phyllis has a habit of sitting by the garden wall and looking down into the valley. This is where she is seen by the German corporal Matthaus Tina. The youngsters get to know each other and fall in love. But the girl's father will not hear of her marrying a German corporal, and threatens to send her away for ever to her aunt's house, which would be like a prison for her. The hussar persuades the young woman to run away with him. He is homesick and, together with his friend, another soldier, he decides to desert, take a boat across the Channel and go to the Continent. Phyllis agrees. At the appointed hour, at night, she goes to the designated place, where the deserter awaits her. But as luck would have it, at that very time and place her former fiancé Gould is passing. He has just returned from Bath and suspects nothing about his bride's betrayal. Phyllis, hidden from his view, sees him and overhears his conversation with his friend, from which she gathers that he has never cheated on her and is coming back to her full of love and hope. In the time between when she sees her fiancé and when her lover arrives as expected, Phyllis's feelings become clearer and she tells the hussar that she has changed her mind. He considers it dishonourable to insist, bows to her decision and leaves with his friend. Phyllis returns home. Gould appears and declares to her that he is already married. The rumour had been quite correct. Phyllis is miserable and sits by the garden wall for even longer than before. Then one day she sees that two graves have been dug at the military camp, and the hussars have formed a line. She then sees her beloved hussar and his friend brought out to be shot as deserters.

The second part of the book, consisting of nine short stories, is written in a conversational style. A few petty townsfolk, returning home, tell each other stories. There is much humour in these stories, as is Hardy's style, but there is also much real, profound drama. To convey in general outline the content of these stories is even more difficult than with the preceding ones, because in doing so one completely loses the impression they create. It is impossible in a dry summary to convey all the subtleties and give a correct understanding of the drama of the situation, just as although one scene of Hamlet might be the greatest exemplar of dramatic style in literature, it cannot on its own convey the character of that great work. One would first have to tell the whole story and be familiar with all the unusually complex and diverse feelings and sensations of the dramatis personae.

Every character Hardy creates is so individual, and so inter-twined with the story itself, that it becomes an inalienable component of the dramatic situation which develops in the story. One can say of these stories, as of Polonius, 'they say, he made a good end'. Hardy always concludes his tales very skilfully with a 'dramatic ending'. For example, the final lines of his 'Melancholy Hussar' are 'The older villagers, however, who know of the episode from their parents, still recollect the place where the soldiers lie. Phyllis lies near.' But a 'dramatic ending' does not always leave a sense of completion. Like Ibsen's plays, many of Hardy's works finish with a question mark.

This collection of short stories, like many of Hardy's works, was sharply attacked by some critics. Certain passages were declared to be indecent. These gentlemen particularly objected to the following sentence: 'That he had been able to seduce another woman in two days was his crowning though unrecognised fascination for her as the she-animal.' It is however strange that a similar phrase could be found in the altogether respectable journal The Spectator 180 years ago. In a letter, supposedly written by a widow, we find the lines: 'There was a young guards officer who had seduced two or three of my acquaintances, and I could not help feeling a little flat-tered when he started paying attention to me.' Hardy has an intense aversion to all conventions 'which serve only to prettify one's shady affairs and keep up appearances'. As Hardy put it: 'To succeed in the Church, people must believe in you, first of all, as a gentleman, secondly as a man of means, thirdly as a scholar, fourthly as a preacher, fifthly, perhaps, as a Christian – but always first as a gentleman, with all their heart and soul and strength.'

In all of Hardy's writings one is struck by his remarkable powers of observation. This ability is clearly manifest even in his very short stories. Each character, each situation is depicted very vividly and distinctly. Unlike with certain other writers, one could not exchange one character for another. For instance, in this little scene: a group of four people set out to sea in a sailing boat; two of them start to feel seasick. Looking at the nauseated features of this old man and young woman, the young woman's beloved notices how they resemble one another and realises that they must be father and daughter.

Av.

Notes

1. Edward Aveling's election to the Board in November 1882 for the Westminster division was supported by H.M. Hyndman and the Democratic Federation and Chushichi Tsuzuki suggests this election campaign saw him 'initiated into the organised Socialist movement'. Following his election Edward said: 'Westminster includes Soho, Peabody buildings, Seven Dials and the voices of the dwellers in such places as these are faintly heard: for over-work and under-pay, hardship and sickness stifle them. I want to speak especially for such as these. The poor, the wronged, the untaught are, above all, my constituents.' Chushichi Tsuzuki, *The Life of Eleanor Marx 1855-1898: A Socialist Tragedy*, Clarendon: Oxford, 1967, p90.

2. This 'compromise' was devised by William Francis Cowper-Temple (1811-1888), a British Liberal politician whose amendment to the Elementary Education Bill assuaged some fears of the Non-conformists that their children would be compulsorily instructed in Anglican doctrine. The clause meant that religious education in board schools would be non-denominational. The LSB confirmed its endorsement of unsectarian religious teaching in 1871 with a resolution moved by W.H. Smith and Samuel Morley which 'was left intentionally vague, no attempt made to define the doctrines and principles to be taught. The interpretation of the rule was left to the good taste and common sense of the teacher'. Hugh B. Philpott, *London at School: The Story of the School Board 1870-1904*, London: T. Fisher Unwin, 1904, pp100-01. The view that these questions contributed to the defeat of Gladstone and the Liberal party in the 1874

general election because of the desertion of Nonconformist voters has been extensively debated and is usefully summarised in Ian St. John, *The Historiography of Gladstone and Disraeli*, Anthem Press: London, 2016, pp135-6.

3. Dissenters were Nonconformist Christians who were adherents to Protestantism, but outside the Anglican church. Nonconformity was closely associated with the Liberal party in the nineteenth century.

4. *The Pilgrim's Progress* was, of course, written by John Bunyan.

5. John Laird Mair Lawrence, 1st Baron Lawrence (1811-1879) was a former Viceroy of India who became first chairman of the LSB between 1870 and 1873. Sir Charles Reed (1819-1881) was a London-born Nonconformist businessman who as a Liberal represented Hackney in Parliament between 1868 and 1874. Reed was elected to the LSB and became its chairman in 1873, an office he held until his death in 1881. Dr Joseph Angus (1816-1902) was a Baptist minister and educationalist elected to the LSB in 1870. Samuel Morley (1809-1886) was a London-born Congregationalist who as a Liberal sat as MP for Bristol between 1868 and 1885. He served on the LSB in between 1870 and 1876. William Henry Smith (1825-1891) was a newsagent and politician, and Conservative Member of Parliament for Westminster between 1868 and 1885, He was elected to the LSB in 1871. Smith latterly served in several Conservative governments. Thomas Henry Huxley (1825-1895) was a renowned biologist and evolutionist who served on the London School Board between 1870 and 1872.

6. The donor of the annual prize for Scripture was Francis Peek (1834-1899), not a factory owner but a wealthy tea and coffee merchant who served on the LSB between 1873 and 1879. Peek gifted £5,000 in 1876 to establish prizes, awarded by the Religious Tract Society, for annual Bible examinations in LSB schools.

7. Robin Betts dates the coalescing of two distinct parties on the LSB to the second election of 1873: 'the Progressives, devoted to expansion and efficiency of the Board schools, and the Moderates, containing a number of clergy (some of whom were mainly concerned to protect the voluntary schools from board school competition) and also a group dedicated to keeping the local rate low...'. Robin Betts, *Dr Macnamara 1861-1931*, Liverpool University Press: Liverpool, 1999, p59.

8. Here the authors were probably referring to the socialists who stood as candidates, some as stated members of the Social Democratic Federation, the Independent Labour Party or on a 'Labour' ticket, but clearly independent of the Progressive 'slate' in the 1894 LSB election: Daniel Hennessy (Chelsea); Mary Bridges Adams (Greenwich);

Annie Thompson (Tower Hamlets); G.A. Gibson (Marylebone); J.E. Dobson (East Lambeth); H.W. Hobart (Finsbury); Thornton Smith (Southwark); Rose Jarvis (Hackney); George H. Young and Edith Lanchester (West Lambeth). Lanchester's candidature was interesting given her friendship and employment with Eleanor Marx Aveling. Yvonne Kapp, *Eleanor Marx: The Crowded Years (1884-1898)*, Lawrence and Wishart: London, 1976, p621. Lanchester polled 3,969 votes, finishing ninth in a six-member division. Soon after the elections, Harry Quelch, editor of *Justice*, the weekly newspaper of the Social Democratic Federation, emphasised the near doubling of the socialist vote since 1891. He attributed the failure to secure at least one seat to: 'the fact that many of their most advanced friends, to whom they could reasonably look for support, had been led away into giving their support to the Progressives. It was simply the old conflict between the Church and Nonconformity over again.' *Reynolds's Newspaper*, 2 December 1894, p3. Three Fabian Society members were elected standing on the Progressive 'slate': Graham Wallas and Stewart Headlam (Hackney) and the Rev. W.A. Oxford (Westminster).

9. Electors in the LSB area could cast votes equal to the number of seats in the multi-member division where they were registered. The LSB area was made up of eleven divisions from which came fifty-five elected members making up the Board. Women ratepayers were entitled to vote and be nominated for election to the Board and in 1894, four women Progressives were elected. The turnout of forty per cent was double that of the 1891 election.

10. The LSB 'compromise' on religious instruction composed by Smith and Morley in 1871 operated without any significant controversy until challenged by board member Athelstan Riley (1858-1945), who was backed by the board chairman, the Rev. Joseph Diggle (1849-1917), in November 1892. Riley, a high-church Anglican, insisted that in teaching Scripture children should be instructed that Christ was God, and that this could only be undertaken by those who had received training in the principles of religion. The matter was discussed repeatedly during 1893 and 1894, significantly disrupting the essential work of managing London's schools. Thomas Macnamara (1861-1931), a protagonist in the dispute in his capacity as editor of the National Union of Teachers' journal, latter commented on these events: 'During the years 1893 and 1894 a terrible "religious" warfare raged at Board meetings. What it was all about most people could never quite understand. During the two years the proper work of the Board was almost entirely neglected; the weekly meetings would

have justified the reading of the Riot Act; the number of memo-
rials and protests ran the printer's bill for 1894 up to ten thousand
pounds, and all London looked on helpless and ashamed', Thomas
R. Macnamara, 'Three years of Progressivism at the London School
Board', *Fortnightly Review*, November 1900, Vol 68, Issue 407, p791. A
Board circular requiring teachers to affirm their Christian dogma in
their Scripture teaching was issued in the spring of 1894, creating a
major dispute with the Metropolitan Board Teachers' Association,
which protested against the instruction on the grounds that it questioned teacher professionalism and set up a possible 'test' under
which staff could be dismissed. Even within the Anglican community there was division on the Board's circular, with backing from
the London Diocesan Conference but not the Bishop of London,
who considered it a 'great mistake'. J.E.B. Munson, 'The London
School Board Election of 1894: A study in religious controversy',
British Journal of Educational Studies, February 1975, Vol. 23, No. 1,
p12. The religious instruction issue took centre stage in the election
campaign of 1894 and featured prominently in the influential publication, *The Case Against Diggleism*, produced by the Progressives
School Board Election Council during the summer of that year.

11. Following the 1894 election the religious instruction controversy
faded, leaving teachers to continue much as before. Macnamara
1900, p792. After the Progressive victory at the 1897 election the
circular, 'which had already long been a dead letter', was quietly
withdrawn from the board's standing orders. Philpott 1904, p110.

12. The authors' reference here to 'Radical supporters of the present
government' relates to those Liberal elected members, supporters
and sympathisers – sometimes called 'Radicals' or 'Advanced
Liberals' – who wanted the government to implement its full programme of political and social change agreed at its conference in
1891. One such was Arthur Herbert Dyke Acland (1847-1926), a politician and educational reformer, who served as Education Minister in
the Liberal government of 1892-1895. Under Acland's leadership the
number of children benefiting from free education increased, the
school leaving age was raised to thirteen, and the curriculum liber-
alised. A co-operator and pioneer of the Oxford University Extension
Movement, Acland's syllabus for evening schools, *The Life and Duties
of a Citizen*, 'reflected his belief in the democratic power of education'. Anne Oakwell, 'Acland, Sir Arthur Herbert Dyke (1847-1926)',
Oxford Dictionary of National Biography, Oxford University Press:
Oxford, 2018. Acland was one of the few Liberal ministers exempted
from criticism by the Fabians George Bernard Shaw and Sidney

Webb, in their broadside of November 1893 against Gladstone's government. They wrote that Acland 'has been one of the successes of the present Government, and has done pretty nearly as well at the Education Office as Sir William Harcourt will allow' (Harcourt was Chancellor of the Exchequer). 'To Your Tents, Oh Israel', *Fortnightly Review*, November 1893, Vol. 54, No. 323, p578.

13. Ada Maria Jane Elizabeth Johnson (1872-1947), Cambridge-born daughter of a University College cook who attended the Park Street Board school in the city before matriculating to Newnham College in 1889. Johnson graduated with a first-class mathematics degree in 1893 and went on to postgraduate study in Germany.

14. The litany of neglect and underfunding of board schools by the Moderate administration of 1891-1894 was well-publicised during the election campaign of 1894. As well as creating a state of near paralysis, critics accused the board of deliberately undermining the state system in favour of the Anglican voluntary schools. Athelstan Riley's remarks of March 1892 were quoted as evidence of this: 'So long as we are forced to pay rates to the exclusive support of education to which we are contentiously opposed...so long as our own money is taken to establish and develop rival schools, which are ruining, by excessive competition, the schools which we have maintained so long... an appeal to us to concur in providing the Board schools with the luxuries and refinements of education, to temper as it were the knife which is held to our throats, the very weapon of our own destruction, can hardly be regarded as anything, but a very ill-timed pleasantry'. Quoted in Clem Edwards, 'Diggleism indicted', *The Londoner*, 29 September 1894, No. 2, p4.

15. In December 1888 the LSB had been the first elected authority to consider the wages and conditions of staff employed by contractors tendering for Board work. The board accepted the argument made by members Annie Besant, Rev. Stewart Headlam and Benjamin Lucraft and others that they had a duty to deal only with contractors who paid a fair wage that was recognised in the trade. The board rescinded this policy in the summer of 1892, provoking a campaign led by the Amalgamated Society of House Painters and Decorators. Following the 1894 elections a new 'fair wage' clause was adopted based on the schedule of wages agreed by the London Building Trades Federation and the Master Builders' Association.

16. The Local Government Act 1894 reformed the parlous state of administration in rural England and Wales. Villages with a population of more than 300 had a duty to set up an elected parish council to conduct parochial administration and above this, district coun-

cils were elected to oversee public health and planning issues. Many socialists and radicals were alive to the potential of these reforms, believing the new bodies could become instruments of local democracy against the traditional rural establishment dominated by landowners, farmers and the clergy.

17. This was the village of Netherpool in Cheshire, where at the 1891 Census the population was more than three hundred, made up almost exclusively of navvies working on the Manchester Ship Canal. The navvies departed when the canal was completed at the end of 1893, leaving only one family in Netherpool, who the newspapers amusingly suggested could form their own parish council. *Manchester Courier and Lancashire General Advertiser*, 28 April 1894, p14.

18. One contemporary survey of the first parish council election results found that 'the most striking fact, because it has been so universal, is the reprobation of the clerical power which the rural people of England have deliberately, and with the most unanimity pronounced'. Richard Heath, 'The rural revolution', *Contemporary Review*, February 1895, Vol. 67, p198.

19. It was reported in early December 1894 that the station master at Hatfield railway station had posted a notice stating that the regulation of the Great Northern Railway Company did not permit employees to be members of parish councils. It was believed locally that a number of the railway servants would be elected in the forthcoming election. One of these employees wrote to a newspaper protesting at the infringement of citizen rights, stating that: 'Half the cottages in the old Town are a disgrace ... Horses in the immediate neighbourhood are housed under more sanitary conditions than some of our fellow creatures. The Parish Council Act has come to us as a ray of hope', only to be told by the company that he could not contest the election. He went on: 'I wish to know in the name of humanity and civilization on what grounds? Are we to be sold to the company both body and soul?'. *Herts Advertiser*, 1 December 1894, p7.

20. Parliament opened on 5 February 1895. On that day Eleanor wrote to Natalie Liebknecht from the apartment in Gray's Inn Square that: 'Today Parliament opens: but what will happen no one can say. Everything (politically) is at sixes and sevens'. Georg Eckert (ed.), *Wilhelm Liebknecht: Briefwechsel mit Karl Marx und Friedrich Engels*, Mouton & Co.: The Hague, 1963, p437.

21. Benoit-Constant Coquelin (1841-1909), eminent French actor who first played in London in 1878 at the Gaiety Theatre and returned

many times thereafter. It is highly probable that the authors saw him perform on numerous occasions through the eighties and nineties.

22. The Queen's Speech of 5 February 1895 included proposals to amend the Factory Acts, reform London local government, disestablish the Welsh church, amend landlord and tenant relations in Ireland, and control the liquor trade, all measures which John Davis describes as 'contentious and intricate and therefore vulnerable in Parliament – by a government with a slender and dwindling majority' that 'indicated that most were being aired to encourage their supporters with little prospect of success'. John Davis, 'Primrose, Archibald Philip, fifth earl of Rosebery and first early of Midlothian', *Oxford Dictionary of National Biography*, Oxford University Press: Oxford, 2018.

23. The authors refer to the Independent Labour Party established in January 1893.

24. In July 1894 the Progressive-controlled London County Council began a review into the possibility of establishing municipal pawnshops, often described as 'poor man's banks'. The idea was enthusiastically supported by Robert Donald, editor of the Progressive-supporting weekly journal *London: A Journal of Civic and Social Progress*, who argued that municipal pawnshops were feasible and would provide the poor with loans on comparable terms to those of the well-off who went to banks for credit. Donald proposed the Paris Mont de Piété as a model for the LCC to follow. Robert Donald, 'Why not municipal pawnshops?', *Contemporary Review,* August 1894, Vol. 66, pp177-91, and 'How to municipalise the pawnshops', *New Review,* December 1894, Vol. 11, No. 67, pp581-93. In April 1896, almost two years after commencing the investigation, the LCC decided that the proposition of municipalising pawnshops was impractical.

25. Thomas Hardy's *Life's Little Ironies* was published in February 1894 to generally favourable reviews. Eleanor told Natalie Liebknecht that the book was 'delightful' and Edward had earlier written positively about Hardy's *Tess of the d'Ubervilles*. Eckert 1963, pp437-8, Tsuzuki 1967, p252.

LETTER TWO

February 1895

The letter begins with a discussion of parish council elections in England. Socialists welcomed the establishment of parish and rural district councils in 1894, believing they would help extend democratic practices to backward rural areas where the interests of landowners, farmers and clergymen traditionally held sway. Encouraged by the first tranche of elections to these new bodies apparently demonstrating that agricultural workers and others were prepared to challenge the squirearchy, Eleanor and Edward hoped this would be just the first stage in the transformation of the countryside.

They similarly regarded the initiatives of progressive municipal bodies, such as those of the London County Council, as worthy of support. Such innovations materially improved the lives of workers, made clear the potential of political action by labour, and presented a model for how society could be differently organised.

In contrast, market capitalism was presented in this letter as giving rise to urban and rural poverty, slum housing, inadequate health care, dangerous places of work and greedy venture capitalist enterprises, exemplified by the account of the Sapphire and Ruby Company of Montana.

With what appears to be some relish, the letter gives a detailed account of Annie Besant's involvement since 1889 in the Theosophical Society, drawing heavily on an expose recently published in the Westminster Gazette. *Having closely collaborated with Besant in his days in the National Secular Society which ended in an acrimonious break in 1884, Edward took the leading part in composing this account of what he regarded as her delusions and those of Theosophical Society members, whom, he reports, she considered 'idiots and fools'.*

As in their contribution of January, one senses the influence of Eleanor in the concluding literary review section of this second letter, with two of her favourites receiving attention. The death of Robert Louis Stevenson is marked with a eulogy to his work, which Eleanor regarded as 'natural and complete' and 'close to genius'.

Eleanor also applauded the recent novel by friend Clementina Black, An Agitator, telling the story of a workers' leader's involvement in an industrial dispute, which she said was 'the only true picture of a strike in England that I have come across in fiction'.

In our previous letter we reported on various elections which had been taking place recently in England, including on the elections to the new parish councils. Of course, it is impossible to describe these innumerable elections in detail, but we think it is worthwhile to inform our readers about certain overall results. The most important consequence of the parish council elections was a return to the old ways of doing things. In the distant past, boroughs and villages in England enjoyed self-government in the fullest sense of the term, but this then changed little by little, and for a long time the people were almost completely deprived of self-government, and even forgot about their erstwhile rights. They began to talk about parish councils as some innovation invented by radicals. In fact, however, the English people have simply regained what they had previously enjoyed.[1]

Voting by show of hands, it seems, is not favoured by the workers and their supporters. Several resolutions condemning this method of voting even as a preliminary measure had already been passed, since it represents a violation of the principle of the law on ballots. The following concrete case shows better than any abstract considerations how necessary it is in fact to make changes in this respect. At one electoral meeting a squire was put forward as a candidate. The usual method of voting by show of hands did not at first go that candidate's way, but when he stood up and stared pointedly at the benches at the back where the workers were sitting, a mass of hands was immediately raised.[2]

The results of the parish council elections for Norfolk, a typical agricultural county, are very characteristic of this present time. Of 230 parishes, thirty-nine did not have the minimum population of 300 required to gain the right to one's own parish council. Great interest in the elections was noticeable everywhere, and in forty-nine parishes the electoral struggle was very heated. There were only two cases where the farmers and officials of the parish seemed indifferent to the elections and did not turn up to a meeting consisting almost entirely of the local working population. Having waited an hour for these gentlemen to appear, the workers at the meeting moved to the vote and elected three agricultural workers: three ordinary workers, one farmer and the local postmaster, to the parish council.[3] But the most outstanding fact, without any doubt, must be the disappearance from rural life, as far as it is reflected in parish council elections, of the clergymen who had previously played such a prominent part in village affairs. In one village where the blacksmith and two workers got the largest number of votes, the clergyman got only three votes and immediately declared the meeting to be a biased and scandalous assembly.[4] In ninety-two parishes for which we have full information about the professions of the elected council members, 185 are workers, 165 are farmers, only seventeen are clergymen and twenty-two are 'gentlemen' – presumably, the local squires. Most of the elected workers (25.8 per cent) are agricultural workers, which can be accounted for by the fact that Norfolk is a mainly agricultural county. For every one gentleman councillor there are nine workers and for every vicar – eleven. It should not be forgotten that previously the clergyman and the squire were, so to speak, the village autocrats. Consequently, the election results outlined above are of enormous significance as an important step in freeing the people from the heavy yoke they are under, and, of course, the creation of the parish councils has played its part in this.[5]

There have been some very characteristic episodes in these elections. In one village, for example, the vicar ordered the schoolmaster to leave his post on the grounds that at a parish meeting the teacher had dared to call the clergyman to order.[6] In one parish a travelling whelk-seller – whelks are eaten by the very poorest people – was elected against the local brewer.[7]

As for the elections to the boards of guardians[8] and the parish administrations, we shall discuss only the results for London, as the most reactionary city. In both sets of elections the reactionary parties gained a majority, especially in the elections to the parish councils, in London known as vestries. This happened because

the working class is still not fully conscious of the power that
the new regulations have given it. A few years ago the members
of the vestries were various petty shopkeepers, not for the most
part distinguished for their honesty. For them parish business was
just a cover for wheeling and dealing, which meant that no honest
person would want the stigma of being a member of a vestry.[9] The
result of this state of affairs was an increase in child mortality
in the most densely populated boroughs, through which two of
London's main streets run. This increase in mortality is entirely
the result of the negligent attitude of the members of the administration towards their responsibilities. The Augean stables of
London urgently demand to be cleared out. We have miles of filthy
streets, densely inhabited by people who are both physically and
morally sick. Myriad courtyards and alleys fill the space between
the main thoroughfares, and in slum dwellings the inhabitants live
and die in cramped closets, eating meagre and unhealthy rations
and poisoning themselves with noxious beverages. The streets
stink, the courtyards and alleyways that come off them smell even
worse, not to speak of the buildings themselves, overcrowded with
poor inhabitants. Up to now not one serious step has been taken by
the parish administrations to alleviate this state of affairs, which,
unfortunately, is the norm for life in London. Nonetheless, to the
credit of London County Council we should say that it has to an
extent tried to relieve poverty. Over the past six years (1889-1895)
the construction of around one thousand new improved dwelling
houses for the poor population has been started or completed, and
a large building for looking after homeless paupers was built. Many
landlords who own property in the poorest and worst districts of
London have been obliged by the council to repair and improve
their buildings, in which the poor of London reside. This has been
done, albeit very reluctantly. Certain sanitary projects have also
been carried out by the council. The course of the Thames has been
cleaned up, and common bleak is again being caught in stretches
where previously there was only filth on the surface of the water,
gushing out of waste pipes. Among the other useful things done by
the LCC we should mention the setting aside of 1,000 more acres
of land for open spaces and parks, called 'the lungs of London'. In
addition, the reign of the contractors is over, as the council now

employs its own workforce directly. A gigantic undertaking to construct a tunnel under the Thames for goods and pedestrians is now half-finished and all this can be credited to the LCC.[10]

A report on the situation of the poor and sick in workhouses was published recently. It would have produced a feeling of national indignation in the hearts of the English had they not already become accustomed to reading reports of this nature. This report was published by Smith, Elder and Co. and for all those concerned with the fate of the poor and sick, it makes very interesting reading.[11] What is revealed in the report creates a depressing and horrific impression, but the worst of it is that this report is not the result of some official investigation, but a private initiative. The local authorities, it would seem, wanted to conceal this state of affairs. However, the systematic investigation carried out by certain newspapers, and in particular the *British Medical Journal*, has cast light on these shady matters. The reports of those sent by their editors to examine these institutions show that everywhere conditions are very poor. There is inadequate isolation of inmates with infectious diseases, poor care or even no care at all, and dreadful sanitary conditions. Here, for example, is how things stand in Haverfordwest, Pembrokeshire, in Wales. On narrow beds made up of three planks, on straw mattresses three inches thick, lie sick paupers from sixteen parishes. There is just one untrained nurse looking after them during the day, at night there is nobody. Thus these helpless sick people, old men and women, mostly covered in bedsores, lie in their uncomfortable beds for hours in the dark – the lights are put out at night – without any care, unfed and filthy! There are unlucky idiots and harmless lunatics here as well. In the orphanage for poor children the stone floor is not even covered with matting on which babies could crawl. In Bath, Somerset, one of the most fashionable English towns, with its squares and boulevards filled with wealthy Anglo-Indians, retired officers and unmarried ladies dressed in silks and velvets, the conditions in its hospital for the poor are as bad as everywhere else. In the hospital there are sixteen wards with 230 beds, mainly filled with the seriously ill. During the day, for the entire hospital, there is one trained nurse and two assistants on duty from six in the morning to ten at night. At night there is just one nurse for 230 beds. It has to be asked: why, given the developed system of inspection which exists in local government, was it left to private individuals to expose all these abuses? These facts raised a certain fuss in the papers and, indeed, some of the more assiduous Members of Parliament will carry out an Inquiry in the House of Commons, but, if the past is any guide, it is hardly likely that anything substantial will be done in this regard. In England we are used to these periodic exposures of various horrors and short-lived bursts of indignation. In 1865 something similar was exposed in the London hospitals for the poor, but it did not lead to any improvement in the way hospitals were organised in rural areas.[12] Maybe, given the new composition of the boards of guardians following the elections, something will be done.

In official reports, explosions in mines are always 'accidental'. But if you talk to miners 'unofficially', you discover from them that the great majority of these 'accidents' in mines could have been avoided if those who are responsible for ensuring that all the precautions and regulations around working with machinery, ventilation etc. are observed, really carried out their job properly. But there is an exception to the rule about official accounts of mining accidents, and that is the report on the terrible disaster in the coal mines near Pontypridd, Glamorgan, in Wales. This report recommends prosecution of the mine management, the agent and the company itself for non-compliance with the regulations laid down in the Coal Mines Regulation Act.[13] Of course, a powerful coal mining company, with the help of money and influence, can escape the reach of the law, but nonetheless it should be said that here in England the position is somewhat better than in Austria. Almost the day after the dreadful catastrophe in Pontypridd, which cost 288 lives, a similar disaster happened in the county of Larisch, Austria. But in Austria there was not even an attempt to prosecute those responsible, even though there, as in England, the accident resulted from the negligent attitude of those in charge towards their responsibilities.[14]

The imposing name of the 'Sapphire and Ruby Company Montana', supported by gentlemen and aristocrats with similarly imposing names, has not stopped that company and its transactions from being somewhat 'shady'. This case is fairly typical. The subscribed capital was £450,000, a small part of which, £25,000, was allocated for working the mines. This means that £425,000 has disappeared. Among the founders of the company are such figures as the Earl of Lorne, the Count of Leinster, the Earl of Breadalbane, the Count of Portland, Lord Chelmsford, Sir Francis Knollys (secretary to the Prince of Wales), one or two more baronets, and various other figures from English high society. Of course, these founders should bear legal liability towards the other shareholders. But when the time came to investigate how things stood, the shares of all these gentlemen were concealed and at the recent general meeting of the company, chaired by Lord Chelmsford, this noble lord stated that the board of directors stood accused of having exploited big names as a trap, and then addressed the shareholders, asking that they be 'lenient' towards the directors. One of the most disgruntled shareholders involved in the investigation commission could only reply that the directors in this case had shown surprising naïveté, and that the consequences of their actions were such as to raise suspicions that the whole company had been formed solely to swindle people out of their money. Since this disgruntled shareholder has now been appointed to the board, in all probability the other shareholders will hear something about what has happened to their capital.[15] The English aristocracy has often been involved in setting up all manner of industrial companies. A letter written as far back as 1574 by the Earl of Leicester shows that even then the aristocracy was not averse to taking part in 'Muscovite enterprises'. The earl declared that if he had had another £10,000 in his purse, he would have invested the lot.[16]

There is bad news from Ireland. The potato harvest has failed, and this means that by the end of January the entire harvest will have been eaten and the Irish will be threatened with famine and an inability to sow for next year, given the complete absence of potatoes. Despite the fact that in one of the leading newspapers an article appeared in December depicting the misery of the Irish and in effect calling for assistance to them, nobody in England has responded to that call.[17] This is a sad, but very significant fact. It is quite possible that the wealthy classes in England will excuse their indifference to the Irish with the claim that they need to provide assistance at home. But they do not do that either. Alas, poverty in

England is increasing all the time, and this is a shameful fact which cannot be denied. For example, in 1894 alone the London police recorded 444 cases of attempted suicide: in round figures there are about as many successful suicides. The number of the very poorest people in our massive city is constantly around 100,000, and it should be borne in mind that not all of them get recorded in the lists of private charities. There are reckoned to be 30,000 prostitutes, but in all probability the figure is twice that. The homeless and unemployed outside of the working classes who have not yet entered the ranks of the criminals number around 70,000; there are around 100,000 regular workers without current employment, 12,000 criminals in prison and another 15,000 outside prison. Around 70,000 people commit petty offences every year. These are the bald figures for London alone. Experts on the question assert that similar conditions exist across the country. According to police figures for 1894, 200 people died from hunger.[18] This figure should have been doubled, to include those cases of death where exhaustion, brought about by chronic undernourishment, was not the least important factor. An individual case or a chance remark can sometimes illustrate the situation better than statistics. A child died in Whitechapel from exhaustion as a result of undernourishment. The doctor who carried out the autopsy made the following meaningful comment on the case: 'We do not usually admit these sorts of cases of exhaustion into hospital, otherwise at this time of year we would have to admit the entire population of Whitechapel'.[19]

Lord Randolph Churchill has been diagnosed with a disease of the spinal cord and the doctors hold out no hope for his recovery. *[Editorial footnote in the original: Lord Churchill has since died.]* In this way a remarkably brilliant political career is coming to an end. In 1886, Lord Randolph Churchill, then thirty-seven years of age, was already serving as Chancellor of the Exchequer in the Tory government and was leader of the House of Commons. Whether he had the necessary qualities to be the leader of one of the ancient political parties is doubtful, to say the least. In any case, he had too much originality, and this originality sometimes expressed itself in ways which were uncomfortable both for his allies and his opponents, as he did not hold back from addressing his critical remarks to them. He was the only one of the Tory leaders who wanted to realise Disraeli's old idea of establishing Tory democracy.[20] For this reason, the Marquis of Salisbury was not too upset when Churchill, presumably wrongly believing himself to be indispensable, quit his ministerial post. Despite this departure and the fact that the official leaders of the Tory Party regarded him with concealed hostility, Lord Randolph Churchill would probably have played a prominent part in political affairs if only he had not suffered from chronic alcoholism. The English papers had hitherto discreetly concealed this sad truth, but now that drunkenness has brought the noble lord to *tabes dorsalis*, the papers can at last call this disease by its real name.[21]

A large scandal has occurred with the Theosophical Society. Russian readers cannot fail to be interested in this, since the history of the Theosophical Society indirectly involves them.[22] The founder of this society is a Russian, Elena Petrovna Blavatsky. The Society was founded in 1874 in New York. In 1878 its headquarters was moved to India. In 1884 Mme Blavatsky moved to England, and was for a time very much in fashion. Everywhere she announced that she was able to produce phenomena of a spiritualist nature. In England there is also a Society for Psychical Research which devotes all its energy to hunting all sorts of spectres. This society proposed to examine the phenomena of Mme Blavatsky and to that end sent a representative, one Mr Hodgson of St John's College in Cambridge, off to India, where these phenomena had been most numerous and vivid. It is beyond doubt that neither the society, nor its representative, were prejudiced against the theosophists.[23] The psychical researchers are hungry for any kind of spiritualist phenomenon and are never happier than when they come across an occurrence which can be considered entirely trustworthy. But alas! That was not the case with the theosophists. Even the theosophists' own house servants gave evidence against them. 'When thieves fall out, honest men come by their own', as the English proverb puts it. Mme Blavatsky had quarrelled with her accomplices, Mr and Mrs Coulomb, and when Hodgson arrived in India he discovered Mrs Coulomb in full flow with her revelations. She was writing articles about Blavatsky in the Madras papers and, worse still, had published letters to her from Blavatsky, full of coded instructions concerning various conjuring tricks they had carried out in India between 1878 and 1883. It was shown beyond all doubt, and even Mme Blavatsky admitted, that her famous 'altar'-shrine in her house in Adyar served as a secret cupboard with a movable back wall. Mme Blavatsky said that this had been done to make it easier to pack up if she were to move house. One could dare compare the late Blavatsky with Reynard the fox – she could never be caught and for every unfortunate circumstance she could find an explanation and people would believe in her again. The shrine hung just above a secret door built into the wall; on the other side of the door was a sideboard with a false back which exited directly into Blavatsky's bedroom. The Coulombs were perfect material for all manner of trickery. The high priestess of the Theosophists once wrote a letter to Mrs Coulomb saying that she had her eye on a very wealthy potential convert, but only a first-class miracle would convince him once and for all. On one occasion, when this intended prize was innocently drinking tea with Mme Blavatsky, the latter, as if by accident, dropped her cup. The cup was smashed to pieces; moreover, it was the only cup of its type. In a previous conversation, Mme Blavatsky had drawn her interlocutor's attention to this fact. Of course, this gave the Mahatma[24] cause to express his favour and sympathy for Blavatsky. The fragments were carefully collected and reverently placed into the shrine, the doors of which were then closed. A few minutes later the doors were opened again and – what a surprise! – in place of the fragments there was a whole cup. The doubting convert was finally convinced. Coulomb states that for that trick two completely identical cups were purchased on a certain day in a certain shop. In the shopkeeper's record book it is actually stated that he sold the goods that day to Mrs Coulomb.

Despite these revelations about its past, the Theosophical Society can still count between three and four thousand members in Europe, India and America, and publishes several magazines in various languages. The three main theosophical magazines are the private property of the three leaders of theosophy: Colonel Olcott, Mr William Judge and Annie Besant.[25] Moreover, the society owns property in New York, Adyar, London and elsewhere. In the recent weeks there have been new scandals in the Theosophical Society. But it seems that no matter how large the scandal, it will not affect either the number of members or the position of the society itself.

This scandal has led to new revelations in the *Westminster Gazette*, but its main interest lies in the fact that the three personages at the head of the Theosophical Society are levelling accusations at one another.

Blavatsky died in London in May 1891. Her mantle was divided, after a certain amount of tussling, between Olcott, the president of the society, Judge, the vice president, and Annie Besant.[26] It should be said, by the way, that all three of them possess the necessary qualities. In Olcott, the element of the madman predominates, in Judge, the element of the con-man, and as for Annie Besant, well, nobody would accuse her of being mad. According to Carlyle, the label of madman can be applied to most of the English, and this does indeed seem to be the case when we consider how the press and the public accept as true everything that Annie Besant says about herself. She poses as the very epitome of truth and virtue, and even today those writers who present irrefutable facts against her nonetheless act as her apologists. Here are some facts which can be cited against the heiress of Blavatsky. On 30 August 1891, three months after the death of Blavatsky, Miss Besant made the following public statement: 'you have all known me for sixteen and a half years, and have never heard a lie from me. And I tell you that after the death of Blavatsky, I started receiving letters in the same hand as the letters I received from her.' These letters were coming through the air from the Mahatmas, who were sending them from the Gobi Desert.[27] To one interviewer who visited her, Miss Besant said that these letters 'came down from on high'.[28] But later, at one of the private gatherings of Theosophists, she admitted that something was not right with these letters. Then she began to accuse Judge of having forged them. Nonetheless, she did not have the courage to declare publicly that what she had said on 30 August 1891 was incorrect and that she had realised she had been deceived. The change in her attitude to Judge, through whom she had received the letters from the Mahatmas, took place shortly after her visit to India and meeting with a certain Chakravarti.[29] One of the writers on the *Weekly Despatch* observed of Annie Besant that with her one should always remember the aphorism 'cherchez la femme', but change it to 'cherchez l'homme'. This means that it is always possible to predict her attitude if you know the man with whom she is in close relations at any given time.[30]

The parallels are there: Deacon Stanley – an ordinary Anglican direction; Doctor Pusey – the outlook of our bastardised form of Roman Catholicism; the Reverend Charles Voysey – theism; Charles Bradlaugh – atheism, Malthusianism, radicalism; Dr Aveling – a few years of scientific pursuits and scientific propaganda; Stead (of the *Pall Mall Gazette*) – general philanthropy; George Bernard Shaw – socialism; Herbert Burrows – theosophy.[31] But alongside these characters who mark the *grandes étapes* of this lady, there were also interregna ruled by less significant kings, such as Chakravarti. Having accused Judge of being a swindler and having declared that she will bring the materials she has gathered against him to England, she suddenly starts to advise that the business be hushed up in the overall interests of the cause, and destroys the evidence that she has. She did not however suspect that there were other copies of the documents she had, and was unaware that these documents had been witnessed in the correct fashion and become the property of the *Westminster Gazette*. This is what Mr Old, a former official of the Theosophical Society who nonetheless continues to believe in theosophy, writes about this matter: 'Miss Besant has in her hands all the proof to support the accusations levelled by her against Mr Judge, but for reasons best known to herself she obliged the whole society to engage in systematic deception and hide the known facts.'[32] And Miss Besant still wants to have the epitaph: 'She believed she was following the truth'!

The articles in the *Westminster Gazette*, written by Edmund Garrett, were subsequently published in pamphlet form with the title 'Isis very much uncovered'. There has been no real answer to this pamphlet. Mr Mead, currently secretary of the European section, declared that it did not deserve an answer.[33] Mr Judge wrote a letter from America unparalleled in the history of epistolatory literature for its stupidity and vulgarity. In the letter he says that he found the articles amusing, gives thanks for the warning, and says in conclusion that he cannot say anything else, other than to reject absolutely all the charges, which he has done.[34] Miss Besant is currently in Australia, and Olcott is in India, and neither one nor the other has reacted to that letter.

You may, of course, ask yourselves: those who remain theosophists and want to continue to do so – what are their brains made of? Let the founder of theosophy herself answer that one. It is to the credit of her own mental capacities that she never disguised her enormous contempt for her victims. 'Idiots and fools' is how she usually described them. But anyone who studies history will surely be interested to observe this movement of the end of the nineteenth century, and draw parallels between it and similar phenomena at the end of the eighteenth century...

In *Investors' Review* there is an article by Mr Wilson: 'Is trade going to revive?'[35] The author is reputed to be well informed about domestic and foreign financial affairs and quite impartial – he was not afraid to attack the shady financial operations of an English bank without any ambiguity.[36] The prices of wheat and cotton are very low, lower than ever before, and prices overall have fallen relative to the previous year. In practice, there is nowhere for capital to go. 'Canada is drowning in debt, Australia has become equally hopeless.' The whole world knows the dismal financial position of the European countries, especially Italy. Those who study history and political economy will of course be interested in the statement with which Wilson concludes his piece: 'The great wealth we possess is increasingly passing into the hands of a minority and the great majority of the population is falling into a position of dependency.'[37]

Two outstanding English literary figures died in 1894: Professor Froude and Robert Louis Stevenson. Froude was the writer who attempted to rehabilitate Henry VIII, and wrote the biography of Carlyle which caused such heated arguments a few years ago. However, despite his study of original historical sources and his narrative style, Froude is not taken seriously by any historical researcher. His superficial and frivolous attitude both to history and to current events and facts, his fondness for presenting facts and events not as they were in reality, but as he would have liked them to have been, led to a new colloquialism being coined: 'Froudacity', essentially a synonym of 'audacity'.[38]

But the greatest loss to English literature was the death of Stevenson, an incomparable storyteller, whose works are so engrossing that they are difficult to put down.[39] Stevenson's style is excellent, he knows how to use words. If genius consisted merely in an enormous capacity for work, then Stevenson would be counted among the geniuses. He himself told of how he worked long and continually on his style in his works, a style which seems to us to be so natural and complete. But there is nonetheless something about Stevenson, hard to define, which brings him close to genius, and surely everyone who has ever read his works would agree. The following four novels can be named as the most representative of his work, around which all the others are grouped: *Travels with a Donkey in the Cevennes*, *The Strange Case of Dr Jekyll and Mr Hyde*, *Treasure Island*, and *Virginibus Puerisque*. The first and last of these works, as well as other similar works by him, in different forms but always in elegant language, express Stevenson's entire philosophy of life, which is both cheerful and beautiful. It is notable that this happy and bright view of life, albeit sometimes imbued with a playful serious-ness, and an amazing fantasy, were the main characteristics of a man who was chronically ill, but who loved life, even though the shadow of death was always hanging over him. In *Dr Jekyll and Mr Hyde* Stevenson is dealing with a very common problem, but one which we are afraid to look straight in the eye: the fundamental duality of human nature. Jekyll, a well-known and much respected doctor, and Hyde, a cruel man-beast, are one and the same person. The tragedy of this position, which is a common phenomenon in nature, and its philosophy are expressed very vividly by the author, but without any moralising conclusions. This work by Stevenson has not only become a classic, but the idea and the title have become very popular in England, since almost every English person thinks it necessary to have this book in his or her small library. *Treasure Island* is one of those books read not only by boys but also by grown men and women, as a result of its absorbing story, beautiful style, and fine characterisations. Such stories give one a whiff of the sea. Stevenson, moreover, had a strange liking for desperate but crippled daredevils. Another peculiarity of Stevenson's novels is the relative lack of female characters in them. However, the two or three female characters which appear in a few works (*Catriona*, *Master of Ballantrae*) show that he could depict women just as well as men. It seems to us that the works of Stevenson will always be favourite reading for the majority – they sell in their thousands now – and the greatest pleasure for some. The space available does not allow us to consider Stevenson's plays or poetry.

In recent times there has been a particular interest in Russian literature, although, unfortunately, Russian works are accessible to us only in English or French translation. The recent publication in English of Sofia Kovalevskaya's *Vera Barantsova* cannot, of course, lessen the interest of the English public in Russian authors.[40] The author of this novel is known to us and the rest of the world as an outstanding mathematical genius, and it may be that reading this novel proves to be a bit of a disappointment. It is most likely that we were expecting too much and should remember that this work had never been revised by its author. But, even taking all that into account, we must admit that Kovalevskaya's autobiography is much more interesting than her novel. The great merit of this autobiography to the English reader is the fact that it depicts Russian life extraordinarily vividly.

If the works of Kovalevskaya mentioned above can be read profitably by the English reading public, then Clementina Black's novel *An Agitator* should be read by anyone interested in the workers' movement.[41] This is a genuinely excellent and strikingly realistic depiction of certain phases of this complex movement. The author's remarkable powers of observation and ability truthfully to depict people and events is testified to by the fact that many people have recognised real figures from the workers' movement in its characters. However, in fact the author is not depicting any particular person but a type, a photographic image of several individuals, put into the same circumstances, and merged together. Thus everybody reckoned that in her hero, Brand, the author is depicting John Burns, because Brand is also an engineer and a leader of the workers. Incidentally, the character of the hero seems to have been taken more from Champion, although that may have been done unconsciously. The story itself is extraordinarily interesting, excellently written and in places infused with an unexpected pathos, the sincerity of which makes a profound impression on the reader.

Av.

Notes

1. Here the authors are referring to the ancient forms of local administration which embodied some democratic elements, including vestry general meetings of householders, but which had been eroded

over time, as a self-perpetuating elite of landowners and clergymen assumed greater control over parochial affairs.

One contemporary radical who stressed the importance of the new parish councils in regaining these historic democratic rights was John Morrison Davidson (1843-1916), whose writing Eleanor considered valuable, as illustrated in her review of Davidson's *The Old Order and the New* in *Time: A Monthly Miscellany of Interesting and Amusing Literature,* September 1890, p1008. Davidson considered the potential of these reforms in *The Villagers' Magna Charta: The Village for the Villagers*, William Reeves: London, 1894.

2. Throughout the nineteenth century radical movements had demanded that elections be conducted by secret ballot and not by a show of hands. This reform was finally introduced in 1872 but did not extend to the provisions of parish council elections set out in the Local Government Act of 1894. Here elections could be by a show of hands or secret ballot if demanded by five parochial voters.

    In the week following the parish council elections of December 1894, the *Daily Chronicle* remarked that 'one thing stands out very clearly from a perusal of the reports of the country papers... the strong dislike of the labourers to a show of hands at Parish meetings, and the difficulty in getting an accurate record when the labourers have the courage to vote. At Kentisbury (Devon) not a single hand was up when the vicar, who was in the chair, put the names. The labourers are naturally afraid of being "spotted" and they resent a method of procedure which seems to them to ante-date the Ballot Act. We are not surprised by this. A correspondent sent us a story of a meeting at which the squire's name was put forward to the meeting with an indifferent response, whereupon the squire rose and fixed his eyes on the backbenches where the labourers sat. The hands then went up in self-defence.' *Daily Chronicle*, 12 December 1894, p4.

3. This occurred at the village meeting of Scoulton, Norfolk. *Norfolk News*, 8 December 1894, p16.

4. These events took place at Terrington St. Clement, near Kings Lynn, Norfolk. The Rev. Marlborough Crosse only secured three votes in the ballot and denounced the meeting as a 'one-sided and scandalous bit of business'. *Thetford and Watton Times and People's Weekly Journal,* 15 December 1894, p8.

5. The authors' stated results for the Norfolk parish council elections approximate those made by Richard Heath in his article 'The rural revolution', *Contemporary Review,* January 1895, pp182-200. For two decades Heath had written extensively on rural affairs based on

his 'pedestrian tours' of England. In 1893 he brought these essays together in a volume, *The English Peasant*, where he gave a warm welcome to the proposal to establish parish councils, believing they would augur 'A day, as joyous as those in the past have been sorrowful...for the Agricultural Labourer, oppressed and depressed for a thousand years.' Richard Heath, *The English Peasant*, T. Fisher and Unwin: London, 1893, pviii. Heath was encouraged by the outcome of these elections and acknowledged the influence of trade unions in mobilising the votes of farm workers. In this the role of the Norfolk and Norwich Amalgamated Labourers' Union was crucial as its secretary, George Edwards (1850-1933) later recalled: 'I held meetings in every village where we had members of the union and explained the provisions of the Act. By the time the first meetings were held to elect the parish councils in many of the villages we had got our men ready as we posted up in the mode of procedure as to nominations and how to carry on.' Edwards paid tribute to the work of the organisers of the English Land Restoration League, who toured Norfolk in a red van encouraging agricultural workers to join the union and elect from their own to the parish council. George Edwards, *From Crow-Scaring to Westminster: An Autobiography*, Labour Publishing Company: London, 1922, p66.

6. The parish meeting at Welney, on the borders of Norfolk and Cambridgeshire, elected as chairman William Baxter, the master at the Church of England school. This gave rise to a protest by Rev. E. Russell Wilford, rector of Welney, who, believing he should be chairman, interrupted the proceedings. Baxter called Wilford 'out of order', a ruling supported by the meeting. Subsequently, the rector dismissed Baxter from his employment at the school. Wilford's actions led to a national protest which forced him to retract Baxter's dismissal. *Daily News*, 14 December 1894, p3.

7. Amos Green (1854-1920), a whelk seller, was elected to Grays (Essex) Urban District Council in December 1894.

8. Boards of guardians were locally elected bodies administering the Poor Law, including workhouse provision of assistance for those in distress or sick.

9. London's unreformed system of local government left the capital with forty-three elected vestries and district boards, each with a poor reputation and a record of low election turn-outs: in 1885 less than one in thirty London electors took part in the vestry elections. David Owen, *The Government of Victorian London, 1855-1889: The Metropolitan Board of Works, the Vestries and the City of London*, Belknap Press: London, 1982, p216. Prefacing its appeal to London's

electors to vote in the vestry polls, the *Daily Chronicle* acknowledged that 'The name "Vestry" has little to commend it to the mass of London citizens in the past. It has stood too often for mere interested cliqueism, and for a disastrous policy of economy in which the lives and health of the citizens and the common good have stood second in importance to the ideal of keeping down the rates.' *Daily Chronicle*, 10 December 1894, p4.

Some improvement occurred during the 1880s with 'the emergence of social politics and the overhaul of London Liberalism', giving the questions of unemployment, housing and labour policy some prominence. John Davis, *Reforming London: The London Government Problem, 1855-1900*, Clarendon: Oxford, 1988, p156. The establishment of the London County Council in 1889 with a reforming Progressive majority, strengthened at the 1892 election, gave new impetus to these modernising forces as increasingly the Council became a model for municipal expansion, enterprise and innovation. Successful new unionist industrial activity and vigorous socialist propaganda meant there was a distinctive socialist presence in the London municipal elections of December 1894. The Social Democratic Federation (SDF) secured nineteen seats on three vestries (Battersea, Camberwell, and Lambeth), while the recently established Independent Labour Party (ILP) won representation at Lambeth and Woolwich. Further successes for the SDF and ILP came in the board of guardians elections, ensuring a socialist view was heard on poor-law issues. Nevertheless, overall, the results for socialists were less than encouraging, and the failure of the Progressives to take control of a majority of London's vestries was disappointing.

10. The London County Council (LCC) inherited land acquired by its predecessor, the Metropolitan Board of Works (1855-1888), for slum clearance but had failed to interest either charities or developers in the sites for new working-class housing. Enabled by the Housing of the Working Classes Act of 1890, the LCC developed schemes to build dwellings on these and other plots of land, including sites of cleared slums at Greenwich and Poplar associated with the Blackwall Tunnel (opened in 1897) and the extensive Boundary Street estate in Shoreditch.

The Council opened a municipal lodging house in Parker Street, Drury Lane in 1893. Here 'for the first time in London, the dosser – who was regarded as a piece of human wreckage of no account – was treated as a human being. The house is clean, comfortable and commodious, with numerous baths and a laundry'. *The London County Council*, London Reform Union: London, 1895, p19.

The LCC took its strategic public health duties seriously, offering financial support to vestries and district boards who wished to appoint sanitary inspectors and enforce orders against neglectful landlords.

The acreage of public parks and open spaces in the LCC area grew from 2,578 in 1888 to 3,647 in 1894. Included in this expansion were Parliament Hill Fields, Hackney Marshes, and Waterlow and Brockwell Parks.

Action by the LCC to improve the condition of sewers meant that by the mid 1890s Thames water was significantly cleaner and there were sightings of freshwater fish in the upper reaches of the river, as the authors note.

The Council's Works Department was established during 1893 to undertake building projects with its own labour employed on pay and conditions recognised by trade unions. John Burns, member of the LCC for Battersea as well as Member of Parliament for that constituency, was instrumental in the founding of the Works Department. In November 1892 Burns wrote in his diary that it was the 'biggest thing yet done for collectivism and which I have as much time, energy and ability for four years as any other piece of work I have yet undertaken'. Quoted in K. Brown, *John Burns*, Royal Historical Society: London, 1977, p67. The prediction of the letters' authors that 'the reign of the contractor is over', proved over-optimistic, however, as the Works Department became wracked by controversy and was abolished in 1907.

11. In June 1894 the *British Medical Journal*, under the editorship of campaigning medical journalist Ernest Hart (1835-1898), began a series of articles on the condition of workhouse infirmaries across Britain. The survey of around fifty workhouse infirmaries exposed major deficiencies in nursing and medical care, including the money-saving employment of inmates to nurse the sick. Kim Price, *Medical Negligence: The Crisis of Care under the English Poor Law, c.1834-1900*, Bloomsbury: London, 2015, pp135-8. Hart brought these articles together in 1895 under the title *The Sick Poor in the Workhouses*, Smith Elder and Co.: London. The articles can be read online at www. workhouses.org.uk/BMJ.

12. In the wake of a number of widely publicised deaths in London workhouse infirmaries during 1865, Ernest Hart (see previous note), then editor of *The Lancet*, exposed poor conditions and practices in these institutions that contributed to the passing of the Metropolitan Asylums Act of 1867. For Hart see P.W.J. Bartripp, 'Hart, Ernest Abraham, 1835-1898, medical journalist', *Oxford Dictionary of National Biography*, Oxford University Press: Oxford, 2018.

13. The explosion occurred at the Albion Colliery in the village of Clifyndd, close to Pontypridd, on 23 June 1894. 290 miners died, making it at the time the worst colliery disaster in Wales. The inquest of August 1894 concluded that the explosion of gas was accelerated by accumulation of dust, but blamed nobody. The barrister appointed by the government to investigate the evidence found that the owners, Albion Steam and Coal Co., should be prosecuted for infringements of the legislation relating to coal mining. The charges against the company were dismissed by a stipendiary magistrate at Pontypridd in October 1894. *The Times,* 18 October 1894, p4.

14. This was the explosion at the mine of Count Georg Karisch at Karwin, near Oderberg, Silesia on 14 June 1894. 200 miners were killed.

15. The Sapphire and Ruby Company of Montana was launched in the autumn of 1891 with a prospectus to raise capital for mining of diamonds in Montana, USA. The founders claimed that if they could purchase several thousand acres of land, the investment would soon yield enormous financial returns. The list of those taking founders' shares included 'two dukes, three marquises, seven earls, over a dozen barons and numerous knights and baronets', obviously presented to reassure potential investors that there was a degree of security as well as the prospect of hefty profits. Patrick Streeter, *Streeter of Bond Street*, The Matching Press: Harlow, 1993, p134.

Within twelve months it was clear that the company was on shaky ground. A deficit of £6,000 and sales of only £168 were shown at the 1893 annual meeting. Instead of holding capital of £450,000 projected at the launch, the company was found to have less than 10 per cent of that figure in actual subscriptions. The Marquis of Lorne and the Dukes of Portland and Leinster, together with promised investments of £370,000, had withdrawn.

The investigative committee asked to look into the affairs of the company presented a damning report revealing that the interest of founder shareholders had been significantly overstated, leaving the enterprise dependent on underwriters from whom the necessary sums to guarantee the future of the business could not be obtained. The report also criticised payments to founding directors vastly disproportionate to their original investment and service to the company. As one financial journalist wrote: 'It would thus appear that the business of the founders, as understood by these noblemen and gentlemen, is the safe, though monstrous old game, "heads I win, tails you lose"'. *Investors' Review*, January 1895, p38.

The assets and liabilities of the failed company were transferred to the Eldorado and Gem Company of Montana in July 1898.

16. Robert Dudley (1532-1588), the 1st Earl of Leicester, who had a large investment in the Muscovy Company, the first major chartered joint stock company.

17. The winter of 1894/5 saw the worst potato crop in Ireland since 1879. The failure particularly affected parts of Donegal, Galway and Mayo, where it has been estimated that 'the crop was a mere one-eighth of its usual yield and a depression in the cattle, cereal and butter prices aggravated the situation'. T.P. O'Neill, 'The food crisis of the 1890s', in E. Margaret Crawford (ed.), *Famine: The Irish Experience, 900-1900: Subsistence Crises and Famine in Ireland*, John Donald: Edinburgh, 1989, p182.

    At first, the Local Government Board resisted pressure to introduce relief to the affected areas, believing it would become a permanent feature. John Morley, the Chief Secretary for Ireland, kept a watching brief on the situation and at the end of 1894, after being told by local government inspectors that the situation was serious, introduced relief works, outdoor relief and seed grants. Virginia Crossman, *Politics, Pauperism and Power in late Nineteenth Century Ireland*, Manchester University Press: Manchester, 2006, pp127-8.

18. These figures were taken from William Bramwell Booth's pamphlet *Work in Darkest England*, Salvation Army: London, 1894, p.vii.

19. This was the case of Rachel Cohen, nineteen months, who died of starvation in Whitechapel in January 1895. Rachel's mother, Sarah, made her living as a slipper maker for which she earned 3 shillings per week. Out of this she had to find two shillings for rent. When Sarah took Rachel to the London Hospital the child was close to death. At the inquest a juror asked the hospital doctor why the child was not taken in for treatment to which he replied: 'It is not the rule to take these cases of starvation in, or we should have the whole of Whitechapel in at this time of the year'. *Lloyd's Weekly Newspaper*, 6 January 1895, p20.

20. Tory democracy was a paternalistic form of conservatism advocating the preservation of established institutions and principles in combination with economic and social policies to appeal to the working class. Benjamin Disraeli is considered to be the originator of Tory democracy, which was later advocated by Lord Randolph Churchill.

21. Lord Randolph Churchill (1849-1895) was a Conservative politician who served in two of Lord Salisbury's governments during the 1880s. Churchill was also Leader of the House of Commons until 1887 and member for South Paddington until his death in January 1895. The

apparent decline in Churchill's mental capabilities in the early 1890s led to speculation about heavy drinking, but 'It was widely believed that his final illness was tertiary syphilis' – hence the authors' reference to *tabes dorsalis* (a complication of syphilis) – 'though it has been suggested latterly that he could have suffered from multiple sclerosis or a brain tumour.' Roland Quinault, 'Churchill, Lord Randolph Henry Spencer, 1849-1895', *Oxford Dictionary of National Biography*, Oxford University Press: Oxford, 2018. See also the essay by John H. Mather, 'Lord Randolph Churchill: Maladies et mort', www.winstonchurchill.org.

22. The Theosophical Society was established in New York in 1875 by Helena Petrovna Blavatsky (1831-1891) and Henry Steel Olcott (1831-1907) with the belief that an ancient wisdom was held by 'Mahatmas', or 'Masters', who could guide the world and assist others in their pilgrimage. Drawing extensively from Eastern religions, theosophists believed there to be a 'cosmic oneness' and an unfolding spiritual evolution of the universe, that would be experienced – over many lives through reincarnation – by those who took a personal 'pilgrimage' guided by the Mahatmas.

23. The Society of Psychical Research was founded in London in 1882. Among its senior figures were a number of men who would also go on to become prominent members of the Theosophical Society. When Madame Blavatsky and Henry Olcott visited London in the spring of 1884, the Psychical Society took an interest in the theosophists' claims that the 'Mahatmas' appeared in astral form. The Psychical Society asked Richard Hodgson, a Cambridge graduate, to investigate. Hodgson's visit to the theosophist headquarters in Adyar, India coincided with revelations by Emma Coulomb who, with her husband, worked for the theosophists, that Blavatsky's claims of 'Mahatma'-guided phenomena was a hoax, which she, Coulomb, and her husband had helped stage. Hodgson's report, published in the journal of the Psychical Society in 1885, upheld the claims of fraudulent activity by Blavatsky.

24. See note 22.

25. Henry Olcott, President of the Theosophical Society, edited *The Theosophist: A Popular Asiatic Magazine* from Adyar, India. Annie Besant took over the editorship of *Lucifer: A Monthly Magazine of Theosophy and Occult Sciences* (London) when Madame Blavatsky died in 1891. William Q. Judge (1851-1896) joined the theosophists' leadership as vice president soon after its formation, and edited *The Path* from New York.

26. Annie Besant (1847-1933) joined the Theosophical Society in May

1889 after reviewing Blavatsky's *The Secret Doctrine* and then visiting her on a couple of occasions. For some time before this Besant had been interested in occult matters, had attended séances – even staging one in her own home – and later claimed in her *Autobiography* that 'since 1886 there had been slowly growing up a conviction that my philosophy was not sufficient; that the life and mind were other than, more than, I had dreamed. Psychology was advancing with rapid strides; hypnotic experiments were revealing unlooked for complexities in human consciousness, strange riddles of multiplex personalities, and, most startling of all, vivid intensities of mental action when the brain, that should be the generator of thought, was reduced to a comatose state. Fact after fact came hurtling in on me, demanding explanation I was incompetent to give.' Annie Besant, *An Autobiography*, T. Fisher Unwin: London, 1908, p339.

27. Besant formally separated from the National Secular Society, to which she had been attached and a leading figure since 1875, following a lecture at the Society's Hall of Science, Old Street, London, on 30 August 1891. In the lecture Besant created a sensation by claiming that she, like Blavatsky before her, had received letters that she took to have been written by the 'Mahatmas'. She told the packed audience: 'You have known me in this hall for sixteen and a half years. You have never known me tell a lie to you. My worst public enemy has never cast a slur upon my integrity. I tell you that since Madame Blavatsky left I have had letters in the same handwriting as the letters which she received. Unless you think dead persons can write, surely that is a remarkable fact. You are surprised. I do not ask you to believe me; but I tell you that it is so.' *Daily Chronicle*, 31 August 1891, p5.

28. The morning after Besant's Hall of Science revelation (see previous note) she explained to a journalist from the *Pall Mall Gazette* that she had made the comment about being in receipt of letters in the same hand as those sent to Blavatsky with the purpose of vindicating the memory of that woman. It had been suggested in the Hodgson report to the Society for Psychical Research (see note 23) that Blavatsky produced personally written letters claiming they came from the 'Mahatmas'. Besant claimed that the handwriting of the letters she had received was identical to those sent to Blavatsky, who was now dead. Besant told the reporter that the report of the Hall of Science meeting in the *Daily Chronicle* had been wrong in talking about her receiving 'messages from an unseen world'. The letters she received were 'precipitated' from the Mahatmas, who were of this world, but had knowledge of natural laws and were able to com-

municate without a postal service or any equipment. Besant told the journalist that she was not able to divulge how 'precipitation' was accomplished, as the Mahatmas only communicated with those who will not reveal their secrets. *Pall Mall Gazette*, 1 September 1891, p2.

29. Gyanendra Nath Chakravarti, a professor of mathematics at Allahabad University with 'a reputation as a mystic, a student of great Indian religious literature, and a skilful hypnotist...Annie Besant was at once fascinated by both his manner and his ways'. Arthur H. Nethercot, *The First Five Lives of Annie Besant*, Rupert Hart-Davis: London, 1961, p404. Besant spent time with Chakravarti during her trip to India in 1893 and it is believed he convinced her that she had been tricked into believing she had received letters from the 'Mahatmas', when they were, in fact, written by William Judge. Besant later accepted that the letters 'were not written or precipitated by the Master, and that they were done by Mr Judge; but I also believe that the gist of the messages was psychically received, and that Mr Judge's error lay in giving them to me in a script written by himself and not saying so...Having been myself mistaken, I in turn misled the public.' Quoted in Edmund Garrett, 'Isis very much uncovered: The story of the great Mahatma hoax', *Westminster Gazette*, December 1894, p63.

30. The linking of Besant's numerous shifts of enthusiasm with 'leading' men with whom she was acquainted became in the twentieth century a popular explanatory device for biographers and memoirists recalling her. The short section in this letter was perhaps the first time this link had been made in published form, and is based on a mixture of Besant's own *An Autobiography*, published in 1893, and personal knowledge.

More recent scholarship on Besant has attempted to provide a more complex account of her intellectual development. For instance, Mark Bevir remarks of Nethercot's Besant biography that it claims that Besant had a need to follow a dominant man, 'with the only evidence for the need being the behaviour it supposedly explains'. Instead, Bevir sees Besant's life as 'a reasoned quest for truth in the context of the Victorian crisis of faith and the social concerns it helped to raise. Besant, with her secularism, Fabianism and theosophy, was very much of her time.' Mark Bevir, 'Annie Besant's quest for truth: Christianity, secularism and New Age thought', *Journal of Ecclesiastical History*, Vol. 50, No. 1, January 1999, pp62-3. Likewise, Ann Taylor's study *Annie Besant: A Biography*, Oxford University Press: Oxford, 1992, avoids recourse to coupling Besant with a commanding man as explanation, and is commended for it by Gareth Stedman Jones in his extended review of her book: 'As [Taylor] shows, [Besant's] progression was not unpondered, as both her critics and admirers like to believe. As for the role of men, the standard picture takes little account of the difficulties confronting a Victorian woman set adrift from the respectability of marriage and driven to fight her battles in public. Besant may have been attracted to Bradlaugh and Stead, but what she most needed from men was companionship in the pursuit of her moral ideals. Certainly, her life had a richly quirky and wilful side. But was it any more quirky than those of her male contemporaries – Shaw, Stead, Wilde or Yeats? This book goes a long way towards rescuing Besant from a condescending double standard.' Gareth Stedman Jones, 'The flight of a clergyman's wife', *London Review of Books*, 27 May 1993, p17.

31. Arthur Penryn Stanley (1815-1881) was Dean of Westminster and leading liberal theologian, known to and admired by Besant.

Edward Bouverie Pusey (1800-1882) was Canon of Christ Church Oxford and a leading light of the Oxford movement in the Church of England. When consulted by Besant about her doubts about the Christian faith he advised her to believe the truth as laid down by the church and to 'pray, you must pray'.

Charles Voysey (1828-1912) was a former Anglican clergyman whose commitment to theism led to his removal from the living as a vicar in Yorkshire. Voysey moved to London and began holding services at St George's Hall, Langham Place, attended by Besant in 1872. Voysey invited Besant to his home in Dulwich, where they had long discussions about their doubting faith. Ann Taylor writes that: 'Always susceptible to men who acknowledged her intellect, [Besant] promoted Voysey to rank of hero, and copied him – as she would others – as closely as she could.' Taylor 1992, p47.

Charles Bradlaugh (1833-1891) was the president of the National Secular Society and editor of its weekly publication, the *National Reformer*, with whom Besant collaborated from 1875 until 1890. Bradlaugh and Besant were convicted of obscenity, but released on a technicality, in 1877 over the decision to publish a pamphlet by Charles Knowlton advocating birth control. Bradlaugh was elected four times as the Member of Parliament for the Northampton constituency, but was denied his seat because he refused to take a religious oath of allegiance. He finally took his seat in 1884. Besant's conversion to socialism in the mid 1880s created a rift with the individualist Bradlaugh and led her to resign the co-editorship of the *National Reformer* in 1887.

Edward met Besant in January 1879 when they were introduced by a mutual friend, the economist J.H. Levy. Besant was impressed with his knowledge of and commitment to science, especially evolution, which she encouraged him to write about in the *National Reformer.* In February 1879 Besant joined the science class Edward taught from his laboratory in Newman Street, with a view to preparing for study at the University of London. Edward quickly became deeply involved in the National Secular Society as author and lecturer, and by May 1880 was elected vice president of the Society. Besant's relationship with Edward was a strong one until 1883, when he began to move towards socialism and, in particular, the ideas of Karl Marx. His increasingly important connection to Eleanor Marx from late 1883 created tensions between the two women, which surfaced in public and did little to abate after Edward and Eleanor set up home together in the summer of 1884.

William Thomas Stead (1849-1912) was a campaigning journalist who edited the *Pall Mall Gazette*. Stead worked with Besant in the Law and Liberty League after 'Bloody Sunday' in November 1887, a demonstration that was met with police brutality, in which at least one, and possibly two, were killed. Besant wrote a review of Blavatsky's *The Secret Doctrine* in *Pall Mall Gazette* (25 April 1889), after which she asked Stead to arrange an introduction to the theosophist leader whom he knew.

George Bernard Shaw (1852-1950) worked with Besant in her socialist years of the mid and late 1880s. Under Shaw's guidance, Besant joined the Fabian Society and for a while took a prominent role promoting its work and attempting to establish an electoral strategy. Their relationship was an intimate one, but Shaw's rejection of Besant's suggestion that they live together brought the affair to an end in 1887.

Herbert Burrows (1845-1922) was a prominent member of the Social Democratic Federation (SDF) who became Besant's 'constant companion' from 1887 and collaborated with her in leading the match girls in the strike at the Bryant and May factory in 1888. Taylor 1992, p189. Burrows was influential in encouraging Besant to join the SDF, which she did in August 1888. Burrows accompanied Besant when visiting Blavatsky and he too joined Theosophical Society in 1889.

32. Walter Gorn Old (1864-1929) was a senior member of the Theosophical Society who was in possession of all the relevant documents concerning relations between Annie Besant and William Judge. Old opposed what he believed to be Besant's concealment of facts that

would expose Judge as a hoaxer of the 'Mahatma' letters referred to by her at the Hall of Science meeting in August 1891 (see note 27). Old released the documents to Edmund Garrett (1865-1907), who published an at-first anonymous critical expose of the Theosophists in a series of articles in the *Westminster Gazette*, and then a pamphlet under his own name in November 1894. This publication, 'Isis very much uncovered: The story of the great Mahatma hoax', *Westminster Gazette*, 1894, was clearly read closely by Eleanor and Edward, doubtless with much pleasure, and provided much of the information for their own account of events, which they described as a 'large scandal' within the Theosophical Society.

33. George Robert Stowe Mead (1863-1933) was a prolific writer on theosophy and esotericism who served as private secretary to Madame Blavatsky.

34. Judge wrote two letters to the editor of the *Westminster Gazette*, 8 and 10 December 1894, both pp1-2.

35. Alexander J. Wilson (1842-1921), a financial journalist, had worked at the *Times, Pall Mall Gazette* and the *Standard* before establishing and editing *Investors' Review* in 1892. In an age when 'the probity of the financial press and financial editors generally left an enormous amount to be desired', Wilson was held in high regard for his honesty and integrity. David Kynaston, *The City of London Volume 2: Golden Years, 1890-1914*, Chatto and Windus: London, 1995, pp178-9.

36. A.J. Wilson's article 'A paralytic Bank of England', published in *Investors' Review* in January 1894, exposed the parlous state of management within the Bank of England. See Kynaston 1995, p96.

37. A.J. Wilson's article 'Is trade going to revive?', *Investors' Review* January 1895, was of interest to Marxists because it described the economy as being in a state of stagnation, the result of a drying up of investment opportunities, overproduction, a surfeit of unused capital and increasing inequality of income and wealth. Wilson predicted conflict between capitalist countries: 'all Europe stands armed, its best energies devoted to the preparation of wars, which shall be the letting loose of hell' (p10). Whole passages of Wilson's article were reproduced in *Justice*, the weekly newspaper of the Social Democratic Federation, with a note that his words 'will strike the readers of *Justice* as what lawyers call "common form" – there is nothing whatever in it new to them. But the appearance of the article is significant as showing that even the "City" is waking up to the truth, as taught by us for so many years.' *Justice*, 19 January 1895, p6.

38. James Anthony Froude (1818-1894), Regius Professor of Modern History at the University of Oxford, author of a twelve-volume history of Tudor England and biographer of Thomas Carlyle.

39. Robert Louis Stevenson (1850-1894) was a particular favourite of Eleanor's.

40. Sofia Kovalevskaya (1850-1891) was a Russian mathematician, poet and novelist who had participated in the Paris Commune and was involved in radical politics. Her novel, *Vera Barantsova,* published in England in early 1895 with an introduction by Sergei Stepniak, tells the story of a young woman who, in the days of the emancipation of serfs, marries a condemned nihilist and shared his exile in Siberia.

41. Clementina Maria Black (1853-1922) knew Eleanor Marx and the Marx family from the late 1870s. By the early 1880s Black had established a minor literary reputation, having published a number of novels, and was well known in the circle of bohemian and radical figures who frequented the Reading Room of the British Museum. Prominent in the late 1880s for her trade union organising work amongst women workers, Black encountered many of the leading figures in the trade union and socialist movements, a knowledge she put to good use in her novel, *An Agitator,* published in November 1894. Telling the story of an engineer, Kit Brand, who leads a strike and goes on to become a Member of Parliament, Black was aware that the story resembled in parts the career of John Burns, prompting a preface in which she denied any attempt at portraiture. Black reiterated this soon after the book was released, telling a reporter that: 'The reviewers seem to be very much hurt by my saying that there are no portraits in it. There is a tendency to identify characters, I find. You must write about people you know. Still, I do not think there is a recognisable portrait in the book'. *Women's Signal,* 31 January 1895, p3. It is almost certain that the paragraph in the letter recommending *An Agitator* was written by Eleanor, who remarks that the character of Kit Brand 'seems to have been taken more from Champion'. Here she was referring to Henry Hyde Champion (1859-1928), who played a prominent part in the early socialist movement. Eleanor recommended the novel to her friend Natalie Liebknecht, saying: 'It is *not* didactic; it is a very good story, contains excellent studies of English working-class types, and presents about the only true picture of a strike in England that I have come across in fiction.' Georg Eckert (ed.), *Wilhelm Liebknecht: Briefwechsel mit Karl Marx und Friedrich Engels,* Mouton & Co.: The Hague, 1963, p437.

LETTER THREE

April 1895

Like their mentor Frederick Engels, Eleanor and Edward invested a good deal of hope in the early reforming work of the London County Council. The recent electoral setback for the Council's Progressives was therefore disappointing, and they attributed it to a parsimonious middle class unwilling to pay for improvements through the rates and an underdeveloped workers' movement.

Keir Hardie's efforts in Parliament to raise the issue of unemployment and the relief of distress is subjected to some sharp criticism in this letter. In a tone characteristic of Edward when denouncing Hardie, the member for West Ham South is accused of not being on top of his brief and of advancing false plans for dealing with unemployment.

Some credit is given to the beleaguered Liberal government for its decision to push forward with factory legislation, even if it was too willing to concede to employers' demands for exemptions from its conditions on safety and overtime. Similarly, the government's decision not to increase the age below which children were allowed to work in factories is seen as lamentable, and partly the result of opposition by northern working-class families who depended on the wage of their children to make ends meet.

When this letter was written, all London was discussing the recently concluded court case brought by Oscar Wilde against the Marquis of Queensberry for declamatory libel. The case collapsed after three days and was followed by Wilde's arrest and subsequent trial, which is commented on in the next instalment.

This letter expresses some interest in a new book of essays by a variety of reforming contributors under the title The New Party. *While advising Russian readers that the idea of a 'new party' was a fiction, the work of some of its essayists is noted with interest, including that*

of Alfred Russel Wallace, the famous evolutionist whom Edward knew
personally.

There have recently been further very lively and important elections in London – the elections to the London County Council
(LCC). We mentioned this body and its activities in one of our
previous letters. Six years ago, in 1889, the Conservative government granted Londoners the privilege of having their own central
representative government. The Londoners were not slow to make
use of this privilege. Over the six years of its existence, the LCC has
undoubtedly done many things for London. In particular over the
last three years from 1892, the Progressive majority on this council,
whose members are unpaid, has voted through many useful measures.[1] But this year's elections have heralded a very strange and
significant reaction. Both parties, Progressives and Moderates
(reactionaries) now have an equal number of representatives on
the new council (fifty-nine each), whereas on the old council there
were eighty-four so-called Progressives and 34 Moderates.[2]

These elections undoubtedly had a political character and
the results are doubly interesting, in that they serve, to a certain
extent, as a harbinger of what might happen at the parliamentary
elections, which are approaching fast. It is also not insignificant
that the question of the purses of London's ratepayers played a very
prominent role. The outgoing LCC had been obliged to raise the
rates to a modest extent in order to cover the many useful measures
it undertook. But if England overall is a 'nation of shopkeepers',
then London in particular is a city of shopkeepers, and even if not
all its inhabitants are involved in trade, most of them are nonetheless infected with the narrow viewpoints of shopkeepers. They are
incapable of going beyond the standpoint of their own pockets and
will not accept anything which does not bring immediate advantages. Therefore Londoners, who can see no further than their
noses, failed to see the benefits that the LCC's reforms could bring
in future and saw only the extra penny taken from the pockets by
revenue collectors. It should however be noted that the real shopkeepers are indeed all on the verge of bankruptcy. Perishing in a sea
of competition which knows no bounds in London, like drowning

men they grasp at straws. In this case the straw is any reduction in the rates, however insignificant.[3] This circumstance is also used by the Moderate party, which is luring the shopkeepers with a promise of a rates cut. But to get a complete picture of the reaction we are witnessing at present in London, we should not forget that London has lagged far behind not only the other cities in England, but also its main continental rivals among the European capitals. At a time when such cities as Berlin and Vienna are at the forefront of the movement to improve the conditions of the working classes and constitute the centre of those movements in their respective countries, London is in almost the last place in this movement, and this is particularly vividly expressed in these recent election results.

Leaving aside the question of the rates, let us take a look at what are the main contradictions in the politics of the two contending parties, the Moderates and the Progressives. The Moderates want to see London divided into numerous boroughs, each of which will be run by its own council, concerned only with its local affairs. Moreover, in this regard the object of the Moderates' particular concern and attention is the borough known as the City of London, where the most repugnant forms of competing corruption hold sway. People do not live here, they just have businesses here, and it is run by a Corporation of traders and brokers who know of no gods other than profit and dividends. The Progressives stand for centralisation, for uniting all of London's administration under a body elected by the citizens on the widest basis. The Progressives would like once and for all to slay the monster that is the City, which squeezes the people of London, and oblige it to return to the people the thousands and millions of pounds it has swallowed up.[4] The Moderates protect the system of private contracts, despite all the evil that it causes in subcontracting and exploitation of workers. The Progressives strive for a position where the council does its business without seeking to enrich individual figures or giving patronage to profiteers. For example, they want certain spaces, currently open only to the privileged castes, to be equally accessible to all, particularly London's children. Immediately prior to the elections they managed to get the well-known space Lincoln's Inn Fields open to the public. These 'fields' had hitherto been a closed, fenced-off space, covered with fine lawns and luxuriant trees, growing on the grounds of the palace of Henry de Lacy, Earl of Lincoln, who lived in the time of Edward I. In the seventeenth and eighteenth centuries this area was used solely for duels and for executing traitors like Lord William Russell, whom perverse posterity has constantly tried to recast as a martyr. Nell Gwynne, one of the innumerable mistresses of Charles II, many prime ministers and leading lawyers all lived in buildings which looked out onto the fields. The Progressives were obliged to wage a stubborn struggle over this historic space against the Moderates, who fought tooth and nail to prevent it becoming public property. The council failed twice in its attempts to get the requisite decision from Parliament, but the third time it was luckier. The fields were acquired by the council for the nominal rent of £1 per annum for 661 years, and this agreement has now come into force. However, thanks to the Moderates the council has had to pay £12,000 in remuneration to various lawyers for this victory, as well as £3,000 in court costs.[5]

On all other questions of the vital needs of London's citizens, the Moderates have always been the opponents of the Progressives whenever they have come out against any private monopoly whether it be in street lighting, water supply, trams or markets. On the eve of the council elections themselves, two appeals were issued by the main tramway company and the water supply company. Both appeals in the most plaintive manner called on their respective shareholders to cast their votes for the Moderates. They were not asked to do this as citizens, but as shareholders.[6] If the elections were to result in a large majority for the Progressives then it would be impossible to count on the companies remaining in charge of water supply or horse-drawn tram services, and this would mean losses for the shareholders. It is of course possible that even despite all the force of reaction, the companies will still not be able to seize the monopoly of gas supply, water supply and tram services. Nonetheless, all these companies, thanks to the elections, are now in a position to demand their own prices rather than having to accept those which would have been offered to them by a Progressive council. Of course, this shows the surprising short sightedness of the London shopkeepers, who are unable to see the advantages gained by Birmingham, Glasgow, Manchester and

Huddersfield when their councils took hold of the monopolies of these companies.[7] It was not only the consumers, but also all the staff of the companies, as well as the towns and communities who gained. The reactionaries, incidentally, pay no attention to any arguments and ignore facts. The previous council had eight Acts of Parliament in hand concerning the removal of London's water supply from private companies. The council had striven consistently to gain the right to conclude contracts for water supply on whatever terms it found advantageous. Sir John Lubbock, a fine scholar but a very poor citizen, tried in every way he could to defeat the bill in Parliament which would transfer the capital's water supply to the council.[8] Failing that, he tried to postpone its consideration until after the elections. But he failed, and that is not surprising. At the very time that this was being discussed in Parliament, London suffered a breakdown in water supplies. The supply pipes were continually bursting, and London buildings were experiencing serious water shortages. It was as if they were living in the Sahara rather than in the capital of Great Britain. The building in which we are writing this letter, despite being in the very centre of the city, also had its water cut off during the recent frosts, which lasted for a few weeks in London.[9] Naturally, a lack of water has a very bad effect on the sanitary conditions in the city. To a significant extent these conditions, the result of a private water supply monopoly, are responsible for the current epidemic of influenza which has broken out in London.[10]

We shall now say a few words about the elections themselves. There were 246 candidates for the 118 seats on the council. The Moderates stood 114 candidates, the Progressives 110, and fourteen stood as Independents. The Independent Labour Party stood six candidates, and the Social Democratic Federation, two. These last figures clearly show that the significance of the workers' party in London lags far behind the position in other cities. The elections to the LCC differ from parliamentary elections in two respects. Tenants in rented accommodation cannot vote, which means that as the majority of the working class rents its housing, it is deprived of the franchise. Women, on the other hand, are allowed to vote, but only if they are ratepayers, shopkeepers and so on. We should however add that it is precisely that class of woman voter which is distinguished for its most appalling and vicious reactionary ideas. The result of this state of affairs is clear to everyone. Overall the Moderate vote increased by 9,000 compared with 1892, and the Progressives lost 27,000. The total poll for the ILP was a very modest 957, while the SDF polled even less, on 342 votes.[11] The turnout figures show that no more than half the electorate took part in voting, and this serves to show the uncommonly indifferent attitude of the working classes.[12] But we repeat – London is not England.

We are still faced with the problem of unemployed workers. Only a fundamental change in the overall conditions which give rise to this dismal phenomenon can put an end to the growth of the army of the jobless. As the years go by this chronic disease is taking on an increasingly acute form. In 1867 the peace of London's capitalists was disturbed to a considerable extent by marches of the unemployed and open-air meetings involving many hundreds of people. But that was as far as it went. The same year an uncommonly severe winter and the unceasing agitation on the unemployment question obliged Parliament to take a few measures.[13] In 1893, when Gladstone was asked in Parliament to appoint a special commission to look at the question, his response was a very polite but very definite refusal, which at the time did not greatly impact on public opinion.[14] But in 1895 Sir William Harcourt's response to virtually the same request was to agree immediately, and thanks to the efforts of Keir Hardie MP a commission has now been appointed.[15] Its task will be to investigate the three following questions concerning the unemployed: 1) What is the scale of the distress resulting from the absence of work? 2) What means do the local authorities have to deal with this distress? 3) What legal or administrative changes can be made to do away with the evils stemming from unemployment? The investigation will be carried out first of all in London, and then in other parts of England and Scotland.

The commission has already started work. The first person to be questioned was Sir Hugh Owen, Permanent Secretary to the Local Government Board, a government body responsible for overseeing parish councils, boards of guardians and works commissions.[16] Sir Hugh is a civil service type. He assesses the extent of the distress on the basis of reports from the workhouses which look after the poor and therefore, of course, finds nothing unusual in the current

situation of the unemployed. Sir Hugh spoke out against the idea of
a state institution to search for employment for those that cannot
find it, and against any financial assistance to cover immediate
need. He also sees no need for richer boroughs to assist the poorest
ones, even though the distress is caused in part by the fact that rich
boroughs always try to squeeze out the poor, preventing them from
concentrating there, which causes them to concentrate instead in
other boroughs, thereby making the problem worse.

Another witness questioned by the commission was of a better
type. This was one Mr Hilleary, Clerk to the Board of Guardians
in West Ham.[17] This borough is one of the poorest in London.
Unfortunately for its residents, who requested that it be joined to
London and brought under the LCC, this borough has remained a
separate district, inhabited mainly by unskilled workers. West Ham
is a factory district, containing the largest gasworks in England. It
lies on the lower reaches of the Thames and is therefore close to the
docks and is the gateway to London for the agricultural workers of
Essex. Mr Hilleary, who does not suffer from the official blindness
which afflicts Sir Hugh Owen, expressed the view that the distress
of the working-class population is partly owing to the fact that the
great majority of the needy does not want to resort to public assistance. If they do that, they lose their civil rights. Any citizen who
needs for whatever reason to resort to parish relief loses his rights
as a citizen, i.e., he cannot vote. In addition, Mr Hilleary said that
assistance carries a moral stigma, and to back this up cited facts
which showed that workers would rather die of hunger than go into
the workhouse. At present the only duty of boards of guardians is
to ensure that nobody actually dies of hunger, but not to find work
for those who have none. And despite that supervision, over the
course of this winter hardly a day went past without news of some-
body dying of hunger. These facts certainly show that political
consciousness has developed in the working classes. Mr Hilleary
added that trade unions always have great influence in elections to
West Ham town council, and that the council pays due attention to
any statements by the unions.[18]

Another witness from West Ham, Mr Hills, the chairman of the
Thames Shipbuilding Company, presented his own scheme for
providing assistance to the unemployed to the commission.[19] The

essence of this scheme was to create a relief fund by reducing the pay of those for whom work was found by a certain percentage. The trade unionists of West Ham protested against this scheme. Although his scheme was rejected by the town council, Mr Hills nonetheless presented his scheme to the commission under the title 'A Bill to Organise the Economic Administration of Relief'.[20] The main points of this bill are as follows: 1) the creation of a benefits fund; 2) the participation of the local authorities in this; 3) the participation of the Treasury; 4) the organisation of work for the unemployed, but with nobody working more than six days per week and six hours per day, and with their pay not exceeding two thirds of the local pay norms; 5) only those who have lived in the area for more than one year can count on being found work; 6) the receipt of work or benefits should not involve any loss of civil rights. Many in the Parliamentary Commission are in sympathy with that bill, and only the paragraph concerning wages meets with strong opposition. But we should not forget the old proverb: *timeo Danaos et dona ferentes* ['beware of Greeks bearing gifts']. In this case it is the shipbuilder who is playing the part of the Greek. At the moment there is a lot of talk about building eighty new warships. It is likely that these boats will be built on the Thames and, if this scheme were to be adopted, it would be fully in keeping with the capitalist tendencies of human nature if Mr Hills and co. were to use it to reduce their workforce's wages.

Naturally enough, the most interesting evidence to the commission was expected from Mr Keir Hardie, whose efforts had brought the commission into existence in the first place.[21] Mr Hardie spoke as a man thoroughly familiar with the unemployment question, and boasted that if the government were to listen to him, the problem would be solved entirely satisfactorily. However, things did not turn out like that. It became clear from his words that he did not understand the problem he had set out to resolve at all. All his proposals were not only unsatisfactory, but also impractical. Moreover, he astonished the members of the commission with his conclusions about the number of unemployed, which in his opinion equals five and a quarter million. Maybe that is indeed so, but there is no doubt that the methods used by Keir Hardie to investigate and gather statistics do not stand up to criticism. In the commission he showed a woeful ignorance of facts which he should have known. It turned out, for example, that he had no idea of the conditions in cities such as Durham, Leeds or Sheffield, nor was he familiar with the measures taken in those cities to deal with the distress of unemployment. He admitted that he had no practical details about how relief was organised because, for some unknown reason, he had always refused to take part in any commissions or committees concerned with these questions.

Some time back, before there was any question of any commission, Keir Hardie was strongly advocating the construction of warships, but subsequently, in his speech in the House of Commons on the commission, he forgot all about warships and started talking about building colonies in England and allocating uninhabited scrubland for that purpose.[22] By the time he was invited to speak to the commission, his thinking had taken another leap and he was already talking about allocating £100,000 from the Treasury, to be matched equally by funds raised locally. There was not a word about warships, scrubland or colonies: just £200,000 could, in his opinion, alleviate the distress. But from this it is already clear that our brilliant orator is a poor accountant. He was clearly very surprised when members of the commission better versed than him in mathematics pointed out that if they were to take his figure of five and a quarter million unemployed, of whom at least three quarters would have families, and divide the sum of £200,000 between them, there would be no more than 9d per family. And this is to last for six weeks, the period laid down by Hardie himself. When he was asked what would happen after the six weeks had expired and all the money had been spent, he answered, without thinking: 'Another £200,000 will be allocated.' From the £100,000 of Treasury funds Mr Keir Hardie modestly demands £40,000 for the Borough of West Ham, presumably with an eye to the forthcoming general elections.[23]

Other suggestions were also made to the commission. The Lord Mayor of London, quite separately from the commission, organised some works in order to give work to the unemployed.[24] Additionally, some ancient Acts of Parliament which gave the guardians the right to rent land and give out allotments were pulled out of a chest and thrown to the local authorities to keep them happy.[25] In the meantime, the commission is supposed to compile a detailed report on the state of affairs.[26] Readers may naturally ask: what attitude has John Burns, the well-known workers' leader, taken to the commission and the unemployment question? Unfortunately, he has up until now confined himself to caustic criticism of all the proposals made. His main argument has been that all these measures would serve only to demoralise those whom they are intended to help.[27] This would be an entirely understandable argument from a politician of the old Manchester School, but it is incomprehensible coming from a political figure in the workers' party.[28] All those who understand the workers' movement realise, however, that both these workers' leaders have failed to exploit this most favourable opportunity which had been presented to them. At the moment this commission on the workers has the attention of the whole civilised world. It is listening to what is being said at the commission. It would have been so important if only all the inadequacies of the way work is organised had been stated loudly and boldly there, with an indication of a possible practical way out of these difficulties...

We have little space left to discuss other parliamentary news. The Liberal government has been going through fairly hard times, but has nonetheless weathered the storm. The most remarkable success chalked up by this government was on the issue which posed the gravest danger to it. An apparently simple proposal was made to postpone a session in order to examine the question of introducing a five per cent import duty imposed in India on English cotton manufactures. If the proposal to postpone the session had been adopted, this would have been in effect a censure of the policy of the government, which had put a five per cent import duty on Lancashire cotton goods and had tried to neutralise its protectionist effect by imposing a similar duty on the produce of Indian factories. There is no doubt that the government would have interpreted the passing of the above-mentioned postponement as a vote of censure, and would have stood down. The matter mainly concerned the interests of the Lancashire cotton spinners, who were not unduly concerned about the bankruptcy of India. The government, however, could not see things the same way and could not permit a situation in which Lancashire cotton traders continued to enjoy the privilege of not paying any duties while other branches of English industry seeking markets in India were not exempt from them.[29]

Almost up to the last minute the defeat of the government seemed almost inevitable. All the forces of the Tories and the Liberal Unionists had come together against the government on this question. Moreover, there was the danger of a split within Gladstone's own party, owing to the defection of the Lancashire Liberal MPs. Balfour, the leader of the opposition, should have led the vote, as they say. But on the very evening when the debate was due to take place, Balfour was struck down with influenza, and this timely malady kept him at home. One illustrated newspaper depicted him lying in bed, covered up to his throat with a blanket, with one eye closed and the other one watching.[30] It is well known, incidentally, that Balfour himself objected to the proposed tactics, the real originator of which was Chamberlain.[31] This vulgar politician and even more vulgar man is losing his status in the eyes of his Tory allies day by day. The senior Tories – aristocrats, of course – look down on him as an ill-educated parvenu, while the young ones see him as a figure standing in the way of their plans and ambitions. Chamberlain is after the position of Chancellor of the Exchequer. Both he and Goschen in this regard show a fairly shameless urge to shove each other out of the way.[32] But Chamberlain's keenness to overturn the government at any cost led to precisely the opposite result. The government received 304 votes against 109. But Chamberlain was not among the 109. He had however been seen in the division lobby. He tried to hide away, not wishing to pass through the doors where a bailiff stands loudly calling out the names of all members who are voting. However, the doors from the division lobby to the floor of the House are always closed after the MPs have passed through them. Where did Chamberlain go? It is a mystery! Like all the other members, he entered the lobby, but did not leave it. He could not have gone back onto the floor of the House, so what had happened to him? This serious question was officially raised in Parliament and the honourable and esteemed Speaker was obliged to explain that there were other places, familiar to all MPs, where one can hide from divisions. The Commons erupted in laughter which did not die down for some time, and this laughter was repeated up and down the country when it became clear that Chamberlain, embarrassed by the fact that he would have to vote with a Falstaff army of cotton traders plotting in their own interests, had hidden in the lavatories during the voting.[33]

The first reading of the bill on disestablishing the church in Wales has already taken place, but, as always in England, the battles around it should be expected only on the second reading. It is highly likely that the elastic consciences of the Nonconformists (Dissenters) belonging to the Liberal Unionist Party will allow them on this occasion to vote with the government.[34] Then there is another very important measure which affects the workers – a bill to supplement and extend the Factory Acts.[35] The main clauses of this bill relate to those trades which are hazardous to life and health. There is an article in it requiring mandatory registration and declaration of all accidents and illnesses resulting from that line of employment (industrial diseases). After several years of stubborn agitation, laundries, docks and bakeries will at last be covered by these laws. The bill directs that all places where work takes place should be registered, and places responsibility on employers for the workplaces and even for outwork given to workers to perform at home. Moreover, girls from thirteen to eighteen are prohibited altogether from working overtime. For women over eighteen, overtime is reduced from forty-eight days per year, which it had been previously, to thirty, and overtime is to be permitted only three days a week rather than five as before. In certain branches of industry, where overtime was permitted for ninety-six days per year, this figure is reduced to sixty. One sad absence from the bill, however, is any mention of a minimum age for children sent to work in factories. Since January 1893 it has been forbidden to use children younger than eleven for this work. Mr Asquith, the Home Secretary, who introduced this bill into Parliament, recognised that however much the government might want to raise, even if only by one year, the minimum permitted age for children to work in factories, it could not do so. The opposition to this did not come so much from the employers as from the children's parents. This may seem implausible, but it is a sad fact that even among the most politically developed workers of northern England you can find mothers and fathers who stubbornly resist the idea that their children should go to school for an extra year and enjoy the freedom to play and

have one less year of the torture which awaits them in the factories. The reason for this abnormal attitude consists in the fact that
even the combined earnings of mother and father are often insufficient to maintain a family. When the sums children can earn in the
factory are added, then existence becomes bearable. The family of
a Lancashire weaver can often earn between four and five pounds
a week in total. The capitalist system has penetrated so deeply
into the consciousness of its victims that even the best workers of
northern England are prepared to squeeze every last drop out of
themselves and their nearest and dearest with just one goal – to
turn themselves into small businesspeople and become employers
in their turn.

Another important omission in the factories bill is that it says
nothing about the factory inspectorate and would not increase it.
When the above-mentioned Factory Acts were finally brought in
after lengthy agitation, it was very hard to ensure they were strictly
observed owing to the shortage of factory inspectors. One person
very well informed on the factory question told us recently that
although he is in favour of any political reform aimed at improving
the position of the working classes, he believes that at present
the workers would derive more benefit from the appointment of
enough factory inspectors to ensure that the existing factory legislation is observed, rather than from a new factories bill.[36]

The Liberal government has finally shut the doors on any
attempt to establish payment for MPs.[37] There is nothing allocated in the budget for that. And this is quite understandable. The
government has a parliamentary majority of no more than twelve
in the best case. It would hardly be expedient to bring in such a
measure, which would allow some unmoneyed but stubborn MP
to vote as he pleased and spurn the 'golden' arguments the party
ringleaders deploy to sway him.

The question of the House of Lords will soon be debated in
the House of Commons, in the form of bill entitled 'The Houses
of Parliament (arrangement of relations)'. This bill represents an
attempt at defining the whole policy of the Liberal Party towards
the House of Lords.[38] The main proposals of the bill, which will
be introduced by Labouchère, are as follows: 1) a limitation on
the Lords' right of veto on bills presented to the upper house; the

veto will remain in force only for one parliamentary session and will expire when the sessions ends; 2) the House of Commons has the right to confirm a bill and give it the force of law, without taking account of the revisions and amendments made to it by the Lords. The question is – does the government want to accept this proposal? In all likelihood the government will reply that it has its own opinions on this matter and will set out its own policies in this regard. Whatever the case, it could be objected here that this bill is an expression of the ideas put forward at a meeting of the National Liberal Federation in Leeds, and does not diverge at all in its essentials from the political views expressed by certain ministers in their official speeches. The campaign against the House of Lords, you may be sure, is essentially stillborn, despite various inflammatory telegrams and newspaper articles trying to breathe life into it.

One of the major recent scandals, which caused a lot of hubbub in London society, featured two distinguished gentlemen in its leading roles – Mr Wilde and the Marquess of Queensberry.[39] Mr Wilde became well known several years ago for writing two or three successful plays for the theatre. The Marquess of Queensberry is best known to the English public as a sportsman who laid down the classical rules for the noble art of boxing. Present-day prize boxing bouts are always conducted according to the 'Queensberry rules', which makes them a little less bestial than illegal contests of the same art. In addition, Queensberry is also known as the only titled agnostic and as someone who disrupted a theatrical performance. The case was as follows. Several years ago Tennyson, rather than continuing with his usual craft of composing poetry – at which he was much better – decided to write a play, *The Promise of May*. It seemed to the Marquess of Queensberry's sensitive soul that the playwright was mocking agnosticism, and so, during a performance the marquess stood up in his box and, addressing the audience, loudly declaimed a short speech of protest against the play. We were present at that performance and are quite unable to say which we enjoyed the most – the stupid play or the impromptu protest from the box and the subsequent undignified scene in which the director and his assistants tried to throw the pugilist lord unceremoniously out of the box. However, when he identified himself, they immediately desisted and started grovelling to the very man they had just been trying to throw out.[40] Everyone knew that the Marquess of Queensberry was intending to create another scene on the opening night of a new play by Oscar Wilde at St James' Theatre.[41] When the curtain was lowered and the playwright called onto the stage, the plan was to throw him a bouquet of carrots, onions and other kitchen vegetables. The theatre director got wind of this proposed demonstration and tried to ensure that the agitated lord was not allowed into the theatre on that day. The reason for the uncommon hostility between the Marquess of Queensberry and Oscar Wilde is fairly scandalous in nature. The Marquess of Queensberry suspects Wilde of a vice it is awkward to discuss in the press, and brazenly accused him of it on a postcard left out for him in the club where Wilde is a member. This card could be seen by all the members of this club, which, it should be added, includes members of the female sex. It is easy to imagine the scandal this caused. Mr Wilde went to court and sued the Marquess of Queensberry for libel. The court investigation, as you are probably already aware from the newspapers, led to many piquant revelations about London high society, and ended with the arrest of the plaintiff, Wilde...[42]

The New Party.[43] This is a collection which we can in all good conscience recommend to Russian readers, both for its merits and its inadequacies. It is precisely those inadequacies which will show to everyone interested in the social, intellectual and political movements in English society, what great confusion there is at present in the conceptions of even the most advanced of our intellectuals. First of all, however, we should warn Russian readers not to be misled by the title of the book. There is no new political party corresponding to the descriptions of most of the authors in the collection. It does not exist. Moreover, the very name of that party precludes any possibility of it existing. The 'Isocratic Party', as Grant Allen calls it, does not exist. Grant Allen is undoubtedly a very prolific writer who likes to deal with all manner of themes in his work, but usually touches them only superficially.[44] There are rumours that he gets other people to do his writing for him and just puts his name to it. Whatever the case, there is no doubt that the above-mentioned collection *The New Party* represents an uncommon medley. Among its contributors, besides the novelist Grant Allen, there is the publisher of a workers' newspaper who seriously claims that the new workers' movement has been brought about by the sentimentalism of Ruskin, Dickens, Thoreau and Carlyle![45] Other contributors are the great artist Walter Crane, the very ordinary Liberal Byles, an MP from Bradford, the inventive politician Keir Hardie, the most respected defender of women's rights and campaigner from the Temperance Society Lady Henry Somerset, and a further half dozen assorted clergymen in various stages of ossification.[46] The only figure among the contributors who is genuinely authoritative is Alfred Russel Wallace, known to the whole scientific world as the man who discovered the principle of natural selection at the same time as Darwin.[47] However his article on the 'Social economy of the future' published in this book, interesting as it is, only goes to show that specialists in one branch of knowledge will certainly not always be able to get a clear grasp of another branch. The three main points proposed by the author to solve the social problem are 1) the nationalisation of land; 2) the elimination of the existing relationship between capitalists and workers; 3) the elimination of debt through the destruction of the very mechanisms for its legal enforcement. The confusion in Wallace's mind here is particularly clearly expressed in his second paragraph, where he talks of guaranteeing every worker the possibility to become a capitalist. But at any rate this article is worthwhile reading for everyone who studies current political and social evolution. There are other articles in the volume which are, certainly, fine in themselves, but have no logical connection with any so-called 'Isocratic' party. Of these we would particularly draw our readers' attention to 'London's pauper chaos', which contains many interesting facts and figures, 'Voice from the rural wilderness' and 'History of private property'.[48]

Av.

Notes

1. For the London County Council's reforming activities see Letter 2, note 10.
2. The London County Council election was held on 2 March 1895.
3. In the election campaign of February 1895 critics of the LCC Progressives argued that the council's ambitious social policies were paid for in large rate rises. Sir John Lubbock, a former Progressive

member of the council, claimed that the LCC had turned a 10d in the pound rate in 1888 to 18s 1d in 1895. John Davis, *Reforming London: The London Government Problem, 1855-1900*, Clarendon: Oxford, 1986, p141. Defending the council from such accusations, Sidney Webb stated that once adjustments had been made for amendments to the system of how rates were levied in the days of the Metropolitan Board of Works preceding the LCC, the first six years of Progressive administration (1889-1895) had seen only a 1½d in the pound net demand on London ratepayers. On this Webb wrote: 'What, on this computation, does the London County Council cost the Londoner? According to Lord Salisbury, the Council is a hot-bed of Socialist experiments. Yet the net increase of charge upon each Londoner, after six years of Progressive rule, is positively less than 1d per month, everything included. Surely never was a revolution so cheap'. Sidney Webb, 'The work of the London County Council', *Contemporary Review*, January 1895, Vol. 67, p152.

4. When the Metropolitan Board of Works, the elected system for London-wide administration, which operated from 1855 until it was replaced with the London County Council, was established, it did not extend to the City of London, which retained its ancient system of government. Successive attempts to reform or incorporate City government into London-wide administration were resisted by the powerful livery companies, which by 1880 were responsible for a land and property portfolio of £20m, yielding an annual income of £750,000. Lavish dinners for livery company members were a significant feature of their spending, prompting *Justice*, the weekly newspaper of the Social Democratic Federation (SDF), to comment on the 'corrupt Corporation ... with its vast revenues properly belonging to the whole body of working Londoners, but devoted mainly to selfish purposes of a mere handful of plutocratic non-resident parasites'. 'A commune for London', *Justice*, 2 March 1895, p5.

    The recommendation of a Royal Commission in September 1894 that the City and the County of London (LCC area) be amalgamated as a new authority known as the City of London was not included in the government's legislative plans launched in February 1895, and with the defeat of the Liberals in the general election five months later, it was lost.

5. The acquisition of Lincoln's Inn Fields, the largest of London's squares, had been an ambition of the LCC since 1891. Twice rejected by Parliament, it finally passed through both houses in 1894 on the condition that the council compensated the Square's trustees at a rate higher than they had originally been prepared to meet. Rather

than cause delay, the council accepted the condition and Lincoln's Inn Fields was finally opened by the LCC chairman, Sir John Hutton, on 23 February 1895. Hutton declared that the council now had eighteen parks, thirty open spaces, and sixteen gardens – totalling 3,676 acres, 1,200 of which had been acquired since the 1889 when the LCC came into being. At this time the authors were living only 200 yards away in Gray's Inn Square and would have benefitted from access to Lincoln's Inn Fields.

6. London was one of a handful of large urban areas without its own publicly owned water supply. The eight water companies supplying the capital made good profits because of their ability to levy a rate in proportion to rental values, and not the amount of water supplied. As London grew and the number and size of homes increased, so water company revenue went up. In the mid 1890s New River Company shareholders were in receipt of a 12 per cent dividend on their investment. Sidney Webb, 'London's water tribute', Fabian Tract No. 34, 1898, p1. In 1895 the LCC introduced into Parliament eight bills to buy up the companies, by agreement if possible, if not, by arbitration. The bills were lost when the Liberal government fell in June.

   The LCC Progressives had similar municipalising ambitions for London's tramway service. Opposition to this was led by the Tramways Institute whose chairman, W.I. Carruthers Wain, was also chairman of the London, Deptford and Greenwich Tramway Company. After announcing a dividend of 7 per cent in February 1895, Carruthers Wain urged shareholders to vote Moderate and Unionist to thwart the Council's municipalising plans. *Morning Post*, 22 February 1895, p9.

7. In the second half of the nineteenth century, many towns and cities established their own municipal water and gas services, and later tramway and electricity operations. The Fabian Society made much of municipalisation, believing it gave local authorities essential revenue-raising potential, as well as demonstrating the value of collectivist solutions to urban problems. Sidney Webb's 'The London programme' of 1891 was probably the best exposition of the Fabian perspective and was influential. However, not all socialists believed municipalisation alone was enough. Keir Hardie, leading figure in the Independent Labour Party (ILP) and editor of *Labour Leader*, while supporting municipal services, was nevertheless keen to point out that 'these developments have been made by no one party. Our Conservative towns have them to as full an extent as our Liberal towns ... Many of them have been made from the narrowest ratepayer point of view, not as works to be run for the public benefit

but solely as works to bring in a profit for the purpose of helping the local rates, in many cases at the expense of the sweating of men employed upon them. They are, in fact, merely a form of extended joint stock capitalism, with the ratepayers as capitalists'. *Labour Leader*, 12 November 1898, p372.

8. Sir John Lubbock, First Baron of Avebury (1834-1913), was tutored by Charles Darwin when he was a boy, and he continued to study and write about natural history all his life. Member of Parliament for the University of London seat and chairman of the LCC between 1890 and 1892, Lubbock became opposed to the extension of municipal enterprise, believing it interfered with private capital, enhanced the power of labour and led to dubious accounting methods. Howard G. Hutchinson, *The Life of Sir John Lubbock, Lord Avebury: Volume 2*, Macmillan: London, 1914, pp235-6. Lubbock was prominent in the opposition to municipalisation of the water companies. See Sir John Lubbock, 'London and the water companies', *The Nineteenth Century: A Monthly Review*, April 1895, Vol. 37, No. 218, pp657-64.

9. In April 1895 when the third letter was written, the authors were living in rooms at 7 Gray's Inn Square, let to them by an Inn Master who had access to properties and could charge rent. The editors are indebted to Andrew Mussell, Archivist of the Honourable Society of Gray's Inn, for this information.

10. January and February 1895 experienced some of the coldest weather for nearly a century, leading to deaths of children and vulnerable adults. Under the very heavy frosts pipes froze, cutting off the supply of fresh water to many homes for several weeks. Water carts were a common sight in the capital's streets during February. Questions were raised about the shallowness of the trenching carrying the pipes making them liable to freeze, a charge denied by the water companies. Public hostility to the companies led one director to feel he had to write anonymously when defending his water company's record because 'I dare not sign my name for fear of personal violence.' 'To the Editor of the *Times*', *Times*, 12 March 1895, p14. See also the reprinted letters of complaint by members of the public to water companies in the *Daily Chronicle*, 2 April 1895, p3.

An epidemic of influenza broke out in mid February, lasting until the end of March, and was responsible for hundreds of deaths. One commentator concurred with the verdict of the authors on the possible link between problems with the supply of fresh water and the influenza when he wrote that 'anything which lowers the conditions of health and lessens the resisting power of the community, is a source of peril for the presence of an epidemic; and we cannot but add that it was, to say the least of it, an unfortunate coincidence that at the very time when we were in danger of a recrudescence of influenza in London, there should be no sufficient continuous flow of water to flush the network of sewers and soil pipes which connect almost all the houses of this vast and complicated city; and that, too, at the moment when, after the drains had been blocked with ice for weeks, a gradual thaw set free the sewage, precisely while the change of temperature made any impurity in the air especially undesirable'. 'Influenza and the water famine', *The Speaker: A Liberal Review*, 6 April 1895, p379.

11. Surprisingly, the authors give incorrectly the number of ILP and SDF candidates and their aggregate votes. In fact, the ILP stood seven candidates: Pete Curran - Greenwich (391 votes); Harold Snelling - Chelsea (218); Jack Elliott - Deptford (1,255); Fred Hammill - North Kensington (147); J.W. Helps - Limehouse (84); J.F. Shillaker (44) and J. Morgan (73), both Islington South. Aggregate ILP vote: 2,212.

The SDF stood five candidates: George Palmer (also an ILP member) - Kensington (144 votes); J. Yallop - St Pancras East (83); C.F. Davis - St Pancras North (187); A. Blackwell (26) and C. Groombridge (72), both Islington West. Aggregate SDF vote: 512.

Both parties were disappointed with the returns. Hardie stated that the votes recorded for ILP candidates 'give no indication of the real strength of the movement in London, and to that extent the election has not done the movement any good'. He pointed to the absence of a co-ordinated London-wide electoral approach as a weakness in which 'each branch selected its candidate in haphazard fashion, and in most cases the election campaign was badly organised and loosely conducted'. *Labour Leader*, 9 March 1895, p2. For the SDF the election was a 'ridiculous exhibition' in which local branches brought forward candidates without reference to the national committee's advice that there should only be contests in those constituencies where the local branch was well organised and financially healthy. That this did not happen caused H.W. Lee, the SDF secretary, to write that it was a situation in which 'local autonomy, elevated to a fetish, held full sway'. In St Pancras and West Islington the poll of SDF candidates brought 'the cause of socialism into disrepute and the Social Democratic Federation into contempt'. *Justice*, 9 March 1895, p7.

12. Despite the even split in the number of Progressive and Moderate councillors on the LCC after the March 1895 election, the Progressives were able to command a majority because of support among appointed Aldermen. The Moderates improved their elec-

toral organisation at the 1895 election because of the work of the London Municipal Society, founded in the previous year to counter the influence of the Progressives. Ken Young, *Local Politics and the Rise of Party: The London Municipal Society and the Conservative Intervention in Local Elections, 1894-1975*, Leicester University Press: Leicester, 1975. Spurred on by remarks of Lord Salisbury, the leader of the Conservative Party in Parliament, that the LCC was 'the place where collectivist and social experiments are tried ... where a new revolutionary spirit finds its instruments and collects its arms', the Moderates, in a well-funded campaign, took the message to the electorate that the Progressive council was profligate with ratepayers' money and too often serving the interests of trade unionists who benefited from the Council's labour policy. *The Globe*, 25 February 1895, p4.

13. Between 1866 and 1869 the East End of London suffered catastrophe from the effects of a downturn in the business cycle, an outbreak of cholera, the decline of shipbuilding on the Thames and severe winters. In January 1867 there were 30,000 destitute in Poplar. The poor law system proved inadequate in dealing with widespread distress, forcing poor-law guardians to turn to private charities for assistance. Charitable aid poured in to the East End from London's wealthier districts, about which local clergyman John R. Green of Stepney commented 'some half a million people in the east end of London have been flung into the crucible of public benevolence, and have come out of it simply paupers'. Quoted in George R. Boyer, 'The evolution of unemployed relief in Great Britain', *Journal of Interdisciplinary History*, Vol. 34, No. 3, Winter 2004, p411.

14. With unemployment on the increase from 1890 there was growing agitation amongst trade unionists and socialists for measures to alleviate distress and create work. In London, regular gatherings at Tower Hill during early 1892 and into 1893 attracted the attention of the police and the Home Office, who deployed agents to report on proceedings. Jose Harris makes use of their reports to the Home Office in his *Unemployment and Politics: A Study in English Social Policy, 1886-1914*, Clarendon: Oxford, 1972, pp81-3. Edward spoke at Tower Hill and Eleanor supported SDF demands for the government to act on unemployment. *Lloyds List*, 25 November 1892, p3; *Morning Post*, 24 October 1892, p2.

In response to calls for the government to tackle distress and unemployment, Prime Minister Herbert Gladstone stated in September 1893 that he would do nothing directly as it was 'one of those fluctuations in the condition of trade which, however unfortunate and lamentable they may be, recur from time to time'. HC Deb. 1 September, Vol. 16, cc.1734-5.

15. Keir Hardie (1856-1915), Labour MP for West Ham South since 1892, was prominent in the agitation on unemployment, repeatedly raising the issue in Parliament and speaking at rallies in London and across Great Britain. Adept at exposing blatant hypocrisy and shocking inequality, Hardie used his parliamentary position to reveal the number of deaths attributable to starvation, while at the same time highlighting the decision to grant an annual pension of £4,000 to the retiring Speaker of the House of Commons in 1895. *Reynolds's Newspaper*, 17 December 1893, p5; HC Deb. 23 April 1895, Vol. 32, cc1504-5.

Fearing the electoral effects of growing unemployment in marginal constituencies and the potential for parliamentary defeat on the Address to Parliament in February 1895 – which Hardie threatened to bring about with an amendment on unemployment – the Liberal government conceded that a House of Commons Select Committee be established to investigate the extent of distress through want of work. However, it was soon clear to Hardie that it was merely an excuse for doing nothing. The announcement that Sir Henry Campbell Bannerman would chair the committee confirmed this, as it was known that he did not concern himself with the unemployed issue. This he admitted in a private letter the day before his appointment was confirmed. He wrote to a friend: 'They are going to put me on as chairman on the unemployed committee – a horrible thing. I protested and said I knew nothing about poor law subjects. I had never picked oakum in my life. The grim reply was, "My dear fellow, you'll wish you were picking oakum before you are done with this job"'. Quoted in Harris 1972, p.91n.

The committee's interim report, 'First report from the Select Committee on Distress from Want of Employment', HMSO, March 1895, included the evidence of those referred to by the authors and in the notes below. The committee produced two further reports, the second in May and the third in July 1895.

16. Sir Hugh Owen (1835-1916), who had been Permanent Secretary to the Local Government Board since 1882, gave evidence over three days and subsequently presented a mass of statistical data, denying that the distress was exceptional and insisting that in cases where relief was necessary it could be met within the established system and funding allocation.

17. Frederick Edward Hilleary (1841-1921), Clerk of West Ham Corporation and West Ham Board of Guardians. By the 1870s West

Ham had become the principal industrial area of the metropolis, with a rapidly growing population working in gas, chemical, engineering, metals, food and drink industries. Dock labour, which commenced in 1855 with the opening of the Victoria Dock, continued to expand with the construction of the Albert Dock in 1880.

The winter of 1894-5 saw widespread distress in West Ham. There were accounts of death by starvation in these months, as with the case of George Boik, a 68-year-old nail maker who died in West Ham in November 1894 after applying for relief from the poor law authority and being told that he must enter the workhouse. Boik's death was recorded as being due to 'heart failure, the result of want of food and exposure'. At the coroner's inquest a West Ham juryman said 'If a man is found begging he gets locked up, if starving, he must become a pauper. I think it is a disgrace to the country that men die like this from starvation'. *Barking, East Ham and Ilford Advertiser*, 3 November 1894, p2.

A deputation of the West Ham Trades Council met Lord Rosebery in December 1894 to bring the desperate situation to the attention of the prime minister. When presented with the evidence that at least 5,000 men were unemployed in West Ham, Rosebery expressed disbelief. *Morning Post*, 15 December 1894, p2. In order to demonstrate the accuracy of their claim, the Trades Council conducted a detailed survey of the borough and found they had underestimated the extent of unemployment, which in fact stood at over 10,000. *Labour Leader*, 16 February 1895, p7. The survey was brought together by Percy Alden (1865-1944), warden of the Mansfield House Settlement in Canning Town, who had been a West Ham councillor since 1892, with the foot slogging undertaken by Trades Council delegates. Alden gave evidence to the Select Committee on Distress.

18. The influence of trade unions on the policies of West Ham Council owed much to the pioneering work of Will Thorne, a close friend and comrade of Eleanor and Edward's, and his fellow members of the Gas Workers' and General Labourers Union, which had been founded in 1888. The union backed Keir Hardie's successful contest of the West Ham south constituency in 1892 and played a key role in municipal contests from 1891, when Thorne himself was elected to the council. 'By 1892 there were seven councillors described as Labour members. Two Labour men were elected to the School Board in 1892, and others to the Guardians'. Paul Thompson, *Socialists, Liberals and Labour: The Struggle for London, 1885-1914*, Routledge: London, 1967, p131. Co-ordination of Labour's electoral effort was made possible with the setting up of a United Socialist and Labour

Council made up of the Trades Council, SDF, ILP, and Christian socialists in 1894. By 1898, socialists had a majority on West Ham council. Thompson, pp131-5.

19. Arnold Frank Hills (1857-1927) was the managing director of the Thames Iron Works and Shipbuilding Company at Blackwall. Hills lived in the East India Dock Road close to the works and was regarded as having philanthropic intentions until he brought in blackleg labour to break strikes of engineers and joiners in 1890 and 1891. In the winter of 1893-4 Hills raised £1,000 by public subscription to tackle distress in the district. West Ham Council matched this sum and men were put to work on Wanstead Flats laying out football and cricket pitches. The men were employed for four days of six hours at 4d per hour. A similar scheme was run at Poplar. Hills considered the scheme expensive for the results obtained and proposed an amendment based on piecework for all future projects. This was initially accepted by West Ham Council but following protest by the Trades Council, who rejected payment by results, support was withdrawn. Hills went ahead in the winter of 1894-5 and it was a scheme organised on these terms that he proposed as a model to the Select Committee on Distress in February 1895.

20. Hills submitted a proposed Bill to the Select Committee for London-wide implementation based on local charity, local authority and Exchequer funding. The proposal was discussed in detail by the committee, but was not recommended for implementation.

21. Hardie gave evidence to the committee over two days, beginning with a critique of Sir Hugh Owen's account, which he believed vastly underestimated the extent of distress across Great Britain. Hardie claimed that he had sent out a circular to his contacts in provincial towns and cities who sat on local unemployment committees composed of trade unionists, socialists and in some cases clergymen and other sympathisers. These, Hardie claimed, were able to give a more accurate picture of the distress, which was acute and widespread. There were 10,000 destitute in Leeds, 15,000 unemployed in Liverpool, 8,000 unemployed in Glasgow and 10,000 out of work in his own West Ham. Contrary to the authors' suggestion, Hardie did have information on Leeds, which he had obtained from local ILP leader Tom Maguire. Additionally, the authors misinterpret Hardie's evidence to the committee on the extent of national unemployment. Hardie estimated the level of unemployment at one-and-three-quarter million, and not the five-and-three-quarter million they attribute to him. The figure of five-and-a-quarter million in distress given by Hardie included family members of those unemployed.

Hardie accepted that he had never sat on any boards or committees to do with unemployment and distress, stating, 'I have always refused on principle ... because there were plenty to do that work. I spend most of my time in going about the country making special enquiries from place to place ... I speak from personal knowledge coming into contact with people ... especially those who are interested in trying to solve the problem'. 'First report from the Select Committee on Distress from Want of Employment', p.94.

22. In December 1893 Hardie had raised the possibility of the government 'laying down eight or ten cruisers to be built in different parts of the country'. He stated that each would generate 3,000 new jobs for between eighteen and twenty-four months. HC Deb., 12 December 1893, Vol. 19, cc1179-224.

Hardie had been interested in the idea of resettlement of the unemployed after having read the Rev. Herbert V. Mills' book *Poverty and the State, or Work for the Unemployed,* in which he proposed to transform workhouses into home colonies based on co-operative production. Victor Bailey, 'In darkest England and the way out: The Salvation Army, social reform and the labour movement, 1885-1910', *International Review of Social History,* Vol. 29, No. 2, 1984, pp151-2. Henry Pelling noted that home colonies were a 'hobby horse' of Hardie's. He proposed them in his evidence to the Royal Commission on Labour in 1892 and at the founding conference of the ILP in 1893. H. Pelling, *Origins of the Labour Party,* Oxford University Press: Oxford, 1965, p119n. Hardie raised the issue in the Commons on February 1893 in commenting on the action of the Newcastle Board of Guardians authorising the demolition and rebuilding of the workhouse and making land available for cultivation. Hardie told the Commons that 'this House, as representing the nation, should give those men who are out of work the opportunity of employing themselves through this system of Home Colonisation'. HC Deb., 7 February 1893, Vol. 8, cc691-770.

23. Hardie's proposals were subjected to rigorous interrogation and some hostility by members of the committee. Although it is clear Hardie had not prepared his brief as perhaps he should have done, and consequently at times appeared to be extemporising, he did manage to get across the basic message that the state had a responsibility to relieve the distress and that action needed to be taken immediately. In essence, Hardie put forward the idea that the Exchequer make available £100,000 to be matched by local sources to create an emergency fund to prevent starvation. Hardie was applauded for this by Harry Quelch in the pages of *Justice* when

he wrote: 'We should have thought that Keir Hardie's proposal for the distribution of food to the destitute was at least immediately applicable, and it certainly ought not to require much consideration or discussion. We do not think that by any means he made the most of the opportunity afforded him for stating the case of the unemployed. But his proposal that they should have food anyhow was eminently practical and simple.' *Justice*, 16 March 1895, p1. Some members of the committee attempted to ridicule Hardie's plan, as did the authors, because the sums involved were not sufficient to cover the extent of the need that Hardie claimed existed. However, one member, George Whiteley (1855-1925), the Liberal MP for Stockport, saw merit in Hardie's suggestion, and pointed out that using costings from a similar scheme active in Blackburn, it would be possible to provide twenty-one million meals for those in distress from the initial Exchequer grant of £100,000. 'First report from the Select Committee on Distress from Want of Employment', p76.

24. Sir Joseph Renals, Mayor of the City of London, appealed in early 1895 for subscribers to support the Mansion House Conference on the Condition of the Unemployed, founded in 1892 to relieve distress in the East End. The charity provided temporary employment at Abbey Mills, West Ham, where forty acres of land was to be levelled and drained to provide allotments. *Illustrated Police News*, 2 March 1895, p6.

25. John Theodore Dodd (1848-1934), a radical barrister active in the Poor Law Reform Association, put forward the idea that it was possible under existing legislation for poor law authorities to provide useful and profitable employment for able-bodied inmates of workhouses and unemployed labourers. Dodd claimed that Statute 43 Eliz. c2 (1601) gave parish authorities powers to provide employment for those in need. To do this the parish might become 'manufacturer and merchant'. Similarly, under the Act 59 George III, c.12. ss12,13 (1819) parish officers had authority to buy or hire twenty acres for cultivation; this provision was extended to fifty acres in 1831. Dodd was able to demonstrate that these Elizabethan and Georgian statutes had never been repealed, even when the New Poor Law was introduced in 1834, leaving poor law authorities with the power to initiate job creation through local schemes which could extend into fully fledged 'labour colonies'. J. Theodore Dodd, 'What can the Government do for the poor at once?', *New Review*, August 1893, Vol. 9, No. 51, p196. Dodd gave evidence to the Select Committee on Distress in 1895 and published a pamphlet on the subject: 'To

boards of guardians in rural districts: The winter's distress – How to provide for the unemployed', n.d.

The St Pancras SDF was first to test the currency of the legislation in November 1893 when they brought a summons against the local guardians for failing to implement the ancient acts entitling the able-bodied destitute to remunerative work. Harris 1972, p82. Frederick Verinder of the English Land Restoration League advocated the use of the ancient legislation in *The Church Reformer*, December 1893, pp271-2.

Hardie raised the question of the application of these Acts in Parliament in September 1893 and was told by the president of the Local Government Board that although the two ancient acts remained on the statute book, 'The adoption of schemes for the provision by Boards of Guardians of work at wages would involve abandonment of what has hitherto been regarded as the principle of the New Poor Law (1834), upon which the orders as to out-door relief which have been in force during the last half-century have been based.' HC Deb., 12 September 1893, Vol. 17, cc940-2. In spite of these apparently conclusive rulings, Hardie persisted in pressing the matter with Sir Hugh Owen at the Select Committee on Distress. 'First report from the Select Committee on Distress from Want of Employment', p45.

26. Hardie was unhappy with the very slow progress of the committee in its deliberations. His request for an early order to enable immediate relief to be made was not forthcoming. John Burns, a socialist, who had previously been a member of the SDF and was prominent in the London dock strike of 1889, warned against any curtailment of evidence, believing 'The whole subject ought to be thoroughly gone into'. *Standard* (London), 22 February 1895, p2. When the report was published in March 1895 it offered no recommendations, inducing Hardie's *Labour Leader* to characterise the episode thus: 'On February 5 Parliament reassembled, and suddenly discovered a difficulty. A man in the Commons actually threatened danger unless something was done for the unemployed. On February 7 a committee was granted with instructions to promptly present an interim report. The interim report reported that there was nothing to report, whereupon all breathed more freely and the "Gentlemen of England" no longer feared their dividends.' *Labour Leader*, 4 January 1896, p7.

27. John Burns (1859-1843) had been elected to Parliament in 1892 for the Battersea constituency. His arrival in Parliament at the same time as Hardie gave socialists optimism that they would forge an

effective force for the socialist cause. However, it became clear very quickly that there were major political and personal differences between the two men that prevented collaboration. These issues are explored in the numerous biographies of both men and by A.E.P. Duffy's 'Differing political and personal rivalries in the origins of the Independent Labour Party', *Victorian Studies*, September 1962, Vol. 6, No. 1, pp43-65.

Hardie's friend in the ILP, Joseph Burgess, believed that Burns was opposed to the establishment of the Select Committee on Distress because it gave Hardie and the ILP a public profile on the unemployment question. Following the announcement that the committee was to be set up, Burgess wrote: 'All through this agitation the Government has been assured by Mr John Burns that if they would rely on him, he would pull them through. They found out early this week that Mr Burns is a broken reed. Member after member of the most radical hue intimated to the whips that their seats would not be safe if they voted against Hardie on the unemployed question.' *Manchester Courier*, 9 February 1895, p10. In contrast, Engels, who had respect for Burns, believed that although raising the issue of unemployment was 'quite a good thing', Hardie's tactics had demonstrated 'two colossal blunders. 1. The amendment was formulated quite unnecessarily as a direct vote of censure on the government, so that its acceptance would have forced the government to resign and thus the whole thing was tantamount to a Tory manoeuvre. 2. He chose to be seconded by the Tory Howard Vincent, a Protectionist, rather than a Labour member, thereby completing the picture of a Tory manoeuvre and himself as a Tory puppet ... If Mr Keir Hardie continues to behave in this way, he will soon be laid low.' Engels to Sorge, 9 February 1893, *Marx and Engels Collected Works, Vol. 50, Engels 1892-1895*, Lawrence and Wishart: London, 2004, pp102-3.

Burns's tone and line of questioning to Hardie at the Committee was certainly rancorous. Hardie wrote that Burns 'might have been the permanent secretary to the Local Government Board, so well did he support the view that help given to distressed localities would demoralise the recipients, and that all the machinery already existed for adequately dealing with the unemployed problem'. *Labour Leader*, 2 March 1895, p9.

When the committee voted on the draft report, Burns fell in with the government's position on every issue, including opposing an amendment recommending legislation to remove the disenfranchisement of those who claimed temporary outdoor relief. On this occasion the vote was tied and only lost on the casting vote of the chairman. This episode gave another opportunity for Burgess to castigate Burns for his actions: 'I can only conclude that Mr Burns is sitting on the Select Committee, not as a friend, but as a critic of the unemployed, and that he cares more about preventing anything from occurring which may be regarded as a score for Mr Hardie, than he does for the necessities of the class of which Mr Hardie, much to Mr Burns's chagrin, is the popular Parliamentary champion'. *The Manchester Courier*, 16 March 1895, p6. Burgess later wrote a full-scale study of what he believed to be the decline of Burns: *John Burns: The Rise and Progress of a Right Honourable*, Reformers' Bookstall: Glasgow, 1911.

28. 'The Manchester School' refers to those political, economic and social ideas which emerged out of Manchester in the first half of the nineteenth century, associated with the Anti-Corn Law League, advancing free trade and laissez-faire capitalism. These ideas formed the basis of much Liberal thinking during the second half of the century.

29. In response to a significant budget deficit, the government of India's proposal in April 1894 for a 5 per cent general tariff on all imported goods, cotton exempted, was approved by the British government. At the end of 1894 the duty was extended to include cotton goods, provoking protests from leaders of the industry in Lancashire, who lobbied MPs demanding the duty be repealed. The movement gathered a head of steam and for a while with Liberal Unionist backing, led by Joseph Chamberlain, it looked likely that the government could be defeated on a critical motion which, if passed, would have forced the government out of office. The debate took place on 21 February 1895 and the Secretary of State for India, Henry Fowler, put up a convincing display which ensured a large government majority.

30. On the day of the Indian cotton vote the Conservative party leader in the Commons, Arthur Balfour (1848-1930), was reportedly ill with influenza. A cartoon of Balfour – one eye open, the other closed – by Francis Carruthers Gould (1844-1914) appeared in the *Westminster Gazette* of 22 February 1895, p3.

31. Joseph Chamberlain (1836-1914), leader of the Liberal Unionists in Parliament.

32. George Joachim Goschen (1831-1907), former Liberal Unionist who, unable to work with Joseph Chamberlain, joined the Conservative Party in 1893.

33. Chamberlain's novel dodge to avoid voting in the Indian cotton debate was raised in the Commons the following day, creating

much mirth amongst members. The *Daily News* also had some fun with the story, describing how once the lobbies were closed and sealed at division time, 'there are certain closets which gentlemen of resource and readiness of movement offer prompt release from sudden embarrassment'. *Daily News*, 23 February 1895, p7.

34. The move to end the established Church of England in Wales grew out of Nonconformist demands that all denominations enjoy equality. Disestablishment became official Liberal policy in 1891 and legislation was introduced in 1894 to bring this about. The bill passed its second reading but came to grief at the committee stage as 'Welsh members quarrelled among themselves as to the tithe income to the county councils'. Roger L. Brown, 'The dis-establishment of the church in Wales', *Ecclesiastical Law Journal*, Vol. 5, No. 25, 1999, p261.

35. Pressure from the Trades Union Congress (TUC) on the Liberal government to legislate for the inclusion of workplaces at the time excluded from the Factory Acts came to fruition in March 1895 when Home Secretary Herbert Asquith (1852-1928) introduced the Factory and Workshop Bill into Parliament. Asquith argued that it would 'provide for all classes of workers to whom it applied those remarkable conditions of safety for life and health which are in fact observed by wise employers and well conducted undertakings'. He went on to say that it was the government's duty 'to recognise what he might describe as the quickening of the public conscience in this matter, which, by general consent, could not safely be left to individual initiative and enterprise'. Quoted in David Powell, 'The Liberal ministries and labour, 1892-1895', *Historical Journal*, June 1986, Vol. 29, No. 2, p426.

Significantly, laundries were brought under the Factory Acts, albeit in a limited way following amendment proposed by Unionists in response to employer interests. Nevertheless, the trade unions did welcome the legislation because it generally strengthened and extended that already on the statute book. The Factory and Workshop Act was passed with cross-party support on 6 July 1895 in the final days of that Parliament.

Eleanor was deeply interested in industrial legislation, having written and spoken on the Factory Acts since the mid 1880s. With Edward she wrote 'The factory hell' in 1885 for the Socialist League's 'Platform Series'. A second edition of this was published by James Leatham of Aberdeen in 1891. Drawing on knowledge her father had imported into the first volume of *Capital*, Eleanor 'was able to speak of the hazards of industry, the loopholes in existing legislation and the conditions in many types of workshop with an authority that added immense weight to her political arguments'. Yvonne Kapp, *Eleanor Marx: Volume Two, The Crowded Years (1884-1898)*, Lawrence and Wishart: London, 1976, p41.

36. At the TUC Congress of 1892 the demand came forward for an increase in the number of factory inspectors and for there to be recruitment amongst those within industry who knew factory and workshop life. 'Report of the 25th Annual Congress, Trades Union Congress', Glasgow, 1892, pp58-9. Representatives of the TUC Parliamentary Committee met with Home Secretary Asquith in January 1893 and found him sympathetic to the suggestion that inspectors be recruited from industrial workplaces. 'Report of the 26th Annual Congress, Trades Union Congress', Belfast, 1893, p2. Subsequently, twenty-five assistant factory inspectors were appointed, mostly 'practical working men'. 'The Liberal record and the Liberal programme', *Daily News*, 25 June 1895, p7. These appointments were warmly welcomed by the TUC but were seen as a staging post, because at the 1893 Congress a motion calling for a further increase in the number of inspectors was passed 'so that better inspections may take place in tailoring, bootmaking, and similar sweated trades'. 'Report of the 26th Annual Congress', p49. The number of factory inspectors grew from fifty-five in 1878 to 110 in 1896, including five women inspectors who specialised in workplaces where women workers predominated. T.K. Djang, *Factory Inspection in Great Britain*, George Allen and Unwin: London, 1942, p50.

37. Payment of Members of Parliament had been a demand of radical movements since the early nineteenth century, and socialist organisations as they emerged from the 1880s. The TUC adopted this policy at its Congress of 1891. The measure was seen as essential in increasing the number of working men in Parliament who were unable to fund expensive election campaigns and then, if elected, give up paid employment. There were a number of working-class MPs in the 1890s but these relied on trade union and local constituency support, which was heavily stretched. Payment of MPs was included in the Liberals' Newcastle Programme of 1891, but legislation was not brought forward by Gladstone, who was against the idea. Despite pressure from radical Liberal MPs and the Parliamentary Committee of the TUC during 1893 and 1894, the issue was edged out of the final Liberal session on grounds of the availability of parliamentary time and budgetary restraints.

38. Having had a number of bills rejected by the House of Lords, the mood of radical Liberals was for reform. The National Liberal Federation Conference at Leeds in June 1894 saw a move by

Henry Labouchère (1831-1912), Radical and independent MP for Northampton, to commit the party to measures that would enable legislation passed by the Commons to move to Royal Assent in the event of House of Lords rejection. This was seen as a first step towards abolition of the Lords, and proved too strong for the Leeds delegates, who opted instead to issue a warning to the upper house that reform would result if they continued to block government legislation. Labouchère's bill, referred to by the authors, did not materialise. The policy of the Liberal government of introducing bills into Parliament that it knew would be rejected by the Lords was described at the time as 'filling the cup', a tactic it believed would expose the upper house and unite the country against their powers.

39. As this letter was being written, the first court case involving Oscar Wilde (1854-1900) and the Marquess of Queensberry (1844-1900) had just concluded at the Central Criminal Court in London, on 5 April 1895.

The case of defamatory libel was brought by Wilde after Queensberry left his card at Wilde's club upon which he had scrawled the words 'For Oscar Wilde – posing as a somdomite' (*sic*), or perhaps 'ponce and somdomite' (*sic*).

Queensberry had for some time been aware of the relationship between his son Alfred Bruce Douglas (1897-1945) and Wilde, and had repeatedly attempted to bring it to end with threats of violence. Queensberry also believed that his eldest son, Lord Drumlanrig, was being somehow drawn into homosexuality by Lord Rosebery, for whom he worked as private secretary. When Drumlanrig died in a shooting accident in October 1894, many suspected suicide, the suggestion being that he may have been afraid of blackmail over his relations with Rosebery, who was by then prime minister. Richard Ellmann, *Oscar Wilde*, Penguin: Harmondsworth, 1987, p402. Queensberry, who 'had begun to see homosexuals everywhere ... [and who was] ... quick to go on the rampage', set out to provoke Wilde. Ellmann, p381.

Acting against the advice of friends who counselled him that he should not react to Queensberry's provocation, Wilde went ahead with the libel case. At the initial hearing at Marlborough Street Police Court on 2 March, the steward at Wilde's club who had received the visiting card from Queensberry said that it read 'For Oscar Wilde, ponce and somdomite' (*sic*), at which point Queensberry interjected that the phrase he used was 'posing as a sodomite' – a clarification 'small but telling', according to Wilde's most recent biographer: 'as an accusation it was more nebulous, less serious, and rather easier to defend [oneself against]'. Matthew Sturgis, *Oscar: A Life*, London: Head of Zeus, 2018, p541.

In the event, when the case was heard at the Central Criminal Court in the first week of April, Queensberry's counsel, Edward Carson, turned the case against Wilde by calling a number of witnesses who testified to Wilde's 'acts of indecency with other male persons', with which he could be charged under the 1885 Criminal Law Amendment Act. After three days in court, Wilde withdrew his prosecution, and later on the same day was arrested and subsequently charged under the 1885 Act.

40. Queensberry, president of the British Secular Union, took exception to Lord Tennyson's portrayal of a character in in his play, *The Promise of May*, which opened at the Globe Theatre, London on 11 November 1882. Tennyson's character Mr Edgar was a declared atheist who had a 'habit of delivering didactic lectures in answers to plain every-day questions'. *St James's Gazette*, 14 November 1882, p6. Queensberry attended the Globe on 14 November and during the performance he interjected with a public comment which created a small sensation. The next morning he wrote to a London newspaper with his own account:

> Towards the close of the first act, when the gentleman representing Edgar appeared on stage, I instantly became deeply interested when I perceived the character he, Edgar, had come to represent, or rather, as I took it, most grossly to misrepresent. After listening a few minutes to the sentiments expressed by this gentleman freethinker and atheist of Mr Tennyson's imagination, I became horrified and indignant that, rising in my stall, I simply, in a loud voice, made the following remarks apropos of Edgar's comment on 'marriage': 'These are the sentiments that a professing Christian (meaning Mr Tennyson) has put into the mouth of his imaginary freethinker, and it is not the truth'. This is all I said and I sat down.

Queensberry claimed that during the interval there were 'cries and calls' from different parts of the theatre to explain himself, which he was prevented from doing by being 'forcibly but kindly removed' from the theatre. *Daily Telegraph*, 15 November 1882, p5.

It is interesting that the authors state that they were present at the Globe Theatre on the evening of 14 November 1882 and witnessed Queensberry's intervention. It is not clear if the authors were at the theatre together, but if they were, it is the first definite recorded instance of their connection. Dating the beginning of the relationship between Eleanor Marx (as she was then) and Edward Aveling is problematic. Yvonne Kapp describes Eleanor's 'animated existence in the spring and summer of 1882' and speculates that 'since she was undoubtedly partnered on her social outings, and the character of her interests, the places she frequented, were so similar to those of Edward Aveling, a married man, it is reasonable to assume that he had entered upon the scene'. Kapp, *Eleanor Marx: Volume 1, Family Life (1855-1883)*, Lawrence and Wishart: London, 1972, pp236-7.

41. This was Wilde's play *The Importance of Being Earnest*, which opened at St James's Theatre on 14 February 1895. Queensberry's intention of interrupting the play on the opening night became known, and preparations were made to exclude him. Queensberry delivered his card addressed to Wilde (see note 39) at the Albemarle Club on 18 February 1895.

42. Two of the three socialist newspapers with national circulation commented on Wilde's case against Queensberry (for details of the case, see note 39). Keir Hardie's *Labour Leader* believed 'nothing so revolting as the Wilde case has been made public this century'. In the context of what *Labour Leader* regarded as Wilde's 'lofty contempt for the common people', it commented on Wilde's actions 'polluting the moral atmosphere with an offence, the very name of which, much less the thing itself, is happily unknown to 99 per cent of the same lower orders whom he professed to despise'. *Labour Leader*, 13 April 1895, pp6-7.

Justice remarked that 'vice is spreading in this country.... Nor can it be pretended that it is confined to the wealthy classes or the neurotic artistic cliques. Manifestly we have a moral taint which is common to all the ages and all the stratifications of human society.... We have, whether we like it or not, to recognise and deal with the tendency and do our best to eradicate it in the future by careful teaching of the physical basis of morality. The details of the Wilde case are more revolting by the reason of the pecuniary temptations alleged to have been held out. This inducement will at any rate be removed with the establishment of socialism.' *Justice*, 13 April 1895, p113.

The *Clarion* did not comment on the case.

43. *The New Party* was a book edited by Andrew Reid, a Liberal-sympathising journalist who commissioned several volumes of essays from well-known figures. During the 1880s Reid had edited volumes focusing mainly on the issues facing the Gladstonian Liberal Party, including Ireland and disestablishment. By the early 1890s the influence of socialism was apparent in his work. His *Vox Clamantium: The Gospel of the People*, published in the spring of 1894, included essays from several prominent socialists. He fol-

lowed this up in June of that year with the *The New Party: Described by Some its Members*, Hodder: London, 1894, a collection of essays loosely connected to Reid's ambition to bring together radical liberals and socialists into a new political force, the New Party, which he accepted Grant Allen's designation of as the 'Isocratic Party' (for Allen, see note 44).

In language that Jon Lawrence accurately describes as 'otherworldly and at times frankly ridiculous', Reid argued that the New Party would become 'the most comprehensive, picturesque, historical, ideal, ethical, political party which has ever stepped [sic] foot on God's earth'. It would be 'universal as well as national, its commanding and baptizing objects are SOCIAL. IT IS THE PARTY OF THE INSPIRED PEOPLES.' Jon Lawrence, *Speaking for the People: Party, Language and Popular Politics in England, 1867-1914*, Cambridge University Press: Cambridge, 1998, p202; Reid, p.vi.

It is possible that the establishment of the Isocratic Club in Cursitor St, Chancery Lane in July 1894 was inspired by Reid's project, but otherwise the book's initial reception was muted, possibly attributable to the lavish production of the first edition, which came out with a prohibitive cover price. A commentator in *Clarion* certainly thought so: 'When the book was first published I used to go about my friends asking, "Have you a copy of the *New Party* to lend?" And I used to be answered, "It costs 14 shillings! Who, even in a minstrel's tale, ever heard of such a monstrous sum?"' *Reynolds's Newspaper,* 8 July 1894, p8; *Clarion,* 16 February 1895, p56. It was only when a new and popular edition was issued at a price of 2s 6d in December 1894 that the book attracted any attention. It was reviewed and commented on in *Justice,* 22 December 1894, p2, and *Labour Leader,* 22 December 1895, p6.

The new edition included accounts by Reid of meetings at which he had spoken to large audiences in Liverpool and Ashton announcing the organisation as 'the New Party and the National Union of Socialists'. Clearly Grant Allen's suggested 'Isocratic Party' label didn't stick. *The New Party* (popular edition), 1894, pp307-9. Further meetings were held in Leeds in January, and another at William Morris's Kelmscott House in March. *Leeds Mercury,* 7 January 1895, p7; *Justice,* 2 March 1895, p8. Reid brought out a pamphlet, *The Great Bill,* in the summer of 1895, which was heavily criticised by Hardie in *Labour Leader,* 2 July 1895, p2. See also Reid's reply, 9 July 1895, p2. With the organisation going nowhere and the outcome of the general election still being processed, Reid made a last-ditch appeal for supporters to write to him at his Leyton home with ideas about how to take the movement forward. *Reynolds's Newspaper*, 28 July 1895, p5. It seems certain that nothing came of this, and what there was of the New Party was allowed to fade away.

44. Charles Grant Blairfindie Allen [Grant Allen] (1848-1899) was a Canadian-born writer who emigrated to England and made a name for himself as an essayist and novelist. Influenced by socialism but always too much an individualist to work in organised politics, Allen confessed 'I will do better work for our common cause – in so far as it is common – by holding myself aloof from all societies and say[ing] my say in my own way.' Quoted in Peter Morton, 'Grant Allen: A centenary reassessment', *English Literature in Transition 1880-1920*, Vol. 44, No. 4, p416.

45. The essay, by *Clarion* editor Robert Blatchford (1851-1943), stated that: 'If you asked a London socialist for the origin of the new movement he would refer you to Karl Marx and other German socialists. But as far as our northern people are concerned I am convinced that beyond the mere outline of state socialism Karl Marx and his countrymen have had little influence. No, the movement here; the new religion which is socialism, and something more than socialism, is the result of the labours of Darwin, Carlyle, Ruskin, Dickens, Thoreau and Walt Whitman.' *The New Party*, 1894, pp13-14.

46. Walter Crane (1845-1915), the successful illustrator, designer and artist, joined the socialist movement in the early 1880s. Crane designed the frontispiece for *The New Party* and composed some verse. William Pollard Byles (1839-1917) was a Liberal Member of Parliament for Shipley, Bradford between 1892 and 1895. Keir Hardie's essay was titled 'The Independent Labour Party'. Lady Henry Somerset (1851-1921) was an aristocratic temperance and women's rights campaigner who joined the Fabian Society in the 1890s. She wrote on 'The woman's cause' for *The New Party*. The 'half dozen clergymen in various stages of ossification' were: the Dean of Durham; Rev. C.L. Marson; W.J. Dawson, Rev. E. Potter Hall, Rev. Percy Dearmer, and P.H. Wickstead.

47. Alfred Russel Wallace (1823-1913) was a pioneering evolutionist known to and admired by Edward. He had been founder and president of the Land Nationalisation Society since 1881.

48. 'London's pauper chaos' was written by Alfred Foster, 'A London guardian'; Rev. Potter Hall and J.S. Hamilton wrote 'Voice from the wilderness'; and Walter R. Warren, who worked closely with Andrew Reid (see note 43) in the winter of 1894-5 trying to establish the New Party and the National Union of Socialists, wrote 'History of private property'.

LETTER FOUR

May 1895

The continuing national debate about unemployment, its causes, effects and remedies, again featured in the letter for May. Evidence of the poverty resulting from unemployment is cited from a variety of sources, including Alfred Russel Wallace, charitable societies and trade unions. The obvious failure of the House of Commons committee on unemployment and distress to tackle this question was matched by the complacency of the Royal Commission on the Aged Poor, which was predictably noncommittal on the introduction of any scheme for old-age pensions.

With Lord Rosebery's administration conveying a strong impression of a government that had lost direction, it stumbled from one mini-crisis to another and failed to check the ambition of its Chancellor of the Exchequer, Sir William Harcourt, to introduce legislation that gave local authorities power to prohibit or limit alcohol consumption. Popular feeling against this measure would have a major effect on the outcome of the general election only weeks away.

In its concluding paragraphs, the letter considers the outcome of three cases which had 'recently been before the court of the British people, although only two have also appeared before courts of law'. Oscar Wilde's second trial is set amidst the hypocrisy and conspiracy that swirled around it. Without judging the moral character of his personal behaviour, the letter critiques Wilde's commitment to 'art for art's sake'. In what sounds like Eleanor's voice, it condemns this stance as a denial of the fact that all human culture is inseparable from the living people who created it.

More prosaically, the sentencing of financial swindler and Member of Parliament Jabez Balfour is seen as a justice of sorts for all those who suffered losses at his hands.

And finally, Annie Besant, who did not appear in a court of law, but who nevertheless was subjected to public ridicule for her performance

at the end of April at St James' Hall, in which she defended her belief in
the 'Mahatmas' of theosophy, semi-supernatural sages who had reached
enlightenment and could guide others. It is almost unnecessary to state
that this account came from Edward's pen.

In our last letter we provided some details of the evidence given to
the parliamentary committee on the condition of the unemployed.
Shortly afterwards, the committee published its 'Interim report',
which declared that nothing had been presented at its hearings
which gave it cause to make any definite proposals to the House of
Commons. Further investigations are therefore certainly needed.
The committee, however, is continuing to sit and has been receiving
evidence from various parts of the country which confirms that
most workers are living in chronically impoverished conditions.
But there has now already been a significant decline in any real
interest in this question. Newspapers which had formerly devoted
entire columns to the sessions of the committee, now print just a
few lines about them. It is no surprise that what some of us were
predicting has quite naturally come to pass – in practical terms
the committee has not been equal to its task. The only benefit this
committee has brought has been to uncover a mass of simultaneously very tragic and very interesting facts and figures. However,
this will all be buried in parliamentary blue books and will make
very little, or indeed no, impression on the public at large.[1]

Meanwhile the promoters of various panaceas continue to offer
them to tackle the miseries of unemployment. The establishment
of so-called 'Home Colonies' is being pushed with particular zeal.
A certain Mr Mather for example, is proposing the creation of agricultural training colonies with state aid. These colonies should be
run by the county councils under local government control. The
main essence of this proposed scheme consists of four points: 1)
the land to be worked should be currently uncultivated but capable
of yielding good results if worked properly; 2) the colonies should
also include some parcels of cultivated land, the produce of which
can initially support the workers starting work on the uncultivated
land; 3) the varieties of grain to be produced should be those which
depend mainly on manual labour for their processing, and 4) the

colonies should then also include branches of industry to provide employment for people for the eight months or more of the year when work in the fields is not possible.[2]

However, this scheme for state colonies can no more solve the difficult problem of unemployment, than can Mr Keir Hardie's occasional sums of £100,000.[3] The public recently got to know about such colonies, thanks to the translation into English of Mrs Julie Sutter's book *A Colony of Mercy*. It seems to us that everybody who reads this remarkable work will acquire lifelong immunity against any propaganda for that sort of colony. Some of the conditions which exist in the German colonies have inspired our philanthropists, who now, for some reason, are particularly keen to replicate this approach at home. Every unfortunate who enters one of these colonies of mercy has to sign a contract declaring, firstly, that the clothing he has been 'lent' will only become his property once he has worked to pay off its cost, secondly, that he has no rights to any wages and will only receive food for his work, and thirdly, everything that he receives in addition to food, no matter how much he has worked, is merely a free gift, granted by the benevolent pastor heading the colony, out of the goodness of his heart. Having signed this contract, the pauper then has to work for two weeks without any remuneration at all. Then, for the next month, he receives two pence halfpenny a day. After six weeks, the maximum remuneration he can receive is fivepence a day. It would however be inaccurate to say that he is paid this money. This is a theoretical wage, which is recorded in a book and mostly goes towards paying off the cost of the clothing the pauper is granted on entering the colony. If there is a surplus in the poor prisoner's account book once his time in the colony has expired, then it is still not handed over to him upon his release. Instead, it is sent on to the poor worker's new master, if he has one. Only if there is no new master does the former prisoner receive the surplus himself, and then only once he is already a safe distance away from the colony.[4]

Alfred Russel Wallace, the well-known naturalist, recently presented a most remarkable series of figures, relating to the question of unemployment, the continual growth of pauperism and the impoverished current situation of the working classes.[5] These figures show that over a thirty-two year period (from 1850 to 1882), the number of London paupers in the workhouses, as a proportion of the total population of London, has remained almost unchanged. Meanwhile, the total amount of income tax paid by Londoners, which constitutes a crude measure of the growth in personal wealth, has tripled over that same period. Wallace, moreover, provides an explanation for all the optimistic data which have been amassed on this question and for all the optimistic conclusions which have been drawn from them. It is quite correct that the proportion of paupers has hardly changed, and at the same time the number of inmates in the London workhouses has fallen slightly over the last two or three decades. However, those who conclude from this that the position of the workers has improved are much mistaken, in that they overlook the very important fact that between 1865 and 1885 no fewer than 132 charitable institutions were founded, and a further fifty have been added to their number over the last decade. Meanwhile, the already existing charitable institutions have not only not ceased their activities, but have instead expanded them and increased their funds. Moreover, these 182 institutions do not include various local charitable societies, nor the large Salvation Army organisation, nor the extremely unpleasant 'Charity Organisation Society'.[6] If we bear in mind the enormous sums of money which get bequeathed to these institutions (in 1893 no less than £500,000 was left to charitable institutions alone, quite apart from all the other educational and religious institutions), as well as the constant flow of individual donations intended for the unfortunate victims of fate, then we shall understand why the official figures for pauperism, high though they may be, are nevertheless not rising any further. In this connection we should also mention a fact which should be better known not only abroad, but also at home. Our old established trade unions, which possess very considerable funds, have year on year been spending more and more of these funds on supporting members of the union who have not been able to find work. Meanwhile, these funds are derived from the weekly dues paid by union members in work. This means that the unemployed are maintained by these same workers who are paying out pennies from their own miserable wages. A few years ago, when the Board of Trade asked various trade unions whether they had had to make extraordinary payments to jobless workers from their funds, almost all answered in the affirmative. Here we shall give just a few figures about textile workers, because these figures seem to us to be typical. Over three years, the sums paid out to union members in need have averaged 14/10^d, 18/2^d, and 25/6^d.[7] Meanwhile, most recently, the report of one of the wealthiest trade unions, the Amalgamated Society of Engineers, noted that the number of unemployed members of that union has increased more than ever before and that over the past twenty years, no less than £100,000 has been paid out from union funds to support its members.[8] Most likely, it would be no exaggeration to say that the official figures on pauperism tell only half the truth. It is of course impossible to give a precise account of the number of unknown people who die every day as a result of insufficient food, of lack of clothing and shelter or of having to breathe polluted air, but even according to official statistics the mortality rate in workhouses and suchlike institutions is continually rising and is moreover significantly above the average mortality rate for the population. Thus, if we take the figures for England and Wales as a whole, deaths in workhouses represent the following percentages compared to overall mortality: 1875 – 5.6; 1885 – 6.7; 1888 – 6.9; 1893 – 7.12. In London the percentages are even more damning: 1865 – 9.1; 1881-1888 – 12.2; 1891 – 13.8; 1893 – 15.2. While overall mortality in London has increased by 21 per cent over the past twenty-eight years, the death rate in workhouses has increased by 100 per cent, and the number of suicides in London has also risen by 59 per cent. And all this is taking place amidst the constantly growing luxury and wealth of the upper classes, as the inevitable consequence of that growth.[9]

The budget compiled by Sir William Harcourt, Chancellor of the Exchequer, was far from a simple matter. Excise duties on whisky were reduced, but those on beer were increased. And, thereby, with a stroke of the pen, the Chancellor of the Exchequer turned a deficit of £19,000 into a surplus of £181,000. The opposition's criticism was that 'the government is taking the ale from the poor Englishman and giving whisky to the Irishman'. It is no secret that the concession on this question was granted out of fear that otherwise all the Irish, Parnellites and anti-Parnellites, would turn against the government.[10] Strange though it is for such a moral country as England, many leading members of the Liberal Party have a material interest in a flourishing brewing industry.[11] Of course, all these gentlemen, together with the entire caste of publicans and restaurateurs, are in revolt against the 'Local Veto Bill'. However, they have not done anything up to now to oppose the budget, and so we can infer that there has been some kind of agreement here. We shall not be surprised if all these gentleman brewers, baronets and counts sacrifice what is most dear to them in the whole world – their commercial advantage – on the altar of their political convictions. They have undoubtedly already received their reward for doing so.

The 'Local Veto Bill' is also a pet parliamentary project of Sir William Harcourt.[12] If this bill passes, it will, or course, be a significant blow to the free trade in alcoholic drinks. If the bill passes into law, ballot forms, like the one shown below, will be issued to voters in the constituencies. If a majority votes to stop issuing licences for the drinks trade, or to restrict the number of licences issued, or to ban licensed trade on Sundays, then that rule will come into force. This example of a ballot form will allow readers to become acquainted with this new method of solving social questions which has been introduced in England.

Form of Ballot Paper.
Form of Front of Ballot Paper where no Resolution is already in force.

1	Are you in favour of Total **PROHIBITION** of ordinary Licenses?	YES.
		NO.
2	If there is not Total Prohibition, are you in favour of a **LIMITATION** of the Number of ordinary Licenses?	YES.
		NO.

Form of Front of Ballot Paper in the case of Sunday Closing.

Are you in favour of Total **SUNDAY CLOSING?**	YES.
	NO.

Form of Front of Ballot Paper where a resolution for Sunday Closing is in force:—

Are you in favour of **REPEALING** the Resolution for total Sunday Closing?	YES.
	NO.

In this way a referendum is being organised on a question of interest to the public, and which affects it materially. This is the first example of this sort of consultation of the people in English politics. We are certainly not on the side of the fanatical enthusiasts for temperance, but nonetheless we cannot ignore the appalling growth in mortality connected with the consumption of alcohol, as the following table shows:[13]

	Deaths from drunkenness
1884	1269
1885	1334
1886	1392
1887	1442
1888	1451
1889	1566
1890	2037
1891	2055
1892	1971
1893	2174

We should not, of course, forget that the most important factor here is the miserable living conditions which impel people towards drunkenness rather than the other way around, that is, drunkenness is not the reason for the miserable position of the poor classes.[14] Another factor here is the foul adulteration of what is sold to the great majority as beer and spirits. Readers should also remember that there are no cafes for the workers where they could, together with their wives and children, spend an evening enjoying a harmless glass of beer in a cheerful and pleasant setting. This is something which impresses our workers when they go to Europe to attend international congresses.[15] It is quite possible that this new measure, if it is brought in, will lead to such a new, better state of affairs, because our licensees currently cater solely to those customers who drink often and fast. In other circumstances they would have to change their dirty, foul-smelling drinking dens into more cheerful and pleasant cafes. In any case, the above bill has the great significance that it leaves this important question not in the hands of officials, but in the hands of the people itself. However, on the basis of our own observations in America, where prohibition is widely practised, we doubt whether any prohibitive measures can have any serious effect in reducing the consumption of spirits in the country overall. One of our experiences in America a few years ago was very typical.[16] Having reached Rhode Island after a long and tiring journey, we asked the Negro servant in our hotel whether he could get us a bottle of wine, which we needed to revive ourselves. 'No, massa', he replied, 'but you can ask at reception'. In the Negro's dark eyes we could see hope and approval, and therefore we went down to the reception. These receptions are peculiar institutions to be found in every American hotel. It is where all the guests' keys are kept and where they can get information about anything. We were so incautious as to ask the clerk for wine at the very moment when a new visitor arrived. While this visitor was nearby, the clerk answered all our requests with 'No! It's prohibited!' But his eyes betrayed a cunning which reassured us, and we decided to wait until the visitor had gone, and sure enough, once he was out of sight, the clerk came up to us and whispered, 'What sort would you like?'

The retirement of the Speaker of the House of Commons provided a suitable opportunity for the English people and press to act out a comedy which seemed to afford the actors themselves satisfaction. The columns of the newspapers were filled with all manner of sensational effusions. And what was there not in these effusions! They described the state ceremonies for the standing down of a Speaker in loving detail, they talked of his Cato-like manner of speaking, they wrote with pathos about the deep disquiet and touching sympathy of the entire English nation, praising the remarkable qualities of this retired gentleman. In a word, on this matter England's scribblers showed in all its glory their fondness for all kinds of hysterical exaggeration, and depicted the matter as if there really was something touching and worthy contained within it. In fact, the former Speaker, Mr Arthur Peel (now already a Viscount) was most unpopular. The laws of heredity[17] suggest that he may have had some qualities, but nonetheless this was a dry, uninteresting person, with very narrow views who did not get on well with the Irish Members of Parliament, nor with any others apart from the Unionists. He increasingly used the power he held by virtue of his high position in Parliament, in a quite unjust fashion, in pursuit of his own sympathies and antipathies. But despite this, the House of Commons, like a bunch of schoolchildren honouring their headmaster on his retirement or because he was letting them go home for the holidays, forgot, or thought it unnecessary to recall, those abuses of power he had permitted himself. And even such newspapers as the London *Daily Chronicle*, which in the past had more than once boldly pointed to official abuses by the former Speaker of the Commons, nevertheless shed tears on the occasion of his retirement and gushed forth the same streams of hysterical praise as all the other papers.[18]

The government had wanted to replace the outgoing Speaker with Mr Leonard Courtney.[19] This gentleman belongs to the small bunch of Liberal Unionists[20] who are trying, not without some success, to reconcile the so-called principles of Liberalism with Toryism. Mr Leonard Courtney had fulfilled his official duties as chairman of Ways and Means well. Mr Courtney is what they call in England a 'worthy fellow', strictly honest in his views, but also very narrow. His wooden face is emblematic of his wooden nature. It reminds one of those comic masks used in Christmas pantomimes, which take the blows of the actors with absolutely no change of expression. Mr Courtney would undoubtedly have been elected unanimously by the House, had it not been for Mr Chamberlain. This politician, acting the dog in the manger, would not hear of the appointment of Courtney. After a certain argument which, incidentally, went largely unnoticed, the candidature of Mr Courtney was withdrawn and the Tories and Liberals put up two political nonentities: the unknown barrister Mr Gully and the equally unknown landlord Sir Matthew Ridley. Mr Gully was elected, but the general feeling is that it will be no surprise that if the Tories win a majority at the next election – which seems likely – the post of Speaker will again be vacant and there will be further elections for that position.[21]

There have been fairly serious disagreements between the Tories and the Liberal Unionists, or, rather, between the Tories and Chamberlain. Chamberlain is the heart and soul of Liberal Unionism – a vulgar heart and an equally vulgar soul. Politically, Chamberlain is undoubtedly the most capable person in the ranks of the reactionaries apart from Balfour, but this state of affairs has long been the subject of mockery from the young Tories. Not long ago, *The Standard*, a well-known Tory organ popularly known as 'The Old Lady', expressed this deep-rooted dissatisfaction among the Tories.[22] The newspaper nurtures a natural prejudice against the elevation of a person who was not born into the ranks of its party. This prejudice, no less naturally, is intensified by the fact that Mr Chamberlain, for all his wealth and garish talents, is nonetheless no more than a parvenu.[23] Chamberlain, despite everything, remains a product of the middle classes and the quintessence of the small shopkeeper, for all that he sports an orchid on his lapel. During the by-election in the Warwick and Leamington Spa constituency there were clear rumblings of discontent about Chamberlain pushing himself forward everywhere.[24] The rivalry between Chamberlain and Balfour is very intense, and it is especially intense between Chamberlain and Goschen. Both are trying to push the other aside unceremoniously as they tussle for the post of Chancellor of the Exchequer in a future Tory government.[25]

The Radical government,[26] which overall did not show any particular artfulness, did, however, manage one very adroit measure, right on the eve of the budget. Unexpectedly for everyone, they put forward a bill for 'one man – one vote'. That this bill contained a certain amount of serpentine cunning can be seen from the furious tone of the opposition insofar as the opposition as a whole decided to come out against that bill. The fact is that now no party can hope to benefit from multiple voting at future elections. This system meant that a rich man could sometimes cast up to half a dozen votes in different places in the same elections. The last Tory government specially struck a blow against that system in its Act on elections to the county councils, and the House unanimously resolved to prohibit it in relation to the parish councils. At the present time, the Tories' opponents have very cleverly increased their difficulties by this time completely simplifying the matter and, without mixing in any other electoral schemes, have simply brought forward the idea of 'one man – one vote, one election on one day'. We consider that the Radical government has however made a fatal error by not insisting on separate measures to simplify the registration of electors, on secondary balloting, on election expenses and other measures which would be important for ensuring that popular representation in Parliament has its due significance and serves as the expression of the people's views on issues which are close to its heart.[27]

One of the most important measures taken on social policy – in essence, the only practical social measure – is the Factory Act we wrote about in our previous letter. In the first few days of May the Standing Committee on Trade appointed by the House of Commons started considering this Act.[28] The principles of the Factory Bill regarding workers' health and safety (unfortunately the measures it proposes do not go as far as is necessary in this regard), its rulings on overtime and night work (unfortunately, it does not eliminate this evil completely), and the inclusion of docks and laundries within its remit – all this was accepted both by the Tory members of the Committee and by the Tory press. The St James's Gazette, a real Tory paper, is urging Mr Asquith to intensify the attack he has launched in his Bill. The paper has come out in favour of doing away with overtime for good and has said that the working day for women is too long.[29] Most likely with an eye to the upcoming elections, Mr Asquith has decided to raise the legal minimum age for child labour in factories once again. We expect there to be very heated discussions in the Committee on this question.[30] It seems incredible that after the publication of the Bill, which set at twelve years the minimum legal age for children to be employed in factories for six hours a day, Mr Asquith was visited by deputation after deputation to complain and request that the Bill's stipulations be reduced, so that at least one more year of children's lives could be stolen. Glass factories, iron works, tailors and so on sent deputations asking that their workshops should be exempt from these new regulations on child labour, so that they could continue to exploit it on the former basis.[31] At a conference in Bradford, one of the centres of cloth production, where not only employers but unfortunately also workers strongly opposed extending the period of schooling and the freedom of childhood, one official, Mr Illingworth, stated that he did not think children under twelve should be allowed to perform factory work.[32] Mr Sykes, a schoolteacher, declared that more than 4,000 Bradford children went out to work. The children who attend his school get up at 5.30 in the morning, and do not return home until twelve hours later. Many of them fall asleep in class, and acquire an exhausted look within a few weeks.[33] Mr Drew, speaking on behalf of trade unionists, said that in Bradford industry children (half-timers) had almost completely displaced the adult male workers.[34] Moreover, Dr Kerr reported that he had measured the height of 1,500 children between the ages of seven and twelve in Bradford schools, and found it to be two and a half inches below average. Dr Kerr advocated the complete abolition of child labour.[35]

Back in 1875 Mr Chamberlain said at the Factory Commission: 'Our supremacy, insofar as we have attained it, is not based on overworking our children.'[36] However, observers from other countries would hardly concur with those words. How is it, they would ask, that the British child is subjected to the torment of factory work a year before the French child, two years before the German child and three years or four years before the Swiss child? Further – how can it be that the British child of thirteen can go out to night work, which exhausts his energy, whereas under French law night work is forbidden for boys under eighteen? Clearly, the demands of world trade are more important for you than maintaining international observance of the Berlin agreement on labour.[37] It is time to recall the words of the poet: 'How long, O cruel nation, will you stand, to move the world, on a child's heart?'

There was recently a session of the Royal Commission on the Aged Poor, but the proceedings and resolutions of that commission are every bit as ineffectual in the practical sense as the proceedings of the unemployed committee.[38] Different schemes for state assistance to the aged were rejected on account of various financial and economic difficulties. The minority on the committee, including Chamberlain and Charles Booth, who produced the excellent survey *Life and Labour of the People in London*, declared in its report that all the proposed schemes for establishing old age pensions had not been adequately thought through by their authors. In essence, they put forward two schemes – one, that of Mr Chamberlain, envisages that the workers themselves, through deductions from their wages, establish an insurance fund which will be topped up by the state; the other, that of Mr Booth, envisages that the government should pay a certain sum to every worker who has reached the age of sixty-five. Judging by the discussions in Parliament, this question will arise again more than once.[39]

It is appropriate to mention here the discontent in England, resulting from the continued payment of a £10,000 per annum stipend to the Duke of Saxe-Coburg, who has ceased to be a British subject and has now become a German citizen. If there were suddenly to be some complications leading to armed conflict between Britain and Germany, we would see the strange spectacle of a duke fighting in the German ranks against the country which pays him an annual stipend.[40]

The British people are angry at the Duke of Saxe-Coburg, but the Duke of Cambridge attracts not only the people's wrath, but also their mirth. This has happened on several occasions in recent years. Nominally the Commander-in-Chief of the British armed forces, he has been dubbed the 'umbrella duke' on account of the fact that he opens an umbrella if it rains while he is carrying out his military duties. It is bad enough that his behaviour creates problems at GHQ and that it is inconvenient to have a gentleman who has never served in the forces in charge of the army. But it is even worse that any attempt to carry out military reforms is thwarted by the stubbornness and ineptitude of the Duke of Cambridge. At the commission chaired by the Duke of Devonshire and Lord Hartington, it was suggested to the Duke of Cambridge that the position of Commander-in-Chief should be abolished. Any ordinary, more or less scrupulous person would certainly take that fairly unambiguous hint.[41]

Two industrial disputes, in the boot-making and construction industries, have been resolved with a compromise. However, the issues have not gone away and we expect trouble to break out again.[42]

The May Day demonstrations in London passed off well. There were processions in many cities, but the London ones are of course the most significant. Of the two London demonstrations, the smaller one was the more significant, in that it was organised for the first of May, which was a Wednesday, while the large one takes place on the first Sunday after May Day. The resolutions approved that day by a large crowd in Hyde Park called for an eight-hour working day and for suffrage rights for all adults. Declarations were made from some platforms claiming that these two reforms were the most important immediate steps towards the nationalisation of the land and so on.[43]

The three people who have been most in the news in recent times and have attracted most controversy are Oscar Wilde, Jabez Balfour and Annie Besant. All three have appeared before the court of the British people, although only two have also became involved in a jury trial. In our previous letter we mentioned Wilde and his dispute with the Marquess of Queensberry, which had landed Wilde in the dock.[44] Your readers are presumably already acquainted with the Wilde case, at least in general outline, from the newspapers. In this whole dismal case the behaviour of the public and the press and been highly typical. At first there was an explosion of the most violent outrage, completely unbalanced, at the abominations of which Wilde was accused and, as always happens in England, they prejudged the verdict of the court.[45] Then, when there were disagreements among the jurors and a new court was appointed, the entire undisciplined mob of journalists stampeded like a flock of sheep over to the opposite side, to the other extreme, and began to say that they had been a little hard on Wilde. But most curious of all was that the facts which have now been broadcast to the public had long been known not only to journalists and people in the theatrical profession, but also to the police. The sudden explosion of outrage from the English press and the display of moral indignation in society serve only once again to show the remarkable hypocrisy which reigns in our country. The zeal displayed by the police once public opinion had forced them to act shows, of course, that they too are not above being bought.

But possibly the most curious aspect of this whole comedy as it plays out in the British press and society is the actions of the theatre directors, Mr George Alexander of St James' Theatre, and Messrs Waller and Morell, the present lessees of the Haymarket. Incidentally, Mr Morell is the son of the famous doctor Morell Mackenzie, who treated the late German Emperor Friedrich. Both theatres had been staging Oscar Wilde's plays very successfully, but as soon as the scandal broke out, these two directors immediately deleted the name of the author from all their billboards and advertisements, although they continued to stage his plays.[46] The upright British public, which had previously been keen to see these plays, has stopped going to the theatre. Needless to say, this is a surprising attitude to works of art, the success of which should of course depend on their inherent merits rather than on the moral character of their author. If the theatre directors, impelled by a sudden rush of virtue, had pulled the immoral playwright's plays off the stage, then we might question their good sense but could not doubt their honesty and integrity. But to continue to put on the plays, and fraudulently attempt to make money from them while doing everything to ensure that any success is not ascribed to their author – this is a way of proceeding for which we cannot find the right expression.

However, on the other hand, we see that Oscar Wilde has found the most energetic and serious defence among strict adherents of the Church of England. The Reverend Stewart Headlam, a member of the London School Board, helped find the bail money for Wilde.[47] The publication of freethinking churchmen, the *Church Reformer*, carried an article by another vicar in defence of Wilde which set out that the specific act of which Wilde was accused has to an extent always had a universal character, and that it is only in England that this act is punishable, while in other countries it is considered not only to be no crime, but not even a sin.[48] In the clubs and theatres the failure of the first trial in the Wilde case is attributed to an understanding between the police and prosecution on the one hand, and the accused on the other, and that the truth is that besides Wilde, there are many other people involved in that case with a much higher social status than he has. Scraps of paper bearing the names of various other 'exalted' personages were secretly being passed between the judges and counsel, and these names were, of course, well known to Wilde and everyone else in literary and artistic Bohemian circles. But they were not made public, and this was to the advantage of Wilde and his case. These days, however, when general suspicion has been so strongly stoked, there have been many people who have linked the Wilde case to wholly unrelated facts such as the illness of a prominent statesman or the Prime Minister feeling faint when giving the most

ordinary speech.[49] Opinions may of course differ about how foul
the specific act of which Wilde stands accused actually is, but we
do not think there can be any doubt about the really foul things
Oscar Wilde has done, in our view, his posturing and his teachings
– those are foul! His posturing makes an absurd and unhealthy
impression; this 'art for art's sake' denies the basic truth that art,
nature and everything else we strive to understand do not exist for
their own sake, but for life, and they should deal with it and reflect
it for living people. Moreover, Wilde's teaching, which he cynically
and openly admits, consists in complete indifference towards the
effects, good or bad, of his works, prose, poetry and plays.[50]

Jabez Balfour is currently back with us, to the great surprise of
those who know a bit more than the general public, and to the great
annoyance of various esteemed financiers and statesmen involved
in the case. It is said that the first police officer sent to arrest
Balfour was 'thrown off track'.[51] At any rate, he was recalled and
another officer was sent from Scotland Yard. One way or another,
he was more skilful, or the money and efforts of Balfour's friends
were less effective, but either way he was able to arrest this interesting prisoner. Without a doubt, the Balfour case promises to be
very interesting, not only in its own right, but also because a mass
of people is involved in it besides Balfour. The situation of Balfour
is in many respects analogous to that of Wilde, in that he also
'knows names'. A few words about these 'names': here, as everywhere else, we have an exemplar of English notions of decorum
and an Englishman's honour. When Balfour was at the height of his
financial glory, was an MP, was one of the leading lights in a religious movement and founded churches, he was generally known as
'Spencer Balfour'. Now, when there is not a single person 'insignificant enough to bow to him' he is called Jabez Balfour.[52] We think
that the very religious persons belonging to the class from which
he sprang will insist that his name be chipped off the foundation
stones of those churches he patronised.[53] Those very same working
classes, whose members he swindled, will be invited to perform
this task.

But much more shameful than the fall of these two men is the
fall of a woman who personified a quite special form of decadence
in our decadent age. We are referring to Annie Besant.[54] In the

cases of Oscar Wilde and Balfour there are beyond doubt elements
of tragedy, both in relation to the accused themselves and in relation to the people who were brought down with them. As far as
Annie Besant is concerned, here we have a ridiculous farce in
every respect. In one of our letters we wrote about the accusations levelled against the Theosophical Society published in the
Westminster Gazette. By her words and deeds since returning to
England, Mrs Besant has amplified those accusations. It would
be wearisome to trace all the twists and turns of this farce. Mrs
Besant returned from India and Australia, she gave interviews, and
then she spoke at St James' Hall, where they listened to her with
mouths agape and realised in silence that she was quite unable to
answer the question: 'where is the proof that the Mahatma exists?'
She had tried battling to dominate the Theosophical Society and
had been defeated. But her fall from the pedestal of truth and
virtue, on which she had placed herself, was much more serious.
The *Westminster Gazette,* with merciless accuracy, traced all her
tricks and dodges, all her evasions, and used data and documents
to condemn her not only as a person who cannot be trusted as
an investigator, but as someone who witnessed and covered up
premeditated fraud. In any movement other than theosophy, such
a woman would be condemned in perpetuity by all honest and
straight-thinking people, just as Oscar Wilde has been. But with
theosophists it is a different matter. We shall not be at all surprised
if Mrs Besant still remains head of the Theosophical Society. She
has not been arraigned before a court, and the verdict of the court
of honour has little weight in movements of a purely speculative,
imaginative nature.

Av.

Notes

1. For the early work of the House of Commons Select Committee on
   Distress from Want of Employment see Letter 3, notes 15-27.
      Following publication of its 'First report' in March 1895, the com-
   mittee continued to receive evidence and published two further
   volumes of submissions, but made no substantive recommendations. For a summary of the reports see George Duckworth, 'The

work of the Select Committee of the House of Commons on Distress from Want of Employment', *Economic Journal*, March 1896, Vol. 6, No. 21, pp143-53.

2. William Mather (1838-1920) was Liberal Member of Parliament for the Gorton constituency in Manchester between 1889 and 1895, and a manufacturer of engineering equipment who introduced improvements in conditions in his factory, including a forty-eight-hour working week. A strong advocate of further and higher education, Mather played an important part in establishing Owens College, which would later become the University of Manchester. Geoffrey Tweedale, 'Mather, Sir William (1838-1920)', *Oxford Dictionary of National Biography*, Oxford University Press: Oxford, 2019.

Mather's evidence to the committee in May 1895 was based on a proposal for state-funded training colonies run by county councils. The colonies would bring land out of cultivation back into use, providing employment and new permanent settlements. 'Third report of the Select Committee on Distress from Want of Employment', July 1895, pp292-331. See also Mather's paper included in J.A. Hobson, *Co-operative Labour upon the Land*, Swan Sonnenschein: London, 1895, pp129-40.

3. For Hardie's proposal to spend £100,000 on the relief of distress, see Letter 3 note 23.

4. Julie Sutter (1846?-1924) was born in India of German parents but spent much of her life in England, where she concerned herself with matters of poverty and the needs of the mentally ill. During the early 1890s Sutter visited the colony established by Pastor Von Bodelschwingh in Westphalia and was impressed with the facilities for epileptics and the unemployed. Her account of this visit, *A Colony of Mercy*, published in 1893, was influential in the establishment of the Christian Union for Social Service, which set up a training colony for the unemployed at Lingfield in Surrey in 1896.

5. Alfred Russel Wallace (see Letter 3, note 47) presented detailed information on the increase in poverty and the growth of charitable institutions in a long letter to the *Daily Chronicle* of 5 March 1895, p3. Wallace wrote that these facts, quoted liberally by Eleanor and Edward, served as 'a veritable "handwriting on the wall" denouncing the rottenness of our whole social system... The time has come when our legislators and politicians must grapple with the fundamental causes which permit this mass of unspeakable human misery to continue in one of the richest – if not the richest – country in the world. If they persist in shutting their eyes to the facts, or in declaring that they have no remedy for them, they will assuredly

bring about their own destruction as utterly incompetent rulers. To myself, the rapid spread of socialism offers the only gleam of light amid the prevailing darkness.'

6. Established in 1878 by evangelist William Booth (1829-1912), the Salvation Army's mission was to spread Christianity and charity among the working classes. Booth's book *In Darkest England and the Way Out*, published in 1890, proposed labour colonies and emigration to tackle unemployment. A labour colony was established by Booth at Hadleigh, Essex in 1891.

   The Charity Organisation Society (COS) was established in 1869 to co-ordinate the administration of charity. The COS opposed what it considered to be indiscriminate giving and instead practised a policy of assisting the 'deserving poor' who, with support, could restore themselves to independence. Applicants for relief were considered by the Society's officials, who made an assessment of the moral character and habits of the individual. From the 1880s the proportion of rejected applicants increased, and by 1895 it was close on 60 per cent. Of this, Robert Humphreys wrote: 'Whereas the COS could attempt to use this huge rejection rate as positive evidence of their investigative skill in exposing fraudulent claimants, there was the overriding countervailing factor of it providing ready ammunition for many who were ready to label the COS members as cold-hearted ideologues ... Many people, aware of the Society's harsh reputation, and worried that they too would be labelled by the COS as "undeserving", saw little point in subjecting their family to the humiliation of protracted probing that could all too easily be fruitless.' Robert Humphreys, *Poor Relief and Charity 1869-1945: The London Charity Organisation Society*, Macmillan: Basingstoke, 2001, p71.

   The charitable response to social crises in London in the second half of the nineteenth century is considered in Gareth Stedman Jones, *Outcast London: A Study in the Relationship Between Classes in Victorian Society*, Clarendon Press: Oxford, 1971, especially pp240-61 and 296-314.

7. Unemployed benefit paid by textile trade unions increased from £37,093 in 1894 to £44,676 in 1895. 'Eighth report by the labour correspondent on trade unions, 1894 and 1895', HMSO, 1896, p.xxvii.

8. Unemployment amongst engineers rose to 8.4 per cent in 1894, representing a near trebling from 1891, and the highest figure since 1879. The Amalgamated Society of Engineers (ASE) paid out £138,976 in unemployment benefit in 1894-5, more than 50 per cent of total expenditure and an increase of more than £4,000 on the previous

year. 'Amalgamated Society of Engineers annual report for 1893-4', ASE, 1895, ppvi-vii and xiv-xv.

9. Statistics from Wallace's article.

10. William Harcourt (1827-1904) was Chancellor of the Exchequer in Gladstone's government elected in 1892.

    Harcourt's final budget speech, delivered on 2 May 1895, was considered uncontroversial by the standards of the previous year, when graduated death duties were introduced. It did, however, attract criticism for what was seen (perhaps somewhat absurdly to modern ears) as partisanship towards Irish MPs, whose votes the government needed to survive, in the decision not to renew the duty levied on spirits, including whisky. *Morning Post*, 3 May 1895, p4. In contrast, Harcourt retained the duty on malt liquors such as beer. Harcourt estimated that the 6d per gallon duty on beer would cover the estimated deficit of expenditure over revenue and leave the Exchequer with a surplus of £181,000.

11. During the nineteenth century a number of important brewing families had strong Liberal affiliations, including those with interests in the Bass, Truman, and Whitbread companies. However, the emergence of an influential temperance movement in the second half of the century diminished this interest, as brewers increasingly transferred allegiance to the Conservative Party. By 1900, of the thirty-three MPs who were known or believed to be connected to the liquor trade, only four were Liberals. Peter Mathias, 'The brewing industry, temperance and politics', *Historical Journal*, Vol. 1, No. 2, 1958, p112.

12. Harcourt was the most prominent advocate of a temperance policy within the Liberal government and was instrumental in the Liquor Traffic Local Veto Bill introduced into Parliament in February 1895, that would allow local authorities to conduct referenda to reduce and/or prohibit the sale of alcohol. The bill had not received its second reading when the government fell in June and its unpopularity was said to have been a contributory factor in the Unionist victory at the subsequent general election. In the election campaign the drink trade mobilised 100,000 public houses to canvass 'their working class customers with a regularity and familiarity which few industries could emulate. ... If one can assume that each licensed drinking place swayed one vote, the drink trade provided the Unionist parties with 83 seats in Parliament in 1895.' David M. Fahey, 'The politics of drink: Pressure groups and the British Liberal Party, 1883-1908', *Social Science*, Spring 1979, Vol. 54, No. 2, p80.

13. These figures were taken from the 'Annual report of the Registrar

General of Births, Deaths and Marriages in England in 1894', HMSO, p.xl.

14.   For a survey of contemporary views on drunkenness and poverty, including those with socialist affiliations, see J.B. Brown, 'The pig or the stye: Drink and poverty in Victorian England', *International Review of Social History*, December 1973, Vol. 18, No. 3, pp380-95.

15.   For Parisian workers' cafes, to which it is likely the authors were part referring, see W. Scott Haine, *The World of the Paris Café: Sociability Among the French Working Class, 1789-1914*, Johns Hopkins University Press: Baltimore and London, 1996.

It is surprising in this context that the authors do not mention the more than one hundred working men's and radical clubs in the metropolitan area, especially as both had been regular speakers at their lecture halls since the 1880s. For a discussion of the changing social, educational and political purpose of these clubs see John Davis, 'Radical clubs and London politics, 1870-1900', in *Metropolis: London Histories and Representations since 1800*, David Feldman and Gareth Stedman Jones (eds), Routledge: London, 1980, pp103-28.

16.   The authors set sail for the USA on 31 August 1886 and arrived back in England on 1 January 1887. For the tour see Yvonne Kapp, *Eleanor Marx: Volume Two, The Crowded Years, (1884-1898)*, Lawrence and Wishart: London, 1976, pp135-91.

17.   Arthur was the son of Robert Peel.

18.   Arthur Wellesley Peel (1829-1912) was Speaker of the House of Commons between February 1883 and April 1895. The *Daily Chronicle* editorial praising Peel appeared in the edition of 9 April 1895, p4.

19.   Leonard Henry Courtney (1832-1918) had been an MP for Bodmin since 1876 and deputy Speaker from 1886 until 1892. When Peel announced he would retire, Henry Campbell Bannerman, Secretary of State for War in Rosebery's government, expressed a desire to be nominated, but was told he could not be spared from the Cabinet. With no obvious Liberal candidate, the party supported Harcourt's suggestion that they should back Courtney, who was originally a Liberal but now sat with the Liberal Unionists in the Commons.

20.   Liberal Unionists were Liberals who broke away from the official Liberal party over Home Rule for Ireland.

21.   Joseph Chamberlain, the leader of the Liberal Unionists in the Commons, blocked Courtney's candidature for the Speakership and instructed his colleagues to support the Conservative nominee, Sir Matthew White Ridley. When Courtney withdrew the Liberals put forward William Gully, the member for Carlisle, 'a quiet but imposing looking barrister ... known to few, had no enemies, partly

because he never attended the House'. Peter Stansky, *Ambitions and Strategies: The Struggle for the Leadership of the Liberal Party in the 1890s*, Clarendon: Oxford, 1964, p158. Gully was elected by the House on a vote of 285 to 274 on 10 April 1895.

22. *The Standard,* a Conservative daily with a circulation of 250,000, was regarded as second only to the *Times* as a morning newspaper. It was widely known as the 'Old Lady of Shoe Lane', where the newspaper was printed.

In response to Chamberlain's insistence that a Liberal Unionist candidate be supported by the Conservative association – against their wishes – at Warwick and Leamington Spa where Peel was the sitting MP, *The Standard,* probably at the instigation of Lord Salisbury, wrote that 'Mr Chamberlain may, perhaps, congratulate himself on the adroitness by which he hopes to add one more name to his list of Parliamentary followers, but the advantage will be clearly bought if it weakens the Unionist alliance'. *The Standard,* 2 April 1895, p4. For the Warwick and Leamington Spa dispute, see note 24 below.

23. Joseph Chamberlain (see Letter 3 note 31), a wealthy screw manufacturer who had made his name as mayor of Birmingham, started out his political career as a Radical Liberal but broke with the party in 1886 over Gladstone's Home Rule for Ireland policy. Chamberlain subsequently sat in the Commons as a Liberal Unionist, assuming the leadership in 1891.

Chamberlain's manufacturing background and middle-class origins made him the subject of a good deal of snobbish chatter in Parliament, which was still dominated by aristocratic and landed interests. As his biographer wrote: 'Chamberlain might look like a gentleman, immaculately attired as he was, sporting a monocle instead of middle class spectacles ... All the same, he bore a clear though 'invisible' stigma as a metal manufacturer ... the more respectable statesmen disapproved, while young whigs discussed his aspirations with condescension, and backbench gentry questioned whether he knew the unspoken rules by which gentlemen played the game of politics'. Peter T. Marsh, *Joseph Chamberlain: Entrepreneur in Politics*, Yale University Press: New Haven and London, 1994, p113 and p142.

When the Liberal government fell in June 1895 and the Queen asked Rosebery about Chamberlain's qualities, he remarked that 'the drawback to his great and brilliant qualities and talents was that he was not quite a gentleman'. Leo McKinstry, *Rosebery: Statesman in Turmoil*, Thistle Publishing: London, 2017, p440.

24. Following the split in the Liberal party over Irish Home Rule in 1886, the Liberal Unionists supported the Conservative government of Lord Salisbury and entered into an electoral compact in which the party most likely to defeat the Liberal candidate was given precedence to stand unopposed.

Tensions between the two parties emerged at Hythe, Kent in January 1895 when the sitting Conservative member announced he would not contest the seat in the forthcoming general election because of ill health. Without consultation, the Liberal Unionists announced a prospective candidate, giving rise to a controversy that was only resolved when negotiations at a national level gave the Conservative a clear run.

A similar scenario unfolded in the Warwick and Leamington Spa constituency when the Speaker of the Commons, Arthur Peel, announced in March 1895 that he would retire and stand down from the seat. Chamberlain regarded the seat as 'Liberal Unionist' and with the support of Conservative leader in the Commons Arthur Balfour, offered it George Peel, the Speaker's son. Local Conservatives resented Chamberlain's intrusion, presumption and what seemed to be a plan to expand influence beyond his Birmingham base. Backbench Conservative MPs regarded it as evidence of how they were paying a high price for Liberal Unionist support in opposing Home Rule, which was no longer a central issue. Following Conservative pressure, Chamberlain dropped Peel for Alfred Lyttleton, a friend of Balfour's, who won the seat in a straight fight with the Liberals in a by-election on 23 May 1895. These events are covered in Ian Cawood, 'Joseph Chamberlain, the Conservative Party and the Leamington Spa candidature dispute of 1895', *Historical Research*, November 2006, Vol. 79, No. 206, pp554-77.

25. For Balfour, see Letter 3 note 30. For Goschen, see Letter 3 note 32. In the new government formed in 1895, Chamberlain turned down Lord Salisbury's offer of the Exchequer, preferring instead Secretary of State for the Colonies. Goschen became First Lord of the Admiralty.

26. The authors are using 'Radical government' to denote the Liberal governments of Gladstone and Rosebery 1892-5.

27. The bill brought forward on 30 April 1895 by George Shaw Lefevre (1831-1928), the president of the Local Government Board, to establish the principle allowing only one vote per man in parliamentary elections and for general election ballots to be held on one day, was unexpected.

At this time plural voting was widespread, with qualification based on freehold, residency, occupation and university membership. Introducing the bill in the Commons, Lefevre admitted to having five votes in parliamentary elections – two occupational, two freehold and one university – which he thought unfair, but dwarfed by the twelve votes available to Sir Robert Fowler in the general election of 1874. The abolition of plural voting, Lefevre argued, would bring the law in line with local government, where it had been abolished for borough and town councils in 1882, county councils in 1888 and parish councils in 1894.

Voting in general elections traditionally took place over twenty-eight days, a system widely believed to favour those parties who gained an early advantage.

Lefevre defended the limited nature of the bill – it did not address payment of members, public funding of contests, abolition of disqualification of those in receipt of poor relief – on the grounds that previous attempts to make sweeping changes had been unsuccessful, In the event, the bill did not get a second reading before Rosebery's government fell.

28. See Letter 3, note 35.

29. The Factory and Workshop Bill stipulated that overtime days for women working in ordinary trades be reduced from forty-eight to thirty, and from ninety-six to sixty in seasonal and special trades.

   St James's Gazette expressed the opinion that: 'The Bill can hardly be said to err on the side of strength. Mr Asquith (the Home Secretary introducing the Bill) has been almost too keenly alive to the opposition which any legislation of this kind necessarily arouses, and has compromised a little too much .... Take the question of overtime. Mr Asquith's own view is that overtime ought to be abolished altogether. So is ours.' St James's Gazette, 23 April 1895, p3.

30. Asquith's commitment to raise the legal minimum age of child labour to twelve years was publicly stated, but was eventually omitted from the bill because the government believed it would imperil its other provisions. Britain remained one of the few countries in Europe with a minimum age for child labour of eleven years until 1899.

31. Asquith received many deputations from employers seeking exemption from the legislation. When the employers in the textile industries met the Home Secretary they were accompanied by trade union representatives, one of whom, David Holmes, president of the Weavers' Association and chairman of the Parliamentary Committee of the TUC, defended the system of 'half-timers' under which children of eleven years could work half a day in factories if they attended school for the other half. Holmes said that: 'The system of half-time employment has worked exceedingly smoothly.

There was no objection to it from the employers, and there was none on the part of the workpeople themselves. The children who came under its operation compared favourably with other children, both physically and educationally, and any interference with the system would inflict very serious hardships upon great numbers of people, because the conditions of the cotton trade were such that a parent could not earn as much as would maintain a family.' *Manchester Courier and Lancashire General Advertiser*, 24 April 1895, p8.

32. A message by Alfred Illingworth (1827-1907), Member of Parliament for Bradford since 1880 and a worsted spinner employing one thousand workers, was read at a conference in Bradford on 30 March to consider the employment of half-timers and mothers with children under five years. Despite being well known for his opposition to legislative interference in factory conditions, Illingworth told the conference, 'I am inclined to think that the age of children entering work might be raised to twelve, though this would cause hardship on many parents, especially widows.' *Bradford Daily Telegraph*, 1 April 1895, p3.

33. Thomas Percy Sykes (1855-1919) trained as a pupil teacher in the 1870s before studying at the University of London and becoming a fully qualified teacher working at Great Horton Board School, Bradford. Sykes wrote 'The factory half-timer' for the *Fortnightly Review* in December 1889.

34. William Henry Drew (1854-1933), textile worker, trade unionist, member of the Bradford School Board and leading figure in the Independent Labour Party.

35. Dr James Kerr (1861-1941) was appointed Medical Superintendent to the Bradford School Board in 1893. Kerr carried out medical inspections in elementary schools which revealed the deleterious effects of child labour on health and well-being. In this work Kerr collaborated with Margaret McMillan, a member of the school board, to improve facilities in schools, including the provision of free school meals.

36. In his evidence to the Royal Commission set up in 1875 to investigate the working of the Factory and Workshop Acts, Joseph Chamberlain, then mayor of Birmingham, chairman of the City's School Board and leading manufacturer, advocated increasing the age at which work begun for children, both half time and full time. He said: 'I should say that my experience teaches me that these restrictions would not have the slightest effect in endangering our Birmingham trades. Our supremacy, so far as we have attained to any supremacy, is not dependent on the overwork of our children; and is due, and

will only be retained, I believe, by an increase in the intelligence of our workpeople'. 'Report of the commissioners appointed to inquire into the working of the Factory and Workshop Acts: Minutes of evidence', Vol II, HMSO, 1876, p265.

37. The International Conference on Labour held in Berlin in March 1890 recommended a legal minimum of twelve years for child labour.

38. The Royal Commission on the Aged Poor, under the chairmanship of Lord Aberdore, commenced work in January 1893 and issued its first report at the end of March 1895.

39. The report concluded that the number of aged paupers had diminished and would continue to do so as thrift grew among the working classes through savings banks, insurance and friendly societies. The commission rejected various pension schemes presented to it on the grounds of financial and economic viability.

A number of the commissioners, including Joseph Chamberlain and Charles Booth, declined to sign the report, instead issuing their own minority report which was significantly more critical of the situation in which three in ten of the elderly population were compelled to apply for parish relief.

Chamberlain proposed an insurance-based pension scheme under which individuals would make an initial cash deposit of fifty shillings before the age of twenty-five years and an annual cash payment of ten shillings, entitling them to a pension of five shillings per week at sixty-five years.

Charles Booth rejected an insurance-based contributory pension scheme, and instead recommended a publicly funded system in which all citizens reaching sixty-five years would be entitled to a five-shilling weekly pension.

40. Alfred, Duke of Saxe-Coburg and Gotha (1844-1900), was the second son of Queen Victoria and Prince Albert. On the death of his uncle, Ernest II, Duke of Saxe Coburg and Gotha in 1893, the duchy fell to Alfred, who became a German citizen but retained his £10,000 annual stipend from the British government. This was the subject of a debate in the Commons on 3 May 1895, when Radical Liberal MPs attempted unsuccessfully to end the grant.

41. Prince George, Duke of Cambridge, (1818-1904), grandson to George III and cousin to Queen Victoria, was appointed Commander-in-Chief of the Army in 1865. Dissatisfaction with his role led to a Royal Commission recommendation in 1890 that the post be discontinued when Cambridge retired. Henry Campbell Bannerman, Secretary of State for War in Gladstone's and then Rosebery's administrations,

conducted long and difficult negotiations with Cambridge over his retirement, which eventually came in November 1895. Unhappy with his treatment, Cambridge made representations to the queen and demanded a pension of £2,000 per annum, which Rosebery refused to grant.

42. The dispute in the boot and shoemaking industry was engineered by the employers to impose a standstill on wages for two years and assert control over the introduction of new labour-saving machinery. The lock-out of 46,000 workers, which began in March 1895 and lasted for five weeks, significantly weakened the trade unions in the industry, which were forced to accept many of the employers' demands. See Alan Fox, *A History of the National Union of Boot and Shoe Operatives, 1874-1957*, Blackwell: Oxford, 1958, pp217-37.

At the end of 1894 members of the Master Builders' Association in London gave notice to the trade unions represented on the London Building Trades Committee of their intention to terminate an existing agreement because of their wish to remove clauses relating to union membership and sub-letting of work, both matters over which they believed the trade unions exerted excessive influence. The trade unions responded by advising the employers that their members were prepared to work with non-union men, but they objected to being expected to work alongside those who had acted as strike breakers. On sub-letting of contracts, the trade unions opposed the change because they argued it would lead to 'skimping', poorer work and downward pressure on wages. The latter demand of the employers came as public bodies across the capital were moving away from sub-contracting in favour of directly employed labour. By the third week in April, the unions declared the result of a ballot giving overwhelming authority for industrial action in defence of the established agreement, a move that forced the employers to withdraw their threat and accept an offer of arbitration on points of difference.

43. The authors had played a pivotal role in the May Day demonstration in London since its inception in 1890. (See Kapp 1976, pp364-80; and *The Legal Eight Hours Demonstration in London*, reprinted from the *Workman's Times*, 1 May 1890, in *Workman's Times*, London: 1891.) Both continued to be active organising for the annual demonstrations – Edward especially as chairman of the demonstration committee – and speaking from the platforms.

Since the first demonstration, the authors and many fellow socialists had attempted to persuade the organising committee to hold the procession and Hyde Park meeting on 1 May each year, in line with the decision of the Socialist International Congress of 1889 that this be a 'universal holiday' for workers. However, it had not been possible to win majority support for this amongst delegates from trade unions, radical clubs and other affiliated bodies, because they doubted the willingness of their members to leave work for half a day to participate. Instead, the organising committee opted for a demonstration on the first Sunday in May.

Edward's attempts in early 1895 to persuade delegates that they should support a demonstration on 1 May was again unsuccessful. Disappointed, he announced his decision to resign from the organising committee, preferring to devote his energies to a May 1 event that the socialists had decided to organise, as well as participating on Sunday 5 May.

Approximately five thousand turned up on the Embankment on Wednesday 1 May. SDF and ILP banners predominated, but there was also a significant trade union presence, with contingents representing printer's warehousemen, hammermen, dockers, railwaymen, coal porters and bootmakers. A band of Socialist Sunday School children dressed in red clothing and caps of liberty sang out the words of William Morris's *No Master*. On the back of their wagonettes were the words, 'If the old 'uns can't, THE YOUNG 'UNS WILL'. (*Reynolds's Newspaper*, 11 May 1895, p4; *Justice,* 11 May 1895, p4.)

As the procession approached Hyde Park the heavens opened, but 'bravely the several speakers held forth – Morris, Hyndman, Aveling, Mann, Lansbury and the rest – steadfast a crowd of stalwarts stood around each platform, but it was impossible to withstand the effects of the rain and artic cold by which it was accompanied'. *Justice*, 11 May 1895, p4.

Following the demonstration, the ILP held a carnival at Holborn Town Hall, while the SDF staged a social at the South Place Institute.

The weather was more favourable for the larger demonstration on Sunday 5 May. Edward spoke from Platform Two, where he appealed to those present to join the ranks of those who would henceforth demonstrate on 1 May, when 'it would necessitate the taking of some of the masters' time'. Referring to a speech made by John Burns at Battersea in the previous week in which the MP expressed regret that two demonstrations were to be held, in his view because of the 'extreme men, who wanted to divorce trade unionism from the advanced labour movement', Edward said that 'there could be no divorce without marriage. These two movements were not yet married. They were only in the preliminary stage of courting. Very soon there would be a real wedding, and when they got that union of trade unionism and socialism, they would have a real May Day'. *Daily News*, 6 May 1895, p3.

Eleanor spoke from Platform Four, where her friend Will Thorne took the chair. Eleanor reminded the audience that one of the demands of the demonstration was universal suffrage, 'and in that they must remember to include the women'. *Reynolds's Newspaper*, 12 May 1895, p3.

44. For the trial brought about by Oscar Wilde against the Marquess of Queensberry for defamatory libel see Letter 3, notes 39-42. Letter 4 appears to have been written in mid May, after the first criminal trial against Wilde (26 April to 1 May), but before the second trial (22 to 25 May).

45. Wilde's case was discussed extensively in the press in the run up to both trials, leading some to suggest that he could not possibly get a fair verdict as the jury would inevitably be prejudiced. One biographer of Wilde wrote that, 'with the exception of one daily and one weekly journal, the *Daily Chronicle* and *Reynolds's Newspaper* respectively, the whole of the London press was uniformly hostile to Wilde'. H. Montgomery Hyde, *Oscar Wilde: A Biography*, Eyre Methuen: London, 1976, p229n. See also Michael S. Foldy, *The Trials of Oscar Wilde: Deviance, Morality and Late Victorian Society*, Yale University Press: New Haven and London, 1997, pp48-66.

Wilde's first trial ended with the jury unable to reach a verdict. At the second trial he was found guilty of gross indecency and sentenced to two years' hard labour.

46. Wilde's *The Importance of Being Earnest* opened at the St James's Theatre on 14 February 1895. In the first week of April the theatre's manager George Alexander removed Wilde's name from the programme and all advertisements. The play closed soon after.

When the Haymarket Theatre decided to terminate Wilde's *An Ideal Husband* on April 7, it transferred to the Criterion with the same cast. Wilde's name was removed from the Criterion's publicity but was later restored before it closed on 27 April.

47. Rev. Stewart Headlam (1847-1924) was a widely respected and influential Christian socialist who founded the Guild of St Matthew and edited the *Church Reformer* from 1884 until 1895.

Headlam was asked by Wilde's friend Selwyn Image to stand surety for Wilde following the end of the first trial when the jury was unable to reach a verdict and a retrial was ordered. The judge set Wilde's bail at £5,000, half of which Wilde himself guaranteed. Headlam and one other offered the remainder in equal amounts. Following the subsequent guilty verdict Headlam wrote: 'I became bail for Mr Oscar Wilde on public grounds: I felt that the action of a large section of the press, of the theatrical managers at whose houses the plays were running, and his publisher, were calculated to prejudice his case before his trial had begun. I was a surety, not for his character, but for his appearance in the court to stand trial. I had very little personal knowledge of him at this time; I think I only met him twice; but my confidence in his honour and manliness has been fully justified by the fact that (if rumour is correct) notwithstanding strong inducements to the contrary, he stayed in England and faced the trial'. Quoted in H. Montgomery Hyde, *The Trials of Oscar Wilde*, Dover Publications: New York, 1973, p220.

48. The author of the *Church Reformer* article was Selwyn Image (1849-1930), who had worked as a curate in London before resigning from holy orders in 1882 to become a designer. Image was a close friend of Headlam and worked alongside him in the Guild of St Matthew. Image took the press to task for its prejudiced and sensationalist coverage of Wilde's case and demanded the law under which the prosecution was taking place be repealed. He wrote: 'With morality, *qua* morality, the law has no concern whatever. It punishes a drunkard, not for the sin of drunkenness, but only when [he] commits an assault or causes a public obstruction; it punishes a thief, not for the sin of stealing, but because he forcibly interferes with his neighbour; but it punishes the man who indulges in this form of sensuality for the mere sensuality itself', *Church Reformer*, May 1895, p107. Following Wilde's sentencing Image wrote again commending his 'manly courage' during the trial and asserting that his career was not over. *Church Reformer*, June 1895, pp126-7.

49. Rosebery was unwell from late February until the end of May. During a speech at the National Liberal Club on 9 May Rosebery broke off mid-sentence and was unable to regain his thread for at least a minute.

   The accusations regarding Rosebery's sexuality and connection to Wilde are discussed fully in the most recent biography of Rosebery, by Leo McKinstry 2017, pp405-27.

   The claim that there was a cover-up during the Wilde court cases because of connections to people in prominent positions is discussed in Foldy 1997, pp21-30.

50. Prior to the publication of these letters the only known comment from either of the authors on Wilde was that of Eleanor's to sister Jenny in July 1882 when she wrote:

   'I have been asked to go this afternoon to a "crush" at Lady Wilde's. She is mother of that very limp & nasty young man, Oscar Wilde:

who has been making a d.d ass of himself in America. As the son has
not returned & the mother is nice I may go...' Olga Meier (ed), *The
Daughters of Karl Marx: Family Correspondence, 1866-1898*, Penguin:
Harmondsworth, 1984, pp154-5.

While we cannot be sure that the remarks on Wilde's 'posturing',
belief in 'art for art's sake', and 'complete indifference towards the
effects, good or bad, of his works, prose, poetry and plays' were
penned by Eleanor alone, they are in a similar vein to her comments
of July 1882, and support Ruth Robbins's persuasive argument that
Eleanor was always serious about things that mattered and objected
to Wilde's 'public persona as an apolitical, purposeless, dandified,
useless aesthete'. Ruth Robbins, 'The genders of socialism: Eleanor
Marx and Oscar Wilde', in John Stokes, (ed.), *Eleanor Marx 1855-1898:
Life, Work, Contacts*, Ashgate: Aldershot: 2000, p100.

51. Jabez Spencer Balfour (1843-1916) was founder of the Liberator
Building Society and associated land and property development
companies that enjoyed widespread support in the Nonconformist
and temperance movements.

Balfour, a Liberal Member of Parliament for Burnley, was exposed
in 1892 as being behind a huge financial swindle that led to him
absconding to Argentina to avoid arrest.

He was eventually apprehended and extradited, arriving at
Southampton in the first week of May 1895. Charged with falsi-
fying accounts and fraudulently applying funds of companies in
the Liberator group, Balfour was found guilty at the Old Bailey
and given a fourteen-year prison sentence. For more on Balfour,
see Esmond J. Cleary, 'Jabez Spencer Balfour, 1843-1916, building
society executive and property developer', in David J. Jeremy
(ed.), *Dictionary of Business Biography: A Biographical Dictionary of
Business Leaders Active in Britain in the Period 1860-1980, Vol 1 (A-C)*,
Butterworths: London, 1984, pp129-34; and David McKie, *Jabez:
The Rise and Fall of a Victorian Rogue*, Atlantic: London, 2004.

52. Here the authors have picked up a point made some months
earlier in the 'Critical comments' section of *Justice*, the Social
Democratic Federation weekly: 'We all know that Jabez Balfour is
a most disreputable person. But is he the same as the Honourable
Nonconformist Liberal J. Spencer Balfour, MP? If so, we should
much like to know why, since he has become disreputable, the
whole respectable world should call the late Mr J. Spencer Balfour,
MP, Jabez Balfour. That respectable daily journals should drop the
"Mr" may be intelligible, but why should they change J. Spencer
to Jabez? This is a mystery of Respectability. But Respectability is

great and must prevail even in names'. *Justice*, 15 December 1894, p1.

53. This happened in at least one case, the Croydon Workhouse Infirmary, where in 1893 the guardians ordered Balfour's name to be removed from the memorial stone. *Reynolds's Newspaper*, 8 October 1893, p8.

54. For Annie Besant and theosophy see Letter 2, notes 22-34.

LETTER FIVE

July 1895

Rosebery's Liberal government fell in the third week of June, when it was defeated in a parliamentary vote on defence spending. Because no dissolution of Parliament was called, Lord Salisbury formed a coalition government of Conservatives and Liberal Unionists, the composition of which attracted accusations of nepotism and favouring vested interests. By the second week of July a general election campaign was underway, which, it was clear to all, would be won by the Conservatives and Liberal Unionists.

With trade union and socialist forces caught unprepared for a general election, there was no agreed common strategy for the representation of labour's interests, resulting in diffuse and sometimes contradictory efforts. The letter continues the theme of singling out the Independent Labour Party for special criticism, suggesting its electoral strategy was 'tantamount to suicide'.

The letter marked the death of Thomas Henry Huxley, the renowned evolutionist, and the knighthood of actor Henry Irving, both known and admired by Edward, who was the likely author of these passages.

Eleanor contributed an extensive section to reviews of a number of 'New Woman' novelists, whose work she welcomed, while cautioning against what she called the 'woman question' being seen as separate from 'the questions of all humanity'.

In our previous letter, expecting that the course of political events would be slow over the summer period, we suggested that this time we would be able to concentrate our attention entirely on an examination of literary and theatrical productions. But our plans have been thwarted by events. *L'homme propose, Dieu dépose.* On this occasion the providential role was played by those sorts of political clashes that are often quite unforeseeable. As you are already aware, we have had a change of government.[1] The Liberals have left the stage to be replaced by the Conservatives. It was not necessary to have prophetic powers to predict the outcome of the elections, since it was obvious to everyone that the Liberals did not stand a chance. Even under the electoral conditions which exist in England, the working-class vote is a very important factor which both the traditional political parties need to take into account. The great majority of the working classes who take part in or are interested in politics continue to think that the Liberal Party, thanks to its historical position, will be obliged to make more concessions to the working classes and go further to meet their aspirations than the Conservative Party. Without a doubt, that has been the case in the past, and therefore even these days the working classes have expected further concessions from a Liberal government. And this has not been an entirely vain hope. However, when it came to certain immediate measures which the working classes had expected would be enacted, they indubitably suffered a disappointment. For example, in relation to certain privileges demanded by the working classes, and in relation to the conduct of elections, the Liberal government took no decisive steps either towards resolving the question of payment for MPs or towards lessening the burden of election expenses, which come entirely out of the candidate's pocket. For example, before a candidate can get onto the ballot paper, he must pay the Returning Officer a certain sum to defray his share of the expenses. Usually that sum equals £100, but in many cases can be twice as much. It is clear that a poor man, supported only by poor men, has little chance of even becoming a candidate, let alone of getting elected.[2]

Our Russian readers will already know the composition of our new government from the newspapers. It should be borne in mind that the number of different official post-holders which make up the administration is usually around thirty or a little more. Of their number, a smaller group go to make up the Cabinet itself, which is the internal executive and decision-taking authority which considers and decides the direction of the government's overall policy. The Cabinet consists of eleven (the minimum number), seventeen or even nineteen members. Our present Tory Cabinet has nineteen members, and Lord Salisbury combines the positions of Prime Minister and Foreign Secretary.

Lord Salisbury had to admit that on this occasion it was very difficult for him to put together a government.[3] Every first minister taking up his post is of course surrounded by a whole crowd of hangers-on, who want not only to serve their country but also to get on the payroll, anticipating remuneration for their work. All this crowd reminds one of a flock of hungry sparrows expecting to be fed. It is just as noisy and quarrelsome, and just as quick to show offence, as the sparrows. Those who are disappointed or dissatisfied, pushed aside by their luckier fellows, get furious with extraordinary ease and seek revenge for their bad luck. Lord Salisbury had to take account of that. He needed, on the one hand, to satisfy the real Tories, and this for him was an affair of the heart, if we can talk of hearts in connection with Tories, those embodiments of cynicism. On the other hand, he had to take care to keep Chamberlain's supporters happy, and that could not have been any labour of love for him. We have already written before about the disdain with which the real aristocrats regard the upstart Chamberlain, who has smuggled himself into their society and usurped their rights.[4] This Birmingham man upsets his rivals among the real Tories not only with his bad manners, but also with his unashamed stubbornness and sharpness. It is said that Lord Salisbury, obliged to concede to the demands of the new coalition Cabinet to replace some of his former Tory colleagues with his new allies, wrote letters of explanation, packed with the most amicable sentiments, to each of those whom he sacked from the Cabinet. It is even said that the letter he wrote to Lord Knutsford, whose position in the Colonial Office was taken by Chamberlain, brought tears to the eyes of the noble Lord.[5] But not annoying the mass of the people is of course the greatest matter of concern at the moment.

The first thing which strikes one about this diverse government is the influence of familial ties in the composition of the Cabinet.

Here, for example, is the family of Salisbury: Prime Minister and Foreign Secretary (salary £5,000 p.a.) – Lord Salisbury himself; First Lord of the Treasury and Leader of the House of Commons (£5,000) – Balfour, Lord Salisbury's nephew; Chief Secretary for Ireland (£4,425) – Gerald Balfour, also Lord Salisbury's nephew;[6]

two further likely members of the administration, Mr Lowther and
Viscount Wolmer are also members of Salisbury's family.[7] Then
there is Chamberlain's family; members of which have the posts of
Colonial Secretary (£5,000), Civil Lord of the Admiralty (£1,000) and
two secretaries' positions at £1,500 a year. Incidentally, we cannot
say that these last two are relatives of Chamberlain in the direct
sense, in that they are not related, but they are nonetheless members
of his family, being his adopted sons.[8] The nepotism expressed in
all these appointments inspired several highly amusing caricatures
by the sharp-witted cartoonist Gould of the *Westminster Gazette*, in
which Chamberlain comes in for particular mockery. One of these
sketches shows a London omnibus, packed with people. Each of
the passengers is depicted as one or another influential member of
the old Tory Party. The bus conductor is Lord Salisbury. A tall thin
woman standing on the street waves her umbrella at the conductor
to stop and let her and her three little boys on. The tall thin woman
is Chamberlain, and the three children are her followers. She
declares: 'We absolutely must get on this bus! If there is no room
for us, then let some of these other gentlemen get off.'[9]

As for the age of the new members of Salisbury's cabinet, although
he has not gone to the extremes of gerontocracy, as Gladstone once
put it, there are still two septuagenarians in his government – the
Lord Chancellor and Lord Cross, who are seventy-two years old.[10]
The latter receives a pension of £2,000 and therefore receives
nothing as a member of the Cabinet. That said, there is little for him
to do in the government, and was only appointed because the queen
wanted it. His job is to carry out her wishes and, they say, take care
of her affairs. The ages of Lord Salisbury, Chamberlain, and Arthur
and Gerald Balfour are sixty-five, fifty-nine, forty-five and forty-two
respectively. Incidentally, one of the objections raised by the Irish
MPs against the appointment of Gerald Balfour as Chief Secretary
for Ireland, apart from the fact that this appointment offends their
national sentiments, is not without its humour: the Irish MPs object
to it because Balfour is the purest embodiment of tedium!

The appointment of Balfour reminds us that there is one
Irishman in the government, although he is an apostate. There are
three Scots in the government.[11]

Of the members of the Cabinet, nine are members of the House of Lords – the chamber which does not consist of the people's representatives. These nine are all landlords. There are a further four landlords among the rest, who are even bigger landowners, making a total of thirteen landlords in the government. To them we must add four capitalist magnates: Sir Henry James, a barrister, Ritchie and Chamberlain, major industrialists, and Goschen, a money-lender. Not bad! It should not be forgotten that the last of these, Goschen, is the grandson of the famous publisher of Goethe.[12]

The name of Goschen, since he serves as a representative of the largest financial firm in the City, naturally brings to mind the institution known in financial jargon as the 'guinea pig'.[13] This term is applied to a person who lends his name to some commercial company and is named as a director. Such companies, of course, are looking for names which look like pure gold to the uninitiated, and will only accept those names. On the other hand, the guinea pig does not lend his name for nothing, and receives a commensurate fee. Previously religious figures with a certain reputation were considered good names to have, but the rate for them has fallen in recent years. Titled people, especially if the title is hereditary, are highly prized, and the price rises still higher if the title-holder has the right to sit in the Lords. The name of any parliamentarian will also get quite a high price on the guinea pig market. But the price for the name of a parliamentarian who also has the title of minister can reach legendary heights. And, most curious of all, it is precisely those gentlemen who get enormous sums for their 'nominal' – in both senses of the term – services who scream loudest of all and are the first to protest against MPs receiving salaries.

Let us now look at what role in all this is played by the members of our freshly baked administration. The figures speak for themselves. To the credit of Balfour, the leader of the Commons, it should be said that he is not a director of any commercial company. His uncle, on the other hand, is a direct of one such company, and his brother, as if trying to make up the shortfall in the family, is a director of no less than seven commercial companies. As for the rest: the Secretary of State for War is a director of six companies; the President of the Board of Agriculture – four; the Lord President of the Council (the Duke of Devonshire) – four; the Secretary for Scotland – four; the President of the Board of Trade – three; Chamberlain – three, etc.

Six other members of the government are each directors of at least two commercial companies, and another three, not counting Lord Salisbury – one. In total the members of the present government have an interest in at least fifty commercial enterprises, which not only puts the well-being of British citizens at risk, but is also in part gambling with the welfare of the entire state.[14] We shall point to three facts in this respect, which are particularly characteristic, affecting Joseph Powell Williams, Sir John Gorst and Gerald Balfour. The first of these persons, appointed Financial Secretary to the War Office, has, besides his directorships of two companies, a very close relationship with the firm of Kynoch and Co. Members of Chamberlain's family also have a very close connection with this company. There is no doubt that the dismissal of the previous war minister, and as a consequence, the fall of the government, was related to questions concerning the above-mentioned firm.[15] The Tories had not wanted that outcome, unlike Chamberlain, who was perspicacious enough to understand that his position in the present circumstances was very advantageous. If the government were to be dissolved a year or even a few months hence, fortune may have turned against him. This undoubtedly accounts for the indecent haste with which a new bill has been brought before Parliament.[16] It will make anyone who dares say any unpleasant truths during the election period about the sacred personages called candidates liable to various punishments and fines. Another personal motivation behind the publication of this bill is a desire to have a weapon to use against cartoonists.

Now for a second fact. Sir John Gorst, the current Minister for Education, was, together with the minister Mundella, a director of a fairly well-known New Zealand company. Mr Mundella, on account of his directorship, was obliged to quit the Liberal government of which he was a member, while Sir John Gorst, also a director of this same company, is invited to serve as a minister in the Tory government.[17] A bright light on all these commercial operations has been cast by the words of the chairman of the meeting of one of these companies of which Gerald Balfour is a director, namely, the telegraph company. This most honest chairman declared at the meeting – and his words were printed in the company report – that the value of the particular guinea pig that is Balfour is all to do with the services he can render the company from his position as a member of the government. Here are the words of this esteemed chairman: 'There are questions with the government, in regard to which mere technical knowledge of telegraphy would not be so valuable as the service of a man of Mr Balfour's position may render us.'[18] That is clear enough. The Balfour being spoken of here is the brother of the Leader of the Commons.

Taking all the above into account, the activities of Lord Salisbury should provide very interesting material for study from the political, economic and also ethical point of view. His predecessor, the late lamented (politically) Lord Rosebery laid down a rule that members of his Cabinet had to break all commercial ties which might inhibit their freedom of action. The future will tell whether the Conservative government wants to follow that example.[19]

The Tories and the Liberal Unionists are constantly talking about their union. The following little tale shows clearly enough how little stability there is in this poorly concluded union: one of the main Conservative clubs here is the 'Junior Constitutional', to which one of the Liberal Unionists applied for membership a few days ago. He was required to give a written answer to a standard question asked of all new members concerning their political beliefs. He completed this formality and thereafter received this letter, from which we extract the following lines:

> I am very sorry to have to inform you that since our club is a purely Conservative club, no Liberal Unionists may be accepted for membership. This may seem strange, given the current union between the Liberal Unionists and the Conservatives, but you will doubtless have noticed from the speeches of Mr Chamberlain that this union has no guarantees of lasting for long.[20]

The new workers' movement is still not fully formed but is already taking on an ominous character. Before we discuss the position it took in the run up to the parliamentary general elections, we must ask our Russian readers not to forget that we are having to write these letters three or four weeks earlier than you are reading them. In order that our readers should form a more or less clear understanding of the workers' question in England, we consider it necessary to make the following preliminary remarks. The workers in various branches of work in England group themselves into associations called 'trade unions'. Every year since 1837 there has been a congress of delegates of these unions. At the first congress, organised in Leeds, Yorkshire, Robert Owen was in the chair.[21] The delegates at these congresses, besides directly discussing questions of interest to the workers, also elect from their number a small group, known as the Parliamentary Committee, which also acts as the executive authority. It is laid down that this committee will always follow, from one congress to the next, the mandate it was given at the preceding congress, in particular in relation to parliamentary measures which affect workers. At the previous congress in Norwich in September last year, the following important resolutions were adopted:

> If the general elections take place before the 1895 congress, the Parliamentary Committee of Congress proposes, immediately after the dissolution of Parliament, to convene a conference in Manchester of all affiliated unions.
>
> This conference should consider the following questions 1) to establish which bills (measures with important industrial significance suggested by previous congresses) were rejected by Parliament; 2) to determine which of these bills need to be again brought before Parliament for its consideration; 3) work out a programme which will include resolutions passed by Congress. In accordance with this, members of unions will be invited to vote for and support only those candidates who accept the programme of the Parliamentary Committee of the Trades Union Congress.[22]

The most important, vital interest, from the point of view of the new direction of English political life, is undoubtedly the third paragraph of this resolution. We have already pointed out that the main essence of this direction consists in the recognition of the existence of two large classes, the workers and the employers, with interests which are different and even diametrically opposed to one another, and in the formation of a new political party, a labour party, which differs sharply from the two oldest political parties, both of which have a bourgeois character. The ultimate goal of that new party consists, as is already recognised at the present time, in the nationalisation of the means of production and distribution. At the congress in Norwich that resolution was passed by a massive majority. In such circumstances, of course, the decisions of the special conference of trade unions called when Parliament was dissolved, are of great interest. The programme elaborated by that special conference, which represented around one million workers, has only just been published. It consists of twenty points, of which the following are the most notable:

1. Change to the Jury Law and payment of jurors for their services.
2. Employers' liability.
3. Introduction of an eight-hour working day.
4. An obligation on the government to take account of the wage scales and working conditions established by trade unions and publication of all contracts concluded.
5. Change to the Law of Conspiracy.
6. A ban on undermanned shipping.
7. The nationalisation of the land and the means of production, distribution and exchange.
8. Old age pensions.
9. Payment for MPs.
10. Reform of parliamentary procedure.
11. Reform of registrations.
12. Reform of the Poor Law system.
13. The creation of a more effective system for inspecting mines, factories, railways, docks and workshops.
14. The abolition of the House of Lords.

Paragraph 7 of this programme indicates that the conference adopted the above-mentioned decision of the Norwich conference by sixty-six votes to fifty-eight.[23]

As for the Independent Labour Party headed by Mr Keir Hardie, it apparently proposes to continue its course of action which is tantamount to suicide. We have already told our readers about this. At the moment, this party has gathered to decide whether it should get involved in elections or refrain from taking any part in them. The resolutions of the party have not yet been published, but whatever they are, it remains an undoubted fact that the dissolution of Parliament has caught the new ILP, if not entirely without any programme, then at least without a fully worked-out political direction.[24] The Social Democratic Federation, in contrast, has both a programme and policy. Its programme is well defined and clear, and corresponds to the programmes of similar parties on the continent.[25] In recent years the federation has significantly extended its activities. Nonetheless, this party is only able to muster four parliamentary candidates, who stand very little chance of being elected. The ILP is standing about twenty candidates. But the working classes will undoubtedly continue to follow the path which will ultimately detach their fate from the fate of one or the other of the traditional political parties.

From the point of view of working-class politics, the most interesting candidacies are those of Keir Hardie, the SDF leader Hyndman, and John Burns, who agrees on most points with the programmes of one or the other of the two parties but does not belong to either of them.[26] But we think it a better idea to leave a detailed analysis of the results of the elections, their significance, and their most characteristic features, to our next letter.

In between the resignation of the Cabinet and the dissolution of Parliament there were two events of considerable significance to parliamentary affairs but not directly connected with those financial and other measures which needed to be resolved as quickly as possible. The first of these was the rejection by the House of Lords of the Irish Municipal Franchise Bill, and the second was the ratification of the Factory Act. The Irish bill was the third measure relating to Ireland rejected by the House of Lords in the last three years.[27] There are many reasons to be found for the rejection of the Irish bill, but there is only one explanation for the haste with which both parties, as soon as dissolution seemed inevitable, tried to get the factory bill through the committee stage and the Commons. The committee, which consisted mainly of employers, had previously tried to drag out any decision on the bill, but as soon as its members saw that they would have to go back to their constituencies and present themselves to their electorates, they immediately hurried to rush through this unhappy bill, which had been mutilated by both sides, just so that both sides then had the right to say to the workers: 'Look how much we love you, now give us your votes.' The ship-owners had tried to derail it, but in view of the general election they were not indulged.[28]

The final report of the Special Committee to establish the extent of the distress caused by unemployment provides a curious example of the English ability to do nothing while keeping up an entirely virtuous appearance. The committee wrote and sent out thousands of letters and listened to almost as many diverse schemes to deal with unemployment which, as the committee put it, 'must unfortunately be left without the attention and consideration they deserve'. The report expresses the hope that the next parliament will resume the inquiry.[29] The final session of this committee, which had long been in its death agonies, was the only one which came closer to tragedy than to farce. It was addressed by Thorne, the secretary of the well-known National Union of Gas Workers and General Labourers.[30] This union has done much more than any other institution to improve the position of the unskilled labourers and the working classes overall, as well as to spread the international character of the workers' movement. At the final session, Thorne said:

> Under the present system, people who are skilful and capable of working are deprived of the right to work. The introduction of machines is pushing workers out. Rather than being a relief for the workers, the machines are a curse, as they throw them out onto the labour market to compete with each other. The main reason for the fall in the use of labour is the fact that across the country machinery and capital are private property. This problem cannot be resolved under the current condition of society, and it makes absolutely no difference what scheme you adopt, farming, colonies or some other such institution, at any rate you will only remove the problem temporarily: within a short time the workers will be in exactly the same position.[31]

Thorne's observation that machinery pushes out human labour and brings benefits not to the workers but to the capitalists, will soon be shown in the most fateful way in the English weaving industry. A new machine has been invented by an American.[32] A company was immediately set up to exploit this new invention and the new loom is already on the market. Without a doubt the appearance of this loom will deprive several thousand men and women of their jobs. One of the main advantages of this loom is that it saves on labour: one worker, male or female, can easily attend to two or even three such looms. Moreover, once it has been started up, this loom can operate for an hour or more without any supervision whatsoever. Thus, when the workers go off for lunch, the loom continues operating in their absence; when they get back they find it working away. In the same way, after the workers have finished for the day, the loom will continue operating for another hour. These two extra working hours in the day are a direct benefit to the capitalist. They say that 5,000 such looms have already been ordered for England, threatening many thousands of workers with the loss of their livelihoods. The saddest thing about all this is, as Thorne says, that rather than the introduction of this machinery being a blessing for the workers, it is a curse, which directly undermines their existence.

Another invention which threatens to impact in the same damaging way on the position of the workers is a machine for loading and unloading coal onto and off ships.[33] Up to now this work has been done with the use of manual labour, and the coal loaders were unionised. Thanks to this new invention, which will be introduced in other countries as well as England, many hundreds of workers will be deprived of their usual occupations. This new invention can be operated by two adults and one child and in an hour will perform as much work as would normally be done by twelve men over twenty-four hours. There is another fact about machines pushing out living labour power which deserves mention, although more from a social than an economic point of view – horse power is also being pushed out. In England as elsewhere, work performed by horses is increasingly being replaced by machine work, and in future is threatened with being replaced completely by gas and electric motors. In the current London season those entrepreneurs who rent out horses and carriages are literally despairing. They are particularly cursing bicycles.

Many of the prosperous and rich London citizens, who had previously been in the habit of riding on horseback round aristocratic Hyde Park, now prefer to ride bicycles on the pathways of the more plebeian Battersea Park.[34] We may hope that in the near future all London omnibuses will be powered by motors rather than horses. Quite recently a carriage powered by a petrol motor travelled from Paris to Bordeaux at thirteen miles per hour, and already in certain English cities, such as Leeds, there are electric omnibuses operating. At the moment, incidentally, English law does not permit the introduction of mechanical carriages, but the president of the Local Government Board of the outgoing administration had introduced a bill which would have permitted such carriages. Since this bill can in no wise be seen as a party measure, it is quite possible that it will pass without hindrance.[35] Our engineers, of course, are not hesitating to accept the invitation, and we shall presumably soon be seeing traders delivering goods, doctors visiting their patients, farmers taking their produce to markets, tourists etc. all travelling around the country in carriages powered by diverse mechanical and electrical motors and so on.

With the death of Professor Huxley at seventy years of age, a most remarkable figure has disappeared from the scientific and literary horizon not only of England, but of the whole world.[36] Intended for a career in medicine, Huxley, like many other biologists (Darwin, Haeckel and others) undertook his first biological studies during a ship's voyage. Huxley, working as a ship's doctor, soon found his true calling in studying the lives of plants and animals, and fairly quickly rose to the position of professor at the Royal School of Mines, the main state institution concerned with the study of natural sciences. To be sure, this position was not a sinecure, but it nonetheless left Huxley enough free time to pursue his favourite activities – all the more because the position itself tended more to encourage rather than hamper these activities. Many of his subsequent positions were nothing but sinecures – the position of Inspector of Fisheries which Huxley held was undoubtedly a sinecure and a well paid one at that. Of course, in other cases Huxley was able to show the full brilliance of his abilities as a professor, in which capacity he was unrivalled. Although he wrote numerous original works, his main service has been the interpretation and dissemination of scientific theories and ideas. He, more than anyone else, has been responsible for spreading the new biological theory associated with the name of Darwin. He collaborated in the dissemination and adoption of these ideas not only among scientists, but also among the public. He influenced scientists by his highly precise scientific method of applying Darwinist principles in zoology, and he influenced the general public with his clear, unerring and, in the best sense of the word, popular exposition and explanation of the new views.

In this country under certain circumstances there can be a sudden real epidemic of bestowing of titles, creating a whole group of new knights, baronets and so on. As they leave office or assume office, governments reward their retainers in this way. Or at least, they are expected to do so. Thus, for example, poor Lord Knutsford received the title of viscount as a consolation prize for having his bureaucratic feelings hurt by someone else getting his job. On the queen's birthday more titles were handed out. This year, incidentally, our greatest living actor Henry Irving received a knighthood on that day.[37] From now on he is 'Sir Henry Irving'. In the new knight's profession a great deal of importance is placed on that bestowal of title. Everyone knows that as an actor, Henry Irving stands head and shoulders above his other confreres, and that he has access to 'high society', but the importance of his elevation to the nobility consists in the fact that this is the first official recognition of the acting profession. Other professions and branches of knowledge have long received official recognition and it was only the dramatic arts which constituted an exception. The legacy of the old Puritan views and sentiments obliged our middle classes, who provide us with all our ideas and moral concepts, to look down on the acting profession. Legally, the actor is nothing more than a 'rogue and a vagabond'. All those who know Irving personally have, of course, no doubt that he attaches no significance to his new honour, and, in all probability, laughs at his title. Nonetheless he has accepted it as an official tribute to his profession and a recognition of the honoured position which it currently enjoys, a position which he, more than anyone else, has helped it attain.

Besides Henry Irving, who is undoubtedly in the first rank, we have other actors worthy of note. After the Lyceum, which we recommend everyone coming to London should visit, there is the Haymarket, where a visitor will also see fine plays and fine acting. The main actor at that theatre is a first-rate talent and, something very unusual among our actors, he speaks two other languages fluently, besides his native tongue. His wife, in whom he has found a very worthy helpmate in the theatrical world, is also unusually highly educated in her profession, as she studied classics at one of our women's colleges.[38]

For readers interested in the development of the dramatic arts, we can confidently recommend William Archer's two-volume *The Theatrical World* of 1893 and 1894'.[39] Archer is our best theatre critic. He has studied drama not only in England, but also in France, Germany, Scandinavia and Italy, and is distinguished by his great erudition, wide education and fine literary style. As we have already stated, Archer is our best critic of dramatic productions rather than of acting. His book on the dramatic arts may therefore be of interest to Russian readers, although English readers could reproach Archer for being insufficiently critical of the execution of plays and of the acting.

A few words about the latest literary novelties which we think deserve our Russian readers' attention. At the moment a lot is being said and written about the works of women writers. In art, as in sociology, there must not and cannot be a 'woman question' separate from the questions of all humanity. Of course, we should not conclude from this that sex plays no part in these questions. A woman's standpoint is different from a man's. For this reason, and as a result of the artificial conditions in which women live, works by women turn out to be rather one-sided. Even the best works of the latest women's literary school, which incontestably deserve our attention, are not completely free from this defect. It is also striking that the centre of gravity in all these works is marriage and relations between men and women in general. Among the first-rate works by women authors in the recent period is *Gallia*, by Menie Muriel Dowie (Mrs Henry Norman), a novel which unquestionably stands out for its great literary merits and is of profound interest.[40] But in this work, too, as in all the others, although it is written by a woman over thirty, we nonetheless encounter strange discourses and phrases about marital relations which the author puts into the mouths of her young heroines.[41] They quite seriously discuss, for example, how in the future the work of reproduction will be entrusted to healthy men and women who will under-take it for those who are incapable of doing so, etc. etc. Another work, *Keynotes*, also written by a woman, who by tradition calls herself 'George Egerton', belongs to the same category of women's writing.[42] This is a collection of short stories, in each of which the central and, it must be said, excessively predominant character is a woman. George Egerton's works again confirm our words about the one-sidedness of women's writing and the woman's standpoint. This, incidentally, is what the author herself says: 'The life of a woman of middle standing is a constant struggle between instinc-tive truths and cultivated lies. We repress and repress our instincts, and then some day we stumble on the man who just satisfies our sexual and emotional nature, and then there is shipwreck of some sort.' Belinda, the heroine of the third story, is a simple servant. She expressed in a fairly sharp and crude form a feeling which, incidentally, is quite widespread among women, saying, 'If one could only have a child, ma'm, without a husband.' That the author of *Keynotes* is rebelling against conditional morality can be seen among others in the following words: 'I would like to know whether we shall ever be in a position ... to be sure that what we need is also good and right.'[43]

But without any doubt the cleverest of our contemporary women writers is Mrs Craigie, who calls herself John Oliver Hobbes.[44] Incidentally, her surname is no longer Craigie, as she has already managed to divorce and re-marry. The circumstances of her divorce, at any rate, cast a shadow on her husband, rather than on her. Some of the newspapers, which sometimes have flashes of humour, have titled the case of Mrs Craigie's divorce with the name of her first story 'Some emotions and a moral'. This writer has a very sparkling style, and moreover she has the rare and saving gift of seeing not only the tragic but also the humorous side of life, and can take the same dispassionate view of both herself and her sex. Of all the authors we have discussed here, John Oliver Hobbes is undoubtedly one of those we can unreservedly recommend to our

Russian readers. Her most recent work, or, as she calls it, her 'first novel', is *The Gods, Some Mortals and Lord Wickenham,* published by Henry and Co.

Av.

Notes

1. Lord Rosebery's Liberal government was defeated in the House of Commons on 21 June 1895 on a motion critical of the War Office's provision of the explosive cordite for the army. Rosebery resigned the following day, but did not initiate a dissolution of Parliament, forcing Lord Salisbury to form a government of Conservatives and Liberal Unionists. Parliament was dissolved on 8 July, followed by a general election, which was concluded by the first week of August.

   This letter appears to have been written in the second week of July when the general election was just underway. By this time it was already clear that the election would result in a Conservative and Unionist victory.

2. The failure of the Liberal government of 1892-5 to introduce payment of MPs or to enable returning officers' expenses to be met out of public funds was a major disappointment to trade unionists and socialists.

   Representatives of the TUC met Rosebery in November 1894 to state the case for these reforms, which were existing Liberal Party policy, having been agreed at the Liberal Federation meeting at Newcastle in 1891. Rosebery told the TUC that parliamentary time and funding would inevitably limit the ability of the government to implement its full programme, which was taken to mean that reform of electoral law would not happen in the current Parliament. Subsequent efforts to persuade the Chancellor of the Exchequer to allocate funding for these changes in his budget of 1895 were unsuccessful.

3. The Third Marquess of Salisbury, Robert Gascoigne Cecil (1830-1903), Conservative prime minister 1895-1902. Salisbury had twice been prime minister in 1885-6 and 1886-1892.

4. For Joseph Chamberlain see Letter 3, note 31 and Letter 4, notes 21-23.

5. Lord Knutsford was Henry Thurston Holland (1825-1914), who had been Secretary of State for the Colonies in Salisbury's previous government and would have expected to resume that office had not Chamberlain expressed a wish to take on the role. Knutsford's title was elevated to viscount in the summer of 1895.

   In addition to Chamberlain, Salisbury appointed three other

Liberal Unionists to his Cabinet – the Duke of Devonshire, the Marquess of Lansdowne, and Sir Henry James, in recognition of support from that party. The government was commonly referred to as 'Unionist'.

6. Arthur James Balfour (1848-1930), Conservative Party Leader in the Commons since 1892, was the brother of Gerald William Balfour (1853-1945), the Chief Secretary for Ireland. The Balfours were related to the prime minister through their mother, who was Salisbury's sister. On this and other appointments (see note 7), the *Daily Chronicle* commented: 'In other words, four most important posts in the government – its supreme direction, the control of foreign affairs, the leadership of the House of Commons and the working chiefship of Irish affairs – are held by members of a single family, while an Under-Secretaryship is held by the son-in-law of the Premier. We must say that a more audacious piece of nepotism was never perpetrated.' *Daily Chronicle*, 3 July 1895, p6.

7. James William Lowther (1855-1949) was Deputy Speaker of the Commons. His wife was niece to the prime minister.

William Palmer, second Earl of Selborne, styled Viscount Wolmer (1859-1942), was Under-Secretary of State for the Colonies. The prime minister was his father-in-law.

8. Joseph Chamberlain's son Austen Chamberlain (1863-1937) was Chief Lord of the Admiralty.

The sarcastic comment on Chamberlain's 'adopted sons' is a reference to Joseph Powell Williams (1840-1904), Financial Secretary to the War Office and Jesse Collings (1831-1920), Under Secretary in the Home Office, both of whom were, like Chamberlain, Birmingham-based and his long-term supporters.

9. Francis Carruthers Gould's cartoon appeared in the *Westminster Gazette* of 4 July 1895, p3.

10. The Lord Chancellor was Earl Halsbury (1823-1921) who had served in the office twice previously. Lord Cross was Richard Assheton Cross (1823-1914), Chancellor of the Duchy of Lancaster.

11. Lord Ashbourne (1837-1913), Lord Chancellor for Ireland, was born in Dublin.

The Scottish-born members of Salisbury's cabinet were: A.J. Balfour, Lord Balfour of Burleigh (1849-1921), Secretary of State for Scotland; and Charles Thomas Ritchie (1838-1906), President of the Board of Trade.

12. The authors derived this from *Reynolds's Newspaper* (a radical weekly with leanings towards trade unions and labour politics), which offered this on 30 June 1895, p1, on the Cabinet:

It consists of seventeen members of whom nine belong to the unrepresentative chamber. This is government by the House of Lords with a vengeance. These nine peers are all landlords, and of the remainder there are four great landlords – Sir M. Hicks-Beach, Sir M. White Ridley, Mr Balfour and Mr Chaplin – thirteen landlords. The other four are capitalists of enormous wealth – Goschen, the money lender, Chamberlain, the iron master, Ritchie, the manufacturer, and Sir Henry James, the lawyer. There's a popular government. The Tory cry at the general election must inevitably be 'Vote for the landlords and the capitalists'.

George Goschen (see Letter 3, note 32) inherited a substantial financial interest in the merchant bank of Fruhling and Goschen.

13. The 'guinea pig' director was one who served on a company board merely or mainly for a fee – often a guinea – plus a lavish lunch. Politicians and titled noblemen were pursued by company promoters seeking to enhance the respectability and public appearance of a company. Such company promoters were particularly active in the mid 1890s, when the number of registered companies doubled. G.R. Searle, *Corruption in British Politics 1895-1930*, Clarendon: Oxford, 1987, p34.

14. The authors underestimate the number of directorships held by ministers in Salisbury's government, which was in fact sixty-one. A.J. Wilson, 'The company directorships held by Lord Salisbury's ministry', *Investors' Review*, August 1895, pp65-76.

15. During the parliamentary debate on 21 June on the adequacy of cordite supplies to the army, defeat in which led to the fall of the government, Joseph Chamberlain asked a question of the Secretary of War about government orders placed with Kynoch and Co., an ammunition manufacturer located in Witton, a suburb of Birmingham. The subtext of Chamberlain's question was a critique of the government short on its supply of cordite, but slow in placing orders to approved contractors, including Kynoch and Co. Within days, the *Westminster Gazette* revealed the Chamberlain family involvement and that of their business partner J.S. Nettlefold in Kynoch's. Joseph's brother, Arthur Chamberlain, was chairman of Kynoch's, and together members of the Chamberlain family held more than 1,300 company shares. This, the *Westminster Gazette* commented, was clear evidence that while Joseph Chamberlain as a Birmingham MP did have a right to ask a question about a company operating in his city, 'he might have added that his family was interested in it also'. *Westminster Gazette*, 26 June 1895, p2. This issue continued to be the subject of public interest, and was investigated

by the Commons Committee on War Office Contracts in 1900. For this, see Searle 1987, pp52-65.

16. The Corrupt and Illegal Practices Bill (1883 Amendment Act) was introduced in the first week of February 1895 to make those who made false statements calculated to prejudice candidates' chances in parliamentary elections subject to the same penalties as those guilty of illegal election practices. During the second reading of the bill, Joseph Chamberlain spoke of the recent adverse publicity that had suggested that he had a pecuniary interest in a company receiving orders from government. He hoped such accusations would be outlawed in the future. The bill was hurried through Parliament before dissolution.

17. Sir John Gorst (1835-1916) was Education Minister in the Salisbury government. In 1894 Gorst had, with A.J. Mundella (1825-1897), then President of the Board of Trade in Rosebery's government, been examined in an investigation by the Court of Bankruptcy into the liquidation of the New Zealand Land and Mercantile Agency Company, of which both men had been directors. The investigation revealed concealment and misrepresentation by board members, compelling Mundella to resign his government office in May 1894.

18. Before taking office in Salisbury's government Gerald Balfour had been the subject of criticism for his willingness to hold multiple company directorships. Among these was the directorship of the West Indian and Panama Telegraph Company, whose chairman, addressing a meeting of shareholders in November 1893, responded to a question asking why the MP had been appointed to the board – 'Had he any knowledge of telegraphy?'. The chairman replied:

> I am rather sorry that the question of the appointment of Mr Balfour has been raised, because it is a matter we discussed a great deal at this board, and we saw very good reasons for asking him to become a director. As I said, we do not want now the organising talent we required in 1873 and 1874. The system has got into perfect order; it works uniformly. Our servants are all experienced, and we still have on the board Mr Andrews who is quite capable in these matters, as was Mr Weaver. There are, however, other points in a man of Mr Balfour's position which are of importance to us, and I trust you will not extract from me more on the matter than I am now saying. You may depend upon it that the request which was made to Mr Balfour to join us was done in the best interests solely of the company whose affairs we have to administer. There are questions with the government, in regard

to which mere technical knowledge of telegraphy would not be so valuable as the service of a man of Mr Balfour's position may render us. *Westminster Gazette*, 22 December 1893, p1.

Balfour was still director of the company when appointed to Salisbury's Cabinet. *Westminster Gazette*, 3 July 1895, p3.

19. Lord Salisbury did not insist that members of his Cabinet break all commercial ties with companies, and it is generally accepted that his period in office represented a 'recession' in these matters. D.C.M. Platt, 'The commercial and industrial interests of ministers of the Crown', *Political Studies*, Vol. 9, No. 3, 1961, p274. These years saw a number of financial scandals that impinged on the Unionist government. See Searle 1987, pp13-51.

20. Naturally, opponents of the Unionist government had some fun with the diktat from the Junior Constitutional Club, one of the leading Conservative gentlemen's clubs in London. See for instance the remarks of James Hincks, the Liberal candidate for the Worcester seat in *Worcestershire Chronicle*, 13 July 1895, p6.

21. Robert Owen (1771-1858) was a wealthy factory owner who pioneered co-operative movements and socialism. It is possible that here the authors are confusing Robert Owen's Grand National Consolidated Trade Union, an attempt from 1834 to establish a confederation of trade unions, with the Trades Union Congress established at Manchester in 1868.

22. The motion submitted by Ben Tillett's Dock, Wharf, Riverside and General Labourers' Union was not debated at the 1894 TUC, but was referred to the Parliamentary Committee, which convened the special conference of affiliates at Manchester on 11 July 1895.

23. As proposer of the undebated motion at the TUC in 1894 (see previous note), Ben Tillett opened the special conference with a statement outlining the programme to be put to candidates and advising delegates that 'they should stand by their class interests' in the general election'. *Daily News*, 12 July 1895, p7.

The authors were keen to point out that the conference confirmed, by a vote of sixty-six to fifty-eight, the decision of the 1894 TUC to support nationalisation of the means of production.

24. Representatives of the Independent Labour Party branches met in London on 4 July 1895 to decide on their policy where no socialist was standing in the election. It was agreed to advise members to abstain in these circumstances.

25. The Social Democratic Federation published its election manifesto in *Justice* on 29 June 1895, p4.

26. For Keir Hardie see Letter 3, note 15; Henry Mayers Hyndman (1842-1921) was the leading figure in the Social Democratic Federation; John Burns had been MP for Battersea since 1892. He was elected as socialist/labour candidate in 1892, but soon moved towards the Liberals. He joined the Liberal government in 1906 as a cabinet minister.

27. The Irish Municipal Franchise Bill was introduced to correct anomalies and give every ratepayer in Ireland a vote in local council elections. The bill was lost in the first week of July, when the House of Lords decided not to give it a second reading.

28. The Factory and Workshop Act 1895 was passed in the final days of Parliament by agreement of the principal parties. The bill introduced by Home Secretary Asquith in March received the acclamation of the TUC, which stated that if passed in that form 'it would have settled the question of factory and workshop legislation for many years to come'. 'TUC annual report 1895', TUC, p21. However, in the committee stage the bill was heavily amended in response to lobbying by employers who sought exemption from its conditions. The TUC published a comprehensive record of MP voting on the bill and urged its affiliates to scrutinise the division lists 'for their own use in the future'. *Ibid.*, pp130-145.

    A last-minute attempt to dilute the provisions of the bill by shipowners, who claimed the operation of trade in docks and warehouses would be impeded by Home Office supervision when they were already subject to Board of Trade inspection, was resisted by Asquith, who proposed a minor amendment and thus secured passage of the bill to Royal Assent. HC Deb. 3 July 1895, Vol. 35, Cc 148-163.

29. See Letter 3, notes 15-27 and Letter 4, note 1.

30. William ('Will') James Thorne (1857-1946). For Thorne, see his *My Life's Battles*, George Newens: London, 1925. For Thorne's relationship with Eleanor, see Yvonne Kapp, *Eleanor Marx: Volume Two, The Crowded Years 1884-1898,* Lawrence and Wishart: London, 1976; and Kapp, *The Air of Freedom: The Birth of New Unionism*, Lawrence and Wishart: London, 1989, pp81-94.

31. Here the authors paraphrase Thorne's contribution to the committee. For a verbatim record of Thorne's comments, see 'Third report from the Select Committee on Distress from Want of Employment', HMSO, July 1895, pp429-38.

32. This was the Northrop automatic power loom marketed by George Draper of Massachusetts from 1894. Invented by James H. Northrop, a Yorkshire-born engineer who had emigrated to America in the 1880s, the loom required significantly less supervision than previous machines, and therefore reduced labour costs. At first, the loom

was imported from the USA, but in 1902 a works was established in Blackburn to manufacture the loom for the British and imperial markets.

33. The 'steam navvy', a mechanical device equipped with a 'grab' to move heavy loads, was manufactured by Rushton, Proctor and Co. from the 1880s. Thorne described the operation of the 'Navvy' in his own Beckton area in evidence to the Select Committee, 'Third report from the Select Committee on Distress from Want of Employment',p433.

34. During the 1890s cycling boomed, as safety and comfort of vehicles improved and mass production reduced the cost of purchase. By the middle of the decade more than one million people were cycling. In London, 'Battersea Park and Hyde Park were the fashionable places for cyclists of both sexes in London society'. David Rubinstein, 'Cycling in the 1890s', *Victorian Studies*, Autumn 1977, Vol 21, No 1, p49.

   Many socialists took up cycling through the Clarion Cycling Clubs which thrived in the 1890s and beyond. For this see Dennis Pye, *Fellowship in Life: the National Clarion Cycling Club, 1895-1995*, Clarion: Bolton, 1995.

   There is no evidence to suggest that either of the authors joined the cycling craze.

35. The Paris to Bordeaux race took place in June 1895.

   Leeds Corporation introduced electric trams in 1891 and it was widely believed that this would be followed in other cities. Andrew Barr, secretary of the Self-Propelled Traffic Association, predicted reduced overheads in the removal of costs associated with horse-flesh, stabling and stablemen's wages. He said the public would benefit from not having to be confronted with the sight of worn-out horses – 'work-him-till-he drops down dead' – being sent out by omnibus companies. *Pall Mall Gazette*, 11 December 1895, p3.

36. Thomas Henry Huxley (1825-1895), biologist, evolutionist and disciple of Charles Darwin, was known to and admired by Edward from the 1870s.

37. Henry Irving (1838-1905) was the leading actor of his generation, widely respected and admired for his role in elevating the profession.

   The authors, both lovers of Shakespeare, admired Irving's interpretation of the plays, and had known him independently of each other for many years.

38. Herbert Beerbohm Tree (1852-1917) was the actor manager of the Haymarket Theatre. His wife, Helen Maud Holt (1863-1937), known professionally as Mrs Beerbohm Tree, often acted opposite her husband. She had studied Classics at Queen's College, London.

39. William Archer (1856-1924), Scottish-born writer and theatre critic who played an important role in introducing Ibsen to the English public. Archer's reviews in *The World* weekly were brought together as *The Theatrical World*, published in 1894, 1895 and 1896.

40. Menie Muriel Dowie (1867-1945) was already a successful writer when she brought out *Gallia* in February 1895. Creating something of a sensation because of its frankness, *Gallia* was recognised as a pioneering novel because its author 'had gone further in sheer audacity of treatment of the sexual relations and sexual feelings of men and women than ever before. *Gallia* is remarkable for extraordinary plainness of speech on subjects which it has been customary to touch lightly or to avoid, and the anatomy of emotions shows a coolness and daring, and the analysis of character and compromising thoroughness for which the ordinary male reader finds himself unprepared.' *Saturday Review of Politics, Literature, Science and Art*, 23 March 1895, p383.

41. Dowie was in fact twenty-seven years old when *Gallia* was published.

42. George Egerton was the pseudonym of Mary Chavelita Clairmonte (1859-1945), whose six short stories were published as *Keynotes* in 1893. The book included open discussion of women's sexuality and was influential on others contributing to what became known as the 'New Woman' literature in the 1890s.

43. The authors' very loose paraphrasing of Egerton's words can be compared to the original 1893 edition of *Keynotes*, published in London by Elkin Matthews and John Lane. The quoted and translated passages appear in the order given on pages 41, 57, 80 and 40.

44. The successful novelist Pearl Mary Craigie (1867-1906) wrote as John Oliver Hobbes. An unhappy marriage to Reginald Walpole Craigie in 1887 led to separation in 1890 and a much publicised divorce in early July 1895, just as the authors were writing this letter. The authors' statement that Craigie had remarried was untrue; she did not marry again. Following the divorce, there were newspaper reports that she would marry George Moore, author of the novel *Esther Waters*, but this she denied. *Southern Echo*, 27 February 1895, p2.

The authors' comment about the divorce case 'cast[ing] a shadow on her husband' refers to evidence presented in court revealing him as a drunkard, unfaithful and cruel. Recent evidence has revealed that 'not only did Reginald have syphilis; he gave at least a mild case of it to Pearl'. Mildred Davis Harding, 'Craigie [nee Richards], Pearl [pseud. John Oliver Hobbes], 1867-1906', *Oxford Dictionary of National Biography*, Oxford University Press: Oxford, 2019.

LETTER SIX

August 1895

As predicted, the Conservative and Liberal Unionist coalition secured a large majority at the general election. Lord Salisbury would lead the government until 1902.

The Liberal Party suffered a major reversal, which Eleanor and Edward predicted would lead to a split: on one side, the traditionalists who had dominated the party for decades, on the other, the radicals who wanted to attract the vote of workers.

The performance of trade-union-friendly and socialist candidates was viewed as lamentable by the authors. Five trade-union-backed Lib-Lab members lost their seats, as did Keir Hardie, the lone Independent Labour Party member, who Edward and Eleanor blamed for his own defeat as a result of broken promises. The wider ILP's electoral effort was portrayed as disastrous, divisive, and partly responsible for the size of the government's majority.

In contrast, the Social Democratic Federation, to which Edward and Eleanor would soon seek readmission, was commended for its organised campaign and increased vote.

The parliamentary elections in Great Britain and Ireland are over, and the new Parliament is already sitting.[1] The House of Commons now presents a very strange spectacle, of a type never before seen. The benches to the left of the Speaker of the House, where the opposition sits, look either completely deserted or at least very sparsely populated. Meanwhile, the benches to the right, where the party in government sits, are completely packed. The 493 MPs who now occupy the government benches constitute such a crowd that there simply is not enough space for them. Even to find standing room, let alone seats, many have to find a free place

on the balconies or behind the railings downstairs, even though,
parliamentary custom regards, these places as technically outside
the boundaries of the chamber itself. Now, more than ever before,
the inadequacy of the building of the House of Commons is plain
to see. It was constructed on such a small scale that even when the
two competing parties balance each other out completely, there is
not enough room in the chamber if all the members were there
at once. The total number of MPs is 670, and although there is
rarely more than 400 present, the chamber is still too small even
for that number. The Parliament building is undoubtedly beautiful
in the highest degree, but it leaves much to be desired in terms of
its practicality, and the discomforts of the House of Commons are
particularly noticeable now. The size of the government majority
means that some people are suffering other discomforts besides
the cramped chamber. For Mr Chamberlain, for example, and for
members of his family, it is not just uncomfortable but also politically disastrous. There is no doubt that the Chamberlain firm was
counting on a relatively small majority, consisting of a mixed group
of Tories and Liberal Unionists. Such a state of affairs would have
been advantageous to the Liberal Unionists, and Chamberlain
would have gained a lot of power in Parliament as the balance
of forces would have depended on him.[2] But now the mutterings
which were being heard among the strict Tories before the general
elections and which did not die down completely during the elections themselves, are growing louder and louder. 'Why should we
lumber ourselves with such inconvenient allies?', they ask. 'The
elections have shown that we do not need them, so why should we
put up with them?' And when Parliament assembled for its first
sitting, Chamberlain received a rather uncertain welcome. There
was some very feeble applause from somewhere, but then mocking
laughter could be clearly heard and – most unpleasant of all for
Chamberlain! – a fairly ominous silence among the Tories.

Given the huge majority for the government and the seven-year
parliamentary term, the possible consequences of these elections
could be very important. But before we consider them, we would
like once again to discuss the parties which played the most notable
roles in these recent elections. The Tories and Liberals are already
well known. As for the Liberal Unionists, or Chamberlainists as

they are now known, they consist of a small group of Liberals who split away from their former party over the question of Home Rule, to which they object. But since their defection from the Liberals they have on every occasion voted with the Tories. On the other hand, the 176 successful candidates labelled in the newspapers as either Liberals or Radicals contain just as many diverse elements as the Tories and Liberal Unionists. The very fact that some dub them 'Liberals' and others dub then 'Radicals' shows that there are two groupings here. One of them is the old Liberals or Whigs, distinguished by their timid and almost reactionary character, while the other is the 'Young Radicals', prepared to present a definite programme which goes some way to meet many of the demands of the workers, in order to win their votes. The representatives of these two groups, or parties within the party, are Sir William Harcourt and Messrs Asquith and Acland.[3] Besides these parties there are also the Social Democratic Federation and the Independent Labour Party. Both these organisations have the nationalisation of the means of production as the main point in their programmes. Then there are the Irish candidates, who have also split into two parties – the Parnellites and the anti-Parnellites, one of which has in recent times shown serious signs of internal disintegration.

It is rare for any elections to have created such a stir as the present ones. The streets which house the editorial offices of those newspapers which publish election results as soon as they receive them have been so packed with people day and night that they have been impassable. No omnibus or carriage has been able to pass down them, and many elegant members of society have had to make their ways home from some formal evening or dinner on foot, in their evening wear, as travelling by carriage has been impossible.[4] As is usually the case in our country, the announcement of the first election results has had an enormous effect on the subsequent results, because in England we have the highly inconvenient and unjust practice of holding elections in different places at different times, even though the elections are all for one and the same legislative assembly.[5] In other parliamentary countries which have come to this system later, such elections are always held on one and the same day. This prevents the possibility of multiple voting, i.e. voting for one and the same candidate in different places, but, most of all, it does away with the damaging effect of success on electors. In fact, elections are decided in favour of one or the other party in England by a small number of voters – the so-called 'wobblers'.[6] These are people without any fully formed political opinions who generally wait to see which way things are going. These 'spineless' types like to cast to their votes once polling is underway, and cast it in accordance with the way the poll is going. In many places, after the first day of voting, the cities were decked out with enormous hoardings from the Conservatives announcing 'We are winning! Back the winners!' And the flock of sheep to which many of our voters belong immediately transferred its allegiance to the side of the victors and gave them its votes. But this indistinct mass, which in practice decides the outcome of elections in England where there is no second ballot, is in fact far from large. Although the current Tory majority is unprecedentedly great, a close analysis of the voting figures shows that the scales were tipped by a mere 70,000 voters.

We think it will not be without interest to set out the overall position of the parties, firstly, at the general election of 1892, then, after several by-elections, at the time Parliament was dissolved in July this year, and finally, following the general elections this year. Here is the position in tabular form:

At the general elections of 1892

Liberals and Labour	274
Conservatives	269
Nationalists	72
Liberal Unionists	46
Parnellites	9
Home rule majority:	40

At the dissolution of Parliament on 8 July 1895

Liberals and Labour	268
Conservatives	272
Nationalists	72
Unionists	49
Parnellites	9
Home rule majority:	28

Current position of the parties

Tories	339
Chamberlainites	72
Liberals	177
Nationalists	70
Redmondists	12
Total:	670

The Tories gained 90 seats and have a majority of 152.

The following table gives the professions and material circumstances of the members of the new Parliament:

Bankers and financiers	26
Practising and non-practising lawyers	131
Brewers, distillers and wine merchants	19
Architects	1
Civil and mining engineers	12
Coal owners and coal merchants	15
Diplomats and government officials	9
State agents and accountants	4
Farmers and landowners	15
Aristocrats and large landowners	105
Hoteliers	2
Iron goods manufacturers and metal traders	15
Workers' representatives	12
Factory and cotton mill owners	54
Doctors	11
Merchant	35
Newspaper and magazine proprietors	31
Sons and brothers of members of the Lords	41
Printers and booksellers	7
University professors and lecturers	10
Railway suppliers	2
Ship owners and shipbuilders	18
Solicitors, practising and non-practising	19
Jobbers	4
Shopkeepers and traders	16
Schoolmasters	3
Profession not known	5

Let us now look at certain individual election results. It is an interesting fact that many of the elected members have a direct interest in the alcoholic drinks trade, especially if we bear in mind the declaration of Sir William Harcourt in favour of the Local Veto Bill (which we discussed in our previous letter), and that one of the few Liberal gains in the election was that of the brewer who defeated the Conservative candidate, the son of the late Charles Darwin.[7] There again, one of the many victories for the Tories was won in Lambeth North, a London constituency, by the company which patronised Stanley. And Lambeth is a working-class district.[8] For the working class and the entire English nation it is indisputably an indelible shame to have elected this man. The money with which Stanley bribed the Lambeth electorate had been extorted by massacring unarmed Africans who had taken him at his word.

The defeat of the official Liberals is very significant. It is true that Herbert Gladstone won his seat with a small majority, but his opponent was none other than Colonel North – a man who would not be possible in any time or society other than our own present day. North, like Stanley, is a thug, but a financial one.[9] Where the one kills, he steals. He has amassed a colossal fortune with nitrates, of which there are massive deposits in America. His wealth is so vast that he can bribe his way into the most inaccessible topmost circles of English society. He is foisted upon that society by his well-placed friends, because he clears their debts for them. The colonel himself explains his defeat in Leeds by the fact that he dined with 'one very highly placed personage' immediately before the elections.[10] In all other respects the colonel is a coarse beast incapable of articulating a single phrase correctly in English.[11] All his claim to represent the people of Leeds is based on the fact that he has engaged in sports with the people of Leeds and knows how to drink well and copiously.

The defeat of Shaw-Lefevre, the candidate in Bradford, another Yorkshire constituency; of Arnold Morley in Nottingham; of Sir William Harcourt in Derby, of John Morley in Newcastle (all industrial centres), and the victories of Asquith and Acland in their constituencies – all this is highly significant both for the present and future political movement. Shaw-Lefevre is the personification of common official Whiggism.[12] Arnold Morley – no relation of John Morley – is the former Postmaster General, a son of the capitalist-philanthropist and hypocrite Samuel Morley.[13] Not one of the most diehard Tories was as deaf as Morley to any calls to improve the lot of the unfortunate postmen and other public servants under his authority. This reactionary minister suffered a defeat thanks to the efforts of the postmen of Nottingham, who used every means to distribute appeals and leaflets setting out the sins of their official boss. Of course, their profession was of great help to them in this regard, as it made it easier for them to distribute this election literature. Whatever the case, their tyrant was soundly beaten at the elections. His previous majority of 577 was overturned and he lost by 165 votes. The self-satisfaction and lack of political acumen of the so-called Independent Labour Party was revealed here in all its glory in relation to this election. The postmen approached this party for help against their natural common enemy. But here too the ILP continued to expound its insane policy of a general abstention in the elections, while in other places where such a policy could have been justified, the party was far from following it.[14] One thing is said about Morley which is entirely credible and which casts quite a curious light on the way English politicians behave and the elastic consciences of the Nonconformists. At the last general elections, Morley and a certain Conservative put themselves forward as candidates, in different places. Both of them were facing charges of bribery and corruption and so, by mutual agreement of the electors of both parties, it was decided to drop the cases against both of them on condition that the Conservative and the Liberal Postmaster General both gave written undertakings not to stand in any further parliamentary elections. The Conservative, a man of honour, kept his word, whereas Mr Arnold Morley, a worthy son of his father, broke his.[15]

The defeat of Sir William Harcourt was a real fiasco, as the Liberal majority in the 1892 election of 1,961 was turned almost completely into a Tory majority of 1,723. This stunning victory, more than any other, was helped by the fact that the above-mentioned 'wobblers' voted for the Conservatives, and the split between the two groups within the so-called Liberal or Radical party appeared even more sharply. On the other hand, the re-elections of both Asquith and Acland on bigger majorities further underscored the split within the party.[16] When the news arrived at the Liberal Club that Harcourt had been defeated while the two younger candidates had won, the young people – in years or in views – were evidently delighted, because it was the politicians closer to their hearts who had succeeded. The blow suffered at the elections by Harcourt, Shaw-Lefevre and many others whose names are much less well known, will, of course, help the so-called advanced wing of the Liberal Party to 'throw the old guard overboard' and realise their sincere desire to take their places as leaders of the party. Moreover, in the highly improbable event of that party's early return to power, they will also be able to seize hold of those positions which come with large salaries.

In a certain respect, the elections in Newcastle were the most important and interesting. Among the members of the previous Liberal government, the most important Liberal candidate was John Morley.[17] At one time it was supposed that the mantle of Mr Gladstone would fall onto his shoulders. Mr Morley, as Secretary for Ireland, in many respects carried out the wishes of the English workers. He would of course have been the most popular member of the former government, and would probably have been re-elected, had it not been for his unbending hostility to the eight-hour working day. Indeed, this level of antagonism was not what one would have expected from the celebrated author of 'On compromise'. Maybe he acted in that way because he was more honest than many other capitalists, who make verbal claims to support the eight-hour day. But, for whatever reason, the fact remains that Morley was an opponent of the eight-hour day.[18] He was opposed at the poll by a candidate from the ILP, which was quite correct from that party's point of view.[19] And thus, whereas in 1885 he was elected with a majority of 629, in 1886 it was 2,661, at the second election of that year it was 1,024. In 1892 he was elected in second place behind a Conservative whose majority over Morley and his running mate was 3,137. In 1895 an entirely undistinguished Conservative defeated him by 1,000 votes.

The other official election worthy of mention is the election of the Speaker of the House of Commons, Mr Gully.[20] According to the traditions of English politics, almost never violated, if the Speaker stands again as a candidate, whatever his politics, the opposing party will never stand against him in the election. But on this occasion, A.J. Balfour publicly recommended that the Tories oppose Gully in Carlisle. This was inexcusable tactlessness on his part, all the more because the Tories were far from being certain of winning. In the event, Mr Gully's majority increased from 143 to 554, and immediately, as soon as the House assembled, he was unanimously elected as Speaker. Balfour, as Leader of the House, was obliged to say various glowing things about him and, so to speak, take back his own words. All present were silently grinning and biting their tongues. All apart from one Irish MP who, as Balfour was making his laudatory remarks, shouted 'Well, what about Carlisle, then?'

After considering the results of the established parties, it is worth looking at the elections of the so-called labour members. Previously, the labour members, both the candidates and those elected, were, in almost every case, definite supporters of the Liberals. They put their Liberal Party ahead of their class of workers. Now, at the last elections, three of the most prominent of these gentlemen, who formerly represented the most solid working class constituencies, were in each case beaten by the Conservatives.[21] In Lancashire the secretary of the TUC was defeated. However, this candidate, Mr Sam Woods, is not quite like all the others; he is one of those people who represent a transitional stage between the old labour candidates, devoted body and soul to the Liberal Party, and the new school of workers' politicians who do not want to have anything to do with any of the old parties.[22] The other example of evolution in that direction is John Burns who, incidentally, avoided the general rout and was elected for the London constituency of Battersea, even though this time around his majority was reduced by almost 1,000 votes.[23]

The Social Democratic Federation, of which we wrote in previous letters, is a fully organised party which insistently preaches antagonism to the two old parties. It also put forward its candidates and won a total of 3,730 votes – not a large number, but showing fairly significant progress since the last elections, when the total vote for that party was 900.[24] A sense of the party's position towards other politicians, even figures like Burns, is best gained from looking at their election addresses. In one phrase, Burns describes himself as 'a collectivist in political economy', and the rest of his election address consists of semi-approval of the Liberal Party, pointing to such measures as Home Rule, three-year Parliaments, raising the minimum age for child labour, payment for MPs – all of which he shares with the majority of Radicals. Hyndman, the recognised leader of the SDF, attacks the Liberals and Conservatives equally. He proposes the immediate nationalisation and socialisation of the railways, mines, factories and land, advocating the establishment of cooperation for production and distribution in each department under the control of the whole community. Another Lancashire candidate expressed himself still more expansively: 'I am standing against the Tories and the Liberals, reject them both and stand for the complete socialisation of all the means of production.'[25]

We have already discussed the Independent Labour Party. This is a highly heterogeneous group, an opponent of the Tories and the Liberals, but especially the Liberals. In its manifesto it says 'We have no need to speak of the Conservative Party... But the Liberal Party is considered to be, and is, to a certain extent, the party of the people. Does it have the right to this?' This question is followed by an emphatic 'No!' Further: 'The Independent Labour Party has the immediate aim not only of electing workers to the House of Commons, but also of reorganising our entire system of production.' This party decided that in all constituencies where its candidates were not standing, it would abstain from voting.

We have already shown how stupid and damaging this electoral policy is.[26] We should also add that the large sums spent on standing the ILP's own twenty-five candidates did not come from that party's own pockets. The Liberals swear that the funds were provided by the Tories. It is of course worth noting that more than £75 was collected at just one meeting which should, in theory, have consisted only of workers. However, such a large sum could only have been assembled from cheques, banknotes and gold coins, and it is unlikely that the necessary funds could have been found in workers' pockets.[27] But all the candidates were heavily defeated, and Keir Hardie, who had been an MP, is no longer in Parliament. It was the Irish voters who lost him his seat, and they can hardly be blamed for that, since Hardie had broken, most blatantly, all the promises he had made to them in 1892, on the strength of which he had been elected.[28] The total vote given to the ILP seems to be 43,445, which represents around 12 per cent of the poll in those constituencies where they stood candidates.[29] But we should remember that many of those votes are simply deceptive, or, as we call them, 'plumpers', where many votes are given to just one candidate. In many constituencies it is necessary to elect two members, as a consequence of which every voter has the right to two votes. He may give one each to two separate candidates or give all his votes to just one. Usually the herd politicians give both votes to their candidate, and this fact means that we should almost halve the total number of votes received.[30] Moreover, studies of the voting show that, for all its declarations about its antagonism, the new party has taken many more votes from the Liberals than from the Tories. In four large cities the number of Tory votes given to the ILP was 2,828, whereas the number of Liberal votes given to the same party was 5,661.[31] These implacable figures also show that the new party did not gain more votes than previously, and in some cases it even lost votes.[32]

All the information we have goes to confirm that the ILP's policy on elections directly harms its own interests. The party's abstention from participation in elections in many cases suited completely the interests of the Tories and was to a certain extent one reason why we now have such an enormous Tory majority in the House of Commons.[33] Incidentally, there is no doubt that Mr Keir Hardie and even Mr Hyndman will boast (and this is their fatal mistake) that they have thrown the Liberal Party into confusion.[34] It is quite true that the Liberals, or, more accurately, the Radical wing of that party are not putting forward those strong measures which the above-mentioned parties proclaim as their immediate aim. On the other hand, the various reforms that the Liberals have introduced in Parliament are far from running counter to those aims. These reforms are more likely to help in achieving these aims, rather than hinder them. Moreover, even though they are still only hinting at them, the victorious Tories are suggesting measures against the trade unions, which, to an extent, represent the power of the people. Therefore, a serious question is posed for all those politicians of the workers' party who are rejoicing that they have at last managed to strike the Liberals down. Do they imagine that at the next elections they will succeed in getting a majority of their people in the new parliament? If not, then how do they expect to overturn the Tory majority, except by means of that very same Liberal Party whose weakening they are regarding as some kind of victory? And in any case the enormous size of the present Tory majority undoubtedly presents the greatest danger to the so-called advanced movement. Firstly, the Tories are hardly likely to do anything for that movement, and secondly, anything the Tories do is likely to scare the ordinary working-class voter and the above-mentioned 'wobblers'. In all likelihood the advanced Radical wing of the Liberal Party will try, in its turn, to attract workers' votes to its side, tempting them with a programme which addresses their aspirations. If this succeeds, then the advanced direction advocated by Messrs Keir Hardie and Hyndman will of course be put in harness.

The Irish members of the new Parliament are already making their presence felt. At the very moment we are writing this letter, the news vendors out on the street are shouting out the sensational news that one of the Irish members has been temporarily suspended from Parliament by order of the Speaker.[35] Neither hoping for nor expecting anything good for themselves from the current composition of Parliament, the Irish members are very likely to resort to their former Parnellite tactic of open obstructionism. However, there is no great agreement between the Irish members themselves – they are divided between parties and those parties are also split into different groupings. For example, at the start of the elections one of them, Mr Healy, publicly and sharply attacked some of his own colleagues, accusing them of accepting money from the Liberals to finance their own election campaigns.[36] The anti-Irish party was victorious because, it would seem, the Irish ranks showed every sign of facing complete and fatal disorder. But, to the great surprise of everyone unfamiliar with the character of the Irish, at the preparatory meeting of the Irish party it was decided that all its existing representatives should be elected, and Mr Healy was, as they say, left high and dry. It is possible that he himself saw that he had gone too far, since he could not have been unaware that all the funds needed to support the Irish members were in the hands of the people he had attacked, and could not have been taken from them. In all probability the fact that all the Irish MPs face a long and stubborn struggle with their implacable enemies, the Tories, will also help consolidate the Irish party more than anything else.

But what can account for such a complete rout of the Liberal Party and the striking victory of the Tories?

For any superficial observer it seems surprising that even London, for which so much has been done by the Liberal-run London County Council, should fall away from the Liberal Party. But even in London the power of the publicans and keepers of ale-houses over the working classes is very great, followed by that of the clergymen, and both of them are openly on the side of the Tories.[37] The publican backs them because the Liberals pose a threat to his business interests, and the clergyman backs them because the Liberals threaten the interests of the church. The Liberals introduced a bill on the separation of church and state in Wales, that is, they proposed to deprive it of a state income. In rural constituencies, for all the great benefit they derived from important measures introduced by the outgoing government, such as the Parish Councils Bill, the matters of church and drink played their role at the elections.[38] Moreover, the publicans and clergy were joined by the village squires or local landlords, whose interests had also been affected by the Liberal measures to increase inheritance tax on landholdings.[39] All this, of course, had its effect in the elections and contributed to the defeat of the Liberals. But there are undoubtedly also other causes of a more general nature, and, indeed, of greater significance.[40] The most important one is that the Liberal Party encroached on too many interests but at the same time evoked too little enthusiasm. The Liberal Party was forced to resort, reluctantly, to certain measures aimed at pleasing the working classes, although it was not very successful at it. But enthusiasm – such an essential element in any election campaign – was finally destroyed by the departure of such a great figure as Gladstone and the battle waged, albeit secretly, between Lord Rosebery and Sir William Harcourt for the vacant place Gladstone left. Of course, neither one nor the other was capable of generating any enthusiasm and, given the lack of any fighting slogan from the Liberals, this helped cool the voters' attitude towards them. Additionally, even the democratic elements in the old Liberal Party did not decide to come out against the plutocratic element. Everyone knows that 'money is the nerves of war' – the Liberal Party had been founded by titled and capitalist members, and since they hold the purse strings, even the most advanced Liberals chose not to risk losing access to that purse by insisting too strongly on really energetic political progress.

In conclusion, it can be said of the elections that they have revealed the bankruptcy of the Liberal Party in its current form. As for the Tories, they have undoubtedly received a new lease of life. Naturally, they are using their position to ensure they do as little as possible for progress, or indeed, nothing at all.

If the late Disraeli were still alive and in power, then we would have the chance to witness the cynical spectacle of a Tory government granting Home Rule to Ireland. But this is impossible given the current composition of the government. Indeed, with the majority it enjoys, it has no need to buy Irish votes. The Liberal Party will certainly split into the old Liberals of Harcourt's stripe, and the new ones with a Radical tinge, like Asquith. If this second group act sensibly and firmly, they can attract a large majority of the working classes to their side, who are far from sympathising with the politics of either the ILP or the SDF. Moreover, the movement which these two parties represent will probably fade into the background for a long time. If the Tories start carrying out excessively harsh reactionary measures, then there will again be a wave of indignation against them in the country. It is more likely that they will attempt to do nothing. Nonetheless, we can expect turbulence in the world of politics in our country throughout the term of the new Parliament.

Notes

1. The general election of 1895 commenced on 12 July and concluded in the first week of August. Parliament opened on 12 August.

2. Although a Unionist victory was widely predicted, most estimated a majority of between thirty and sixty seats, which would have enhanced the position of Joseph Chamberlain and his Liberal Unionists.

3. For Harcourt see Letter 4, note 10; for Asquith see Letter 3, note 35; for Acland see Letter 1, note 12.

4. Large crowds assembled outside the Fleet Street offices of the major national newspapers, which erected screens to display election results as they were received by telegraph. On some nights traffic was unable to pass through Fleet Street and police were drafted in from nearby stations to deal with the huge gatherings. *Clarion,* the socialist weekly in Fleet Street, reported: 'Late o'nights the offices of the daily papers are besieged by muddle-headed mouthers of both

parties, who howl themselves hoarse and poison the surrounding atmosphere with their beery breath.' *Clarion*, 20 July 1895, p2.

5. The staggered nature of the general elections was acknowledged as contributing to the victories of those parties having early success. In the 1895 contest the Conservatives issued targeted posters calling on electors to follow the neighbouring constituency where they had already elected a Tory candidate. The Liberal weekly, *The Speaker,* criticised the staggered election process that 'sprawls unnecessarily over a fortnight, leaving all the later elections to be influenced by the innate desire to of feeble persons to be on the winning side'. *The Speaker*, 3 August 1895, p117.

6. John Burns, who was returned to the Battersea seat with a reduced majority, estimated that in London '2,500 wobbling voters, more or less drunk, had voted with beer. These had deprived London of something like eighteen progressive members. In the counties 30,000 wobblers out of two and three quarter million men, coupled with 10,000 new voters brought in by the Tories, had been the means of placing a tremendous coalition majority in power'. *Manchester Guardian*, 5 August 1895, p6.

7. Here the authors are picking up a thread from the post-election analysis about the effect of Liberal support for Sir William Harcourt's Local Veto Bill (see Letter 4, note 12). The widespread view was that Liberal identification with the measure had been significant in its loss of seats, including Harcourt's own surprise defeat at Derby. This was confirmed in a survey of 157 unsuccessful Liberal candidates, 134 of whom considered the local veto proposal to have been very harmful to their prospects. *Westminster Gazette*, 13 August 1895, p2.

   The brewing trade organisations produced more than a million leaflets, posters and cartoons during the election carrying the message of defending 'an Englishman's right to personal liberty, against narrow-minded faddist reformers' and protesting the 'middle-class bias of the attacks on the poor man's club, the public house'. David M. Fahey, 'Brewers, publicans and working class drinkers: Pressure group politics in late Victorian and Edwardian England', *Social History*, May 1980, Vol. 13, No. 25, p99.

   Such messages conveyed by the means of posters, used extensively in the 1895 election, were understood by contemporaries to be important in influencing voters: 'Men can refuse to read newspapers, they can absolutely abjure all public meetings, they can bundle the canvasser into the gutter, but unless they shut their eyes they cannot prevent themselves from seeing cartoons, pictures and caricatures which the party billsticker has covered the hoardings and available walls.' 'The general election 1895: The poster in politics', *Review of Reviews*, August 1895, p168.

One poster on the local veto theme was remarked upon as being particularly resonant. It featured 'Rosebery, Harcourt, Morley & Co. putting up the shutters of a public house, notwithstanding the protests made by an intelligent seventh-standard boy, who tells the statesmen "I have come for Father's dinner beer." The boy in the picture is warned off. He goes singing a piece of smart doggerel, of which the meaning is that the rich man may drink at all times at home, but the poor man must never drink at all.' *Manchester Guardian*, 17 July 1895, p4.

Clarion recounted a 'scrap of conversation ... [which] ... gives you the true working-class sentiment towards local veto. It is not so much the deprivation of beer as the intolerance with [the] working man's privilege of visiting his pub which is virtually his club. This is what the fatuous Liberals do not seem to see.' The conversation followed:

'Tell yer wot mate', said a down-at-heel bystander, 'it's local veto wot's upset the Liberal apple cawt.'
'Yus', replied a well-to-do mechanic. 'I voted Liberal lawst time, but I don't again. Not me.'
'Nice state o' things I calls it', growled the other, 'when you cawn't meet your mate and have 'arf a pint because they ses so.'
'That's just where it is, mate', said the mechanic. 'They don't use the public 'ahses. That's why they want to shut 'em up.' *Clarion*, 20 July 1895, p2.

The 'brewer who defeated the Conservative candidate' was Henry Charles Fulford, chairman of the Holt Brewery, Birmingham, who won the Litchfield seat over Liberal Unionist Leonard Darwin by forty-four votes. The result was subsequently voided on petition, forcing a by-election in which a different Liberal candidate was successful.

8. Henry Morton Stanley (1841-1904), the famous explorer known to be guilty of atrocities in Africa since the 1870s, won the Lambeth North seat for the Liberal Unionists. Stanley was backed by many of the large employers in the district, including Sir Henry Doulton, whose pottery factory employed 4,000 workers. Given access to workers at factory meetings, Stanley presented himself as 'one of themselves, a man of their own ranks', in contrast to the young aristocratic Liberal candidate. Alex Windscheffel, 'In darkest Lambeth: Henry

Morton Stanley and the imperial politics of London Unionism', in Matthew Cragoe and Anthony Taylor (eds), *London Politics, 1760-1914*, Palgrave: Basingstoke, 2005, p202. For Stanley's imperialist exploration see Felix Driver, 'Henry Morton Stanley and his critics: geography, exploration and empire', *Past and Present*, No. 133, November 1991, pp134-66.

Local socialists were so alarmed at the prospect of Stanley winning the seat that the ILP and SDF reluctantly pledged support for the Liberal candidate. *Times*, 10 July 1895, p8; *Justice*, 20 July 1895, p1.

9. John Thomas North ('Colonel North') (1842-1896), made a fortune buying and selling nitrate fields in South America during the 1870s and 1880s. Honorary colonel of a regiment of volunteers in Tower Hamlets, North was known for his extravagant lifestyle: 'his great notion of hospitality was to drown his friends in champagne'. 'North, John Thomas', *Oxford Dictionary of National Biography*, Oxford: Oxford University Press.

North contested the Leeds West constituency against sitting member Herbert Gladstone (1854-1930), who had served as minister in the Liberal government elected in 1892, first under his father's premiership and then under Rosebery. Gladstone retained the seat with a significantly reduced majority.

10. In an interview immediately after the election, North revealed that during the campaign he had received 'an invite from the Prince of Wales to go to Sandringham, so, of course, I couldn't help myself. But [the local Unionist committee] didn't like it a bit. I believe it made a difference ... I should have got in if it hadn't been for that'. *The Sketch*, 31 July 1895, p58.

11. On North's death in 1896, *Justice* wrote: 'Colonel North was just an ignorant, conceited, feasting, drinking, horse-racing bully who, had he been a poor man, would have been described as a low, drunken blackguard, but whose millions earned him the title of a "bluff and sturdy Englishman" from the fawning reptile press and the cringing hypocrites and panders by whom he was surrounded.' *Justice*, 1 May 1896, p1.

12. For Shaw Lefevre see Letter 4, note 27.

13. Arnold Morley (1849-1916), the son of wool manufacturer, political radical and philanthropist Samuel Morley (see Letter 1, note 5), had been an elected Member of Parliament for Nottingham since 1880. Appointed Postmaster General in 1892, Morley faced determined postal worker trade unions demanding national recognition and a minimum wage. Morley's refusal to deal with the unions on

a national basis and the victimisation of trade union officials led to a successful campaign by postal workers to remove him from the Nottingham East seat.

14. The authors' hostile comments about the Independent Labour Party's policy of abstention in this context relate to an approach to the ILP made by the Nottingham branches of postal workers' trade unions to support their effort to secure Morley's defeat. The Nottingham ILP voted to retain their abstention policy. *Labour Leader*, 20 July 1895, p8.

15. Following the 1892 general election, petitions were issued by Conservatives against the return of Arnold Morley in the Nottingham East constituency, while Liberals did likewise against the return of Conservative Henry Smith Wright in Nottingham South. In August 1892 the two parties agreed a compact under which both parties withdrew their respective petition on the understanding that neither Morley nor Wright would contest the next general election. When Morley's nomination was put forward in 1895, the *Pall Mall Gazette* exposed the terms of the agreement and then rejoiced at his defeat with the comment: 'The moral of all this is, that if you are determined to do a dirty trick you should satisfy yourself that it will succeed.' *Pall Mall Gazette*, 17 July 1895, p1.

16. In fact, Acland was returned in the Rotherham seat unopposed.

17. John Morley (1838-1923) edited the *Fortnightly Review* and the *Pall Mall Gazette* before entering Parliament as a Liberal in 1883 at a by-election for one of the two Newcastle seats. A convinced Home Ruler, Morley became Chief Secretary for Ireland in Gladstone's short-lived administration of 1886, and then again in 1892-95. For Morley, see D.A. Hamer, *John Morley: Liberal Intellectual in Politics*, Clarendon: Oxford, 1968.

18. Morley's denunciation of the proposal to introduce an eight-hour working day by statute, on the grounds that it interfered with the free working of natural economic processes, put him at odds with the growing band of Newcastle socialists, who in protest declared for the Conservative at the 1892 general election. Socialist opposition to Morley and the Liberal Party intensified in the spring of 1895, when the Newcastle Liberal Association reversed an earlier decision to endorse the candidature, as Morley's running mate, of Arthur Henderson, a local trade unionist, largely because of his working-class origins.

19. The ILP put up Fred Hammill, an engineer, who polled 2,302 votes. Morley finished third in a contest for two seats.

20. For William Gully see Letter 4, note 21.

21. The first Lib-Lab Members of Parliament; trade unionists or supporters of trade unionism who had the backing of Liberal associations, had been elected in 1874. These members maintained an independence on industrial issues but were generally happy to accept the Liberal whip in Parliament. In the 1892-5 government they numbered fourteen members. Only nine were returned at the 1895 general election.

   The authors' reference to 'three of the most prominent of these gentlemen', certainly includes the defeated George Howell (Bethnal Green), Sam Woods (Ince) and probably Randal Cremer (Haggerston).

22. Samuel Woods (1846-1915) was a coalminer who became a leading figure in the Lancashire and Cheshire Miners' Federation and then the Miners' Federation of Great Britain. Woods was returned for the Lancashire constituency of Ince in 1892 with Liberal support. His advocacy of the Miners Eight Hours Bill put him at odds with other miners' union-sponsored MPs, who opposed the legislation. One of these, Charles Fenwick of Northumberland, was voted out of the office of secretary of the TUC's Parliamentary Committee because of this stance and replaced by Woods.

23. For John Burns see Letter 3, note 27.

24. The Social Democratic Federation candidates at the 1895 general election were:

Constituency		Votes
George Lansbury	Walworth	203
Henry Mayers Hyndman	Burnley	1498
William Henry Hobart	Salford South	813
Frederick George Jones	Northampton	1216

25. This was Henry Hobart (1854-1941), a compositor and member of the London Trades Council, who was employed by the SDF's Twentieth Century Press at 37a Clerkenwell Green.

26. The ILP agreed its policy at a meeting of branch delegates at the Essex Hall, Strand, London on 4 July but it did not announce its decision until the following week, when it revealed that twenty-nine candidates would stand (twenty-eight went to the polls) and that in other constituencies members should abstain from voting. The party's manifesto, strong in criticism of the Liberal government's failure to tackle unemployment and fulfil its social and political commitments, rejected arguments from its apologists to the effect that Home Rule and then House of Lords obstruction had prevented

progress: 'We, on our part, affirm that it is not Home Rule nor the House of Lords, which blocks the way, but the composition of the House of Commons. So long as landlords, manufacturers, share-holders, great companies, railway directors, lawyers, military men and other parasites on the industry of the community, monopolise the House of Commons, it is absurd to expect social or labour legis-lation.' *The Standard*, 12 July 1895, p2.

27. On the question of the ILP's election fund, the authors follow the lead of *Reynolds's Newspaper* editor William Marcus Thompson (1857-1907), who claimed that the party was in receipt of money from external sources. Thompson, an established opponent of the ILP and Hardie in particular, alleged: 'We are prepared to state, as a matter of fact, that the Brummagem Tory Party has been going from town to town, supplying nominees of the Independent Socialists with funds to fight the Radical Democracy'. *Reynolds's Newspaper*, 21 July 1895, p1.

For the ILP's part, Hardie denied this and remarked on Thompson's cleverness in using the titles of non-existent organisations, the 'Brummagem Tory Party' and 'Independent Socialists', to evade the law of libel. *Labour Leader*, 27 July 1895, p3.

Thompson repeated the allegation – which was again denied by Hardie – and it is possible that Eduard Bernstein (see note 34 below) also ventured onto this territory, but could make nothing stick. *Reynolds's Newspaper*, 28 July 1895, p1; *Labour Leader*, 17 August 1895, p6; and 24 August 1895, p6.

Full details of donations made to the ILP election fund were pub-lished weekly in *Labour Leader* and the *Clarion*. When the party's final election account was published it was found to be £200 in credit, partly explained by the low election expenses of ILP candi-dates compared to those of other parties. H. Pelling, *The Origins of the Labour Party, 1880-1900*, Oxford University Press: Oxford, 1965, p166. As an example of this, the ILP's Fred Brocklehurst declared expenses of £179 in the Bolton constituency, compared to the £736 of the Liberal and £630 of the Conservative candidates. *Manchester Evening News*, 16 August 1895, p2.

28. Hardie's defeat by a Conservative at West Ham South came as a heavy blow to the ILP, but was the cause of much celebration among his opponents, including the Liberal party establishment, some Radicals and a few labour men. There were cheers at the National Liberal Club when the result was declared; Thompson at *Reynolds's Newspaper* rejoiced and described Hardie's leadership as 'beneath contempt', 21 July 1895, p4 (*Reynolds's* was a Radical Liberal news-

paper and opposed to the ILP because the ILP wanted to pull the the working-class vote away from the Liberals); while John Burns declared that Hardie deserved the defeat, saying that, having thrown out the Liberal and Radical programme on which he was elected in 1892, Hardie had failed to present his new programme to constituents because he knew it would be rejected. *Manchester Guardian,* 5 August 1895, p6.

Hardie's loss of a significant number of Irish votes (estimated at around 600) was widely regarded as important in his defeat, and seen by Eleanor and Edward as deserved since he 'had broken, most blatantly, all the promises he had made to them in 1892'. Roman Catholic priests in West Ham had tried to persuade Irish voters not to support Hardie because they interpreted his attitude to Home Rule as something he was content merely to tack on to the 'tail of the socialist programme', in contrast to in 1892, when he was said to have given the issue priority over others. Caroline Benn, *Keir Hardie,* Hutchinson: London, 1992, p128. Hardie defended his consistent support for Home Rule, but asked constituents to consider the wider interest: 'Do you say it is Home Rule first? I can understand an Irishman in Connemara saying that, but here in West Ham it is labour first'. *Labour Leader,* 20 July 1895, p2.

Hardie's loss of a large part of the Irish vote was only one factor in his defeat, which he reflected had been brought about by an unholy alliance of 'teetotallers and publicans, trade unionists and free labour men, Liberals and Tories, Home Rulers and coercionists' (the latter being a reference to repressive government measures in Ireland). *Ibid.*

29. The ILP's 28 candidates polled 44,321 votes; four SDF candidates polled 3,730 votes; and one independent labour candidate in Aberdeen North, John L. Mahon, polled 608 votes.

30. Contrary to the authors' view that because of 'plumper' votes 'we should almost halve the number of votes received', an analysis of the seven two-member constituencies where ILP candidates stood for election reveals that there were 8,870 'plumper' votes for the party, only one in five of the total votes cast in its twenty-eight contests. Hardie told readers of *Labour Leader* that those who highlighted 'plumper double voting' were seeking to damage the reputation of the ILP, and that he was thankful that 'most of our fights were triangular'. *Labour Leader,* 3 August 1895, p4.

31. These figures were taken from the two-member constituencies of Halifax, Newcastle-upon-Tyne, Leicester, and Bolton, each with a participating ILP candidate. *Daily Chronicle,* 24 July 1895, p5. These

figures approximate those given by Hardie in January 1895, that the ILP expected to take two Liberal votes for every one vote from the Tories. James Keir Hardie, 'The Independent Labour Party', *Nineteenth Century*, January 1895, Vol. 37, p6. *Fabian News* estimated that 'the socialist elector is drawn from both parties in approximately equal numbers, and probably in many cases from the class which has for some years back declined to vote for either party. The outcry therefore raised by the Liberals against the ILP for splitting the party is unfounded.' *Fabian News*, August 1895, p21.

32. In 1895 the ILP contested only three seats in which they had previously stood in by-elections, following the establishment of the party in January 1893. In Leicester, Joseph Burgess's vote of 4,009 was lower than the 1894 by-election vote of 4,402. John Lister's vote in Halifax of 3,818 exceeded his 1893 by-election result of 3,028. And in Bristol East, Sam Hobson's vote of 1,874 was lower than that of 3,558 achieved by Hugh Holmes Gore in the by-election of March 1895.

33. It is impossible to assess the impact of the ILP's policy of abstention in constituencies where the party did not have a candidate. However, using the results of contests where socialists did go to the polls, it can be stated that, notwithstanding the verdict of some Liberal newspapers keen to blame the new third force as decisive, the socialist vote could only have been responsible for Liberal defeats in seven divisions, and a further two where they failed to capture a Conservative seat. *Daily News*, 22 July 1895, p7.

34. Here the authors' argument concurs, not unsurprisingly, with that of Eduard Bernstein, the exiled German social democrat, who published an article in *Vorwarts,* the journal of the Social Democratic Party of Germany, critical of what he described as the ILP's 'rejoicing in the defeat of the Liberals'. This was picked up by the Berlin correspondent of the *Daily Chronicle*, who telegraphed London with a short piece summarising Bernstein's arguments. Two days later Bernstein revealed himself as the author of the article and defended his critique of the ILP, accusing the party of a policy of 'political adventure' that contributes to a reduction in the influence of labour in Parliament. Bernstein asked: 'how will they manage to undo the Conservative majority otherwise than by bringing back into power the very same Liberal party whose smash [they now claim] as a socialist triumph?'. *Daily Chronicle*, 26 July 1895, p7.

Hardie's reply, prefaced with a gentle rebuke of Bernstein for 'pretending to know better than we do ourselves what should be done here', restated the party's verdict on the Liberal Party as a 'poor, played-out spent force ... It is no answer to say that the result has been to return the Tories, who are further removed from us. Even were the Liberals to again return to power, they would only give one more exhibition of their helplessness. Henceforth the battle in this country is collectivism versus private property, and the removing of liberalism is a clearing of the issues'. *Labour Leader*, 3 August 1895, p7.

Similarly, *Justice* took Bernstein to task for his attention to the Liberal Party, 'the most hypocritical and unscrupulous faction that ever gulled a people. Its leaders pretend to be ready to sympathise with and help on socialist ideas wholly and solely for the purpose of rendering the formation of a genuine and powerful Social Democratic Party in Great Britain impossible.' *Justice*, 27 July 1895, p1.

Bernstein replied to this and a subsequent article in *Justice* (3 August) arguing that it was necessary to judge political parties by their ability to assist the 'final emancipation of the workers', and in this 'the Liberals to a far greater extent depend upon the socialist worker than do the Conservatives'. Bernstein expressed fears about what the Conservative government would do to put back the progress achieved by local authorities such as the LCC through measures to weaken local democracy, including a favouring of voluntary over board schools. He concluded: 'I think the elections have shown that the socialists have a better chance when they have not acted ... as the door-opener to the Conservatives'. *Justice*, 10 August 1895, p5.

35. Dr Charles Kearns Tanner (1849-1901), MP for Mid Cork since 1885, was suspended from the House of Commons on August 15 after refusing to withdraw a comment in response to the accusation that the Liberal Party was 'running away from Home Rule'; Tanner said this was a 'lie'. Tanner left the House saying he withdrew 'with more pleasure than he entered the dirty House'. *Times*, 16 August 1895, p9.

36. Timothy Michael Healy (1855-1931), Member for North Louth who wanted the Irish Parliamentary Party to 'return to local constituency autonomy in close alliance with the clergy', attacked pro-Liberal anti-Parnellites, claiming they sold parliamentary seats in the north to the Liberals for £200 each. Healy's opponents 'clung resolutely to the Liberal alliance and perceived the Nationalist cause in terms of Home Rule alone'. Eugenio F. Biagini, *British Democracy and Irish Nationalism, 1876-1906*, Cambridge University Press: Cambridge, 2007, p299.

37. The Liberals lost fifteen seats in London, leaving them with only seven parliamentary seats in the capital, compared to the Conservatives' fifty-five seats. *Reynolds's Newspaper* remarked on

how Tory 'money was poured into constituencies, beer was flowing everywhere without money and without price'. *Reynolds's Newspaper*, 28 July 1895, p4.

38. A bill for the disestablishment of the Church in Wales was introduced in early 1895 but did not complete its progress beyond the committee stage before falling at the dissolution of Parliament in July. For an earlier effort to secure disestablishment of the Church in Wales, see Letter 3, note 34.

39. Sir William Harcourt's budget of 1894 introduced a high uniform rate of death duty, set at 1 per cent on estates worth £100 to £500, up to 8 per cent on estates worth over £1 million.

40. The Liberal election post-mortem threw up a myriad of explanations for the defeat. Between 13 and 28 August, the Liberal *Westminster Gazette* carried an interesting series of articles titled 'Why the Liberals were defeated', based on returns to a survey of Liberal MPs and candidates. *The Speaker* summarised the reasons 'given by those who profess to speak with authority in the newspapers' citing the following: the retirement of Gladstone; the Local Veto Bill; bad trade; church support for Unionists; excellence of Tory organisation; poor Liberal organisation; dread of socialism; the ILP; effects of first polls; the dispiriting effects of Harcourt's attitude to Rosebery; lack of a clear issue to fight on; Irish 'squabbles'; the 'filling up of the cup' policy (see Letter 3, note 38). *The Speaker*, 27 July 1895, p85. See also Paul A. Readman, 'The 1895 general election and political change in late Victorian Britain', *Historical Journal*, June 1999, Vol. 42, No. 2, pp467-93.

LETTER SEVEN

December 1895

With Parliament in recess and uncertainty about how matters political, social and industrial would develop in the new year, the concluding letter is something of miscellany of topical events, featuring trade union conference decisions, quickly broken political promises, parliamentary indiscretions and misjudged government awards of funding.

The letter concludes with an interesting comment on Board of Trade statistics on average wage levels, which are shown to be unrealistically high and misleading. This treatment one suspects to be that of Eleanor who, like her father, had mastered government 'blue books' and was adept at knowing when statistics were being distorted to suit the needs of the administration.

Similarly, Eleanor is also likely to have authored the short note on the struggle for women's admission to Trinity College, Dublin, that rounds off the letter and the series.

The autumn season in our country is always the time when all sorts of associations and learned societies hold their congresses and conferences. Some of these congresses are of general interest, and among these, without a doubt, are the congresses of the railway workers and sailors, in that they touch upon the interests of almost all classes of society. One of the most important questions considered at the railway workers' congress concerned the excessive length of the working day.[1] Nobody can deny that this question is of direct interest not only to the workers themselves, but also to the general public. A great proportion of the railway accidents and disasters, with loss of human life, are precisely the consequence of over-tiredness on the part of railway workers, signalmen and drivers remaining at their posts without a break for long hours.

Over the course of this year alone the railway workers' committee collected fifty incontestable cases of overwork and excessive tiredness. Recently a law was issued making it illegal to oblige signalmen to work over their official hours, but this law, as often happens in such cases when it affects corporations and large numbers of employers, is continually and openly flouted by the railways, which in England are private companies.[2] But the railway workers' unions are energetically fighting against the predominant indifference of the railway companies and their lack of interest in the safety of the people who pay for their dividends. Unfortunately, the unions' efforts are to a certain extent paralysed by the railway workers themselves, many of whom favour long working days and thereby give the railway companies their most potent weapon against the demands of the unions.[3] As for accidents on the railways, although the number of them has fallen in recent years, if we nonetheless take account of the enormous incomes of the railway companies, brought about through improvements in machinery and other equipment, the number of accidents on the railways should still be regarded as too high. For example, in 1874 on the railways one worker in 320 was killed and one in eighty-nine was more or less seriously injured. Twenty years on, in 1894, those figures were one in 796 killed and one in 140 injured.[4]

The congress of the union of sailors and firemen also raised a question of wide interest.[5] Everyone knows that one of the burning questions in England at the moment is the immigration of destitute foreign workers. Many in the British working classes, as the discussions at the recent TUC congress showed, would like to see a law passed through Parliament forbidding what they call the immigration of paupers.[6] But the most enlightened and far-sighted of the workers object on the basis of their class interests to such measures. They rightly consider that the real way to deal with the oversupply of the labour market which necessarily results from the immigration of foreign workers is not proscriptive measures but greater justice in relations between employers and their employees, whether natives or foreigners. Last year the TUC congress came out categorically in favour of banning the immigration of foreign workers, but this year the number of votes in favour of this measure fell significantly.[7] At the congress of sailors and firemen a completely opposed resolution was adopted. This showed that although foreign immigration is causing seafarers no little harm, they have nonetheless in this case managed to rise above purely individual considerations and base their resolution on much broader principles. An Act of Parliament has laid down that there should be 72 cu. ft. of space for every person on a ship. However, this regulation is often violated by ship owners, even when the crews consist entirely of English people. In cases where the crews are comprised of foreign workers, this regulation is never observed. So, at their congress the sailors and firemen resolved to demand that all ships registered in the fleet of the United Kingdom with crews of foreigners and natives of Asia should strictly observe Parliament's regulation about the number of cubic feet of air per person. Further, the resolution calls on the government to recognise the need to confirm in legislation the recommendation of the Royal Commission on Labour that the number of cubic feet of air per person required on ships be increased from seventy-two to 120.[8]

In our last letter we discussed the abundant representation of various industrial companies in the new Cabinet. In our speculative era, it would of course be not without interest to continue this investigation further. We could thereby determine how large is the proportion of those selfless and patriotic politicians in the House of Commons, who simultaneously combine service to the state with participation in various industrial companies whose interests are very often adversely affected by the legal measures voted on in the House. There are 670 members of the Commons, of whom 264 (that is, 39.4 per cent) are directors of various companies, and 153 of this 264 have a direct interest in 556 companies. In the House there are representatives of eighty-one insurance companies, eighty railway companies, forty-eight banks, nineteen breweries, eleven water and ten gas companies. Most of the remaining members are also directly or indirectly interested in various industrial enterprises. Overall, there are at least 667 companies which have one or another relation to the House.

The promises made by the opposition are fated never to accord with its actions when it finally gets into power. In this respect the Tories have displayed striking cynicism. They shamelessly at every convenient opportunity declare that they attach no significance at all to the promises they made when they were fighting against the Liberal government. When the Tories were not in power, one their main reproaches against the Liberal government was that it was not energetic enough, that it was negligent and lazy, especially when it declared a six-month parliamentary recess. What a hue and cry the Tories raised then! They were almost predicting that the state would perish in consequence of such a long break in parliamentary work. And so? Now, after three weeks of parliamentary activity, brought about by the pressing need to decide some urgent matters, the Tories, who had previously protested against such things, have now themselves declared a parliamentary recess, also for six months.[9] As soon as the elections were over, there began the usual process of breaking those promises which were partly responsible for the Tories having been voted into power. Mr Chamberlain, for example, appeared before his voters with a plan for establishing old age pensions. However, we can conclude from the speech by the Duke of Devonshire, who had been the leader of the Liberal Unionists along with Chamberlain when it was supposed that they would be a separate political organisation, that Chamberlain has no desire to insist that his project be adopted by the House of Commons. 'This measure can only be implemented as an experiment and gradually', said the Duke of Devonshire.[10] That, incidentally, is what 'statesmen' always say when there are any measures they intend to kick into the long grass, and certainly do not want to put before the House. In his characteristically philosophical way, Mr Balfour touched on this question, admitting that the government may have to deal with it. In doing so, he let slip the following magnificent words: 'The temptation to regard all these social questions as merely means for election is, of course, very great, but if you love – I won't say your country – but your party, then resist this temptation.'[11]

Another question which played no little role in the last elections was the exclusion of prison-made goods from the general market. Mr Chamberlain played the most active part in this matter.[12] Like Trochu, he obviously 'had a plan'.[13] But whenever he was asked what his plan was, he would answer: 'You are not calling us to the patient, but you expect us to prescribe the medicine'. When he was finally 'called', i.e., found himself in power, his opponents started to badger him at every opportune and inopportune moment to prescribe 'his medicine' for the illness afflicting prison production. Chamberlain would constantly reply that this medicine was ready to hand, but that the government found it necessary to have talks with foreign powers on this question. It is quite possible that this appeal to foreign powers was nothing more than a ruse to win time, since it is known that this question has already been discussed in committee and the experts have already reached their conclusions. Of course, this appeal to foreign powers is all very nice and fully in accord with international courtesies, but has anyone ever seen a case where nations have sacrificed their commercial interests to political niceties?[14]

Bimetallism also became an issue during the recent elections. The voting in Lancashire was of no little significance in this case, not only in quantitative terms, but also because of the view of the large cotton weavers on this question. Some time back, before the elections, Lancashire got interested in the question of bimetallism and organised a monstrous Bimetallic League.[15] Even the workers were infected with the mania for bimetallism, and it is highly likely that the defeat of the Liberals at the general elections was in part the result of this enthusiasm for bimetallism. One must give the Liberal Party representatives their due for standing aside from this craze. Now let us look at its consequences. Following the general election an association was immediately formed to defend the gold standard which was so powerful both economically and commercially that bimetallism, for the moment at least, has been practically killed off.[16] It is most interesting to observe how the speeches of Balfour changed in this regard. In April, before the elections, he declared himself most energetically and categorically in favour of bimetallism, whereas in August, after the elections, he began to say something quite different. It is interesting in that it shows how the political ideas of politicians will change, depending on whether they are in power or not. In April Balfour called the British monetary system, particularly that which exists in India, 'crying stupidity', declared that 'a change to this system is urgently required', and that he did not think that 'the good sense of the nation could permit such a state of affairs any longer'.[17] It would seem that such speeches, promising so much, would give one the right to hope for more or less energetic political activity. And what happened? In August this self-same Balfour declared to the defeated and chagrined bimetallists that he 'did not consider he had the right to insist on this question to his colleagues', that he 'had no grounds to suppose that it would be possible to reach international agreement on this question', and so on. At the same time, outside of politics Balfour is said to be a generally honest and straight person. Politics has a strange effect on people if a person with such a character, incapable of dishonest acts in his private life, will resort to what he would otherwise regard as 'deception' as soon as it is a matter of politics. Some say in defence of Balfour that he is lazy. It is true that he has shown this quality more than once in his political life, and in fact he is much more interested in philosophy and books than in people.[18] But in any case he could still observe the rules of honour not only in his private life but also in politics.

The Liberal government, as is well known, had nominally raised the question of reforming the army, and the previous War Minister put forward a scheme for reforms, intended at last to free the British army of the bad reputation it has in Europe. The new government has cunningly used the question of military reform for its own purposes. The new War Minister has put forward his own scheme for military reform, and in this case has followed the Tories' favourite method, in that his scheme is completely identical to the previous scheme of the Liberal government.[19]

From all the above it is clear that we can fully expect six years of reactionary Tory government. It is additionally beyond doubt that the Tories will make just as few concessions to the people as the Liberals did in the recent period. It will not be at all surprising if the Tories try some half-measures to keep the Irish quiet, or give the workers some meaningless gain in labour legislation long promised by the Liberals. But even if the Tories do all that and more, it will still be impossible to characterise the situation as anything other than reaction. One of the most characteristic signs of that reaction is the instructions concerning national education. The only minister in the previous cabinet who really did anything in that area was Mr Acland.[20] He is now seriously ill and already unable to work. In recent years the reactionaries have expressed a definite intention to take control as many as possible of those areas of education which had been taken away from them. All their activities on the London School Board demonstrate this.[21] Now we can see for sure that over the coming six years of Tory rule the cause of rational education will be sharply reversed. The powerful corporations of clergymen seem already to have drawn up a plan of action on this, and the government will probably follow it very willingly. This plan shows the great cunning of the Church Party.[22] Thus the first part of this plan talks in favour of the complete secularisation of national education, which is obviously in keeping with the spirit of the past quarter century of educational reforms. However, the second part of the programme contains an article which completely contradicts this principle. According to this article, the state will get the right to use its general educational funds to subsidise those schools which will teach specific dogmas. Of course, this advantage will be used only by Church of England schools.[23]

All that remains to be said about the present Parliament concerns just certain parliamentary figures who have managed to draw attention to themselves during this short session. The indefatigable Sir Charles Dilke takes first place in this respect.[24] This able politician advanced very quickly a few years back, and some suggested that he might even make prime minister. He undoubtedly played a most outstanding role in radical politics, but then suddenly there was a major scandal which put an end to his brilliant career.[25] We shall not go into the details of that scandal, but shall just say that it resembles the story of Madame Walter and Suzanne in Maupassant's 'Bel ami'. But the English Suzanne was a married woman. We should, however, discuss the wise decision of the English court which considered this *cause célèbre*. The husband of the English Suzanne demanded a divorce, and the court found in his favour. But the most astonishing thing was that although she was found guilty of a breach of marital fidelity with Dilke, Dilke was not found guilty of breaching his marital vows with her! But nonetheless, Dilke was already considered to be finished in England after that case, just as Parnell had been after his *affaire* with Mrs O'Shea. However, time cures all in England, and although Parnell had committed a blunder from the point of view of English morality he could, had he remained alive, have returned to politics. Dilke was better placed in that respect, in that he, in line with the rules of the Nonconformist conscience, went the opposite way to Parnell and abandoned the woman who had involved him in this unpleasant business, and who, it should be noted, was twenty years younger than him. Dilke created the possibility of regaining his former position by getting married, all the more so because it was immediately after the scandal that he married the widow of the Rector of Lincoln College, Oxford.[26] This lady, with real womanly stubbornness, set about cleaning up her husband's reputation and now, thanks to her devoted assistance, he has managed to get through to the second rank of politicians. Both husband and wife have acted very cleverly by choosing the workers' movement as their cause, and they are advocating for it to this day.[27] The workers pay little or no attention to the requirements of the Nonconformist conscience and have no interest in the court decision regarding the divorce. From the moment the new government was installed, Dilke has simply carried out his duties, which has caused great discomfiture to the new Home Secretary, a wealthy Yorkshire squire with no thoughts whatsoever on workers' concerns, nor on much else, except foxhunting. Dilke has annoyed him particularly with his investigations into fines and deductions from wages, which are made completely unlawfully across the country, particularly in relation to women and girls.[28]

Among the Irish MPs, Mr Healy is undoubtedly the most notable figure.[29] He has very skilfully managed to convince himself and others that he is the only person who is absolutely indispensable for Ireland.

The post of Attorney General is currently held by Sir Richard Webster, who is considered to be a gentleman both *ex officio* and *ex natu*. But he recently attracted a whole torrent of criticism from the Tory press, simply for being so indiscreet as to say out aloud what members of the House tacitly think about one another. Incidentally, in this particular case, so far as we can tell, Webster's comments were groundless. The case was as follows: there were discussions about some railway or other, and one of the members spoke out against a resolution which would have put money into the pockets of the railway company. Sir Richard whispered loudly that this member had been given money to say that. His words were noticed and the whole House was in uproar, so that the honourable gentleman was obliged to take his words back and apologise.[30] Of course, such words from a government official, in receipt of a large salary and huge incomes from his private and legal practices, were more than inappropriate.

We have already mentioned Balfour's carelessness in political matters. The following illustration of this quality has caused no little mirth in England. Here we have a so-called 'Royal Bounty Fund', the capital of which comes from state funds, and is placed in the hands of the leader of the House of Commons to provide benefits and support for writers, male and female, who need and deserve assistance.[31] A few weeks ago everyone was surprised to learn from the newspapers that Mr Balfour proposed to give a grant of £200 from the Royal Bounty Fund to a certain worthy Mr George Brooks.[32] Most people had never heard of that gentleman and were very puzzled as to what his literary services had been. Even those who were well acquainted with all the literary byways had no knowledge of this fellow. Moreover, the papers reported that he would be given this grant in recognition of 'his literary activities and the value of his works, in which he sets out the principles of good governance'. What did this turn out to be in fact? Mr Brooks had quite recently been the most fervent Radical who had been giving public lectures and writing articles which openly condemned the Tories and all their works. He combined his literary output with business, and opened a chandler's shop in the suburbs. We cannot judge the quality of his wares, but throughout his shop, besides the merchandise, he had put printed Bible texts all over the walls. But since neither his writings and lectures, nor his merchandise and Bible texts brought him the income he had hoped for, he turned to the other side, and wrote an outraged pamphlet against the trade unions and suchlike institutions and started to act against the very party from which he had recently been extracting money.[33] This would never have happened if Balfour had taken the trouble to find out something about the person for whom he intended the grant.[34] He could, for example, have enquired about Brooks from his close friend Labouchère, the editor of the radical paper *Truth*, which always tries to expose any fraud and deception.[35] He would have discovered that this fellow, to whose application he had hurriedly responded with the award of a grant, was the most appalling swindler who extorted money from anyone and everyone. He had started with rich Radicals, moved on to rich Tories, and had always tapped rich religious people. He invariably used the same pretext: without the money he was unable either to finish or publish his literary works. His activities had become so well known that several years ago the Charity Organisation Society found it necessary to issue an official warning against accepting any applications from Brooks. Naturally, the Leader of the House of Commons Balfour, having been so careless as to award this same Brooks a grant of £200 from the Royal Bounty Fund for supporting writers, thereby put himself in a very comical and uncomfortable position. The Tory papers are outraged by this and, describing Brooks with certain choice epithets, are demanding that Balfour reimburse the fund from his own pocket the sum he had so thoughtlessly given away.

Every year, the government statistician Sir Robert Giffen publishes his official and voluminous account on wage levels.[36] Giffen is a convinced optimist, who himself receives a large salary. For example, he can declare without blushing that the average wage in recent years has been no less than 24s. 7d. For anyone who is closely acquainted with the conditions and position of the workers in our state, such a declaration is an astonishing distortion of reality, but Giffen compiles his figures solely on the basis of reports concerning labour which is more or less properly organised, and pays no attention to any irregular or out-of-hours work. However, some of the figures Giffen has provided are nonetheless very curious, even though, as we look at his statistical data, we must always bear in mind the above-mentioned optimism of his conclusions. Thus, for example, we see that rates of pay are best in large print works and worst in small print works. The worst-paid labour is in the boot and shoe industry. In distilleries, where such enormous fortunes are made, half of the workforce receives less than twenty shillings per week. The figures for women's wages are even worse in their miserliness, and may serve as the best explanation for the growth of prostitution in our cities. According to Giffen the average annual wage for women equals £34 19s. – that is what is paid in fashion houses. Girls receive on average no more than £5 17s., on which they are expected to subsist.

Among the male professions, postmen are the worst paid. Only 12 per cent of them in England receive 17s. 6d. a week, and many of them get even less than 12s. 6d. a week. The maximum wage for an agricultural worker is 18s. in Scotland and 9s. 6d. in Ireland. In England the average is 13s. A hired soldier receives £42 10s. per year, and an ordinary seaman, £53 5s.

Discussing women's wages has reminded us of the struggle for the rights of women to education which has been waged in Dublin over the last two years. Trinity College, the Dublin college of Edmund Burke and Oliver Goldsmith, has long lagged behind all the other English universities in this regard.[37] Many of the best professors at this college, including Dowden, one of our best literary scholars, have tried energetically to overcome the stubbornness of the old professors, who incessantly repeat their 'non possumus'.[38] The professors who support women's education have recently published their correspondence with their 'ossified' colleagues on this question.[39] These letters show why it has not yet been possible to open the doors of the college to women. The main argument against the admission of women to the college is that once 'a young girl has passed through the gates of the college' nobody can monitor 'which rooms she might enter, and how long she might remain there'. The result, of course, may be no worse than 'early and hasty marriage', but at the moment at any rate such a view of women in the college removes any hope that women will gain access to university education in Dublin, even if they were to agree never to attend lectures unaccompanied by a 'reliable chaperone'.

Av.

Notes

1. The annual conference of the Amalgamated Society of Railway Servants (ASRS) was held at Manchester between 1 and 4 October 1895.
2. The Railway Regulation Act 1893 gave the Board of Trade authority to investigate the working hours of railway workers and where they were found to be excessive to order the company to end the practice. At the ASRS conference of 1895 the general secretary, Edward Harford, urged union branches to make use of the Act, which he believed could be an effective instrument in abolishing system-

atic and gross forms of overtime. *Manchester Courier and Lancashire General Advertiser*, 2 October 1895, p8. In time, the Act was seen by the ASRS as ineffective, because of its permissiveness in allowing companies to claim exemptions to the regulations, and the frequent employer victimisations of union men who brought cases to the attention of the Board of Trade. Philip S. Bagwell, *The Railwaymen: The History of the National Union of Railwaymen*, George Allen and Unwin: London, 1963, p171.

3. ASRS general secretary Edward Harford acknowledged that where working hours had been reduced, it brought hostility from some drivers and firemen who on some shifts had to lodge away from home, but he urged all railway workers to accept the progressive effect of the changes. See *Manchester Courier and Lancashire General Advertiser*, 2 October 1895.

4. The authors quote the statistics for deaths and accidents of railway workers given by ASRS general secretary Edward Harford at the conference which he, in turn, extracted from the annual reports presented to Parliament by the Board of Trade. From the same series Philip Bagwell notes: 'In the quarter of a century between 1875 and 1899, no less than 12,870 railwaymen were killed and 68,575 were injured. In 1875 the 767 men killed represents a proportion of one in every 334 employed and 2,815 injured one in every 89. By 1899 the 531 killed in that year represented a proportion of one in every 1,006 employed and the 4,633 injured one in every 115, revealing the fact that the earlier accident rate was indeed unnecessarily high.' Bagwell 1963, p95.

5. The national conference of the National Sailors' and Firemen's Union was held in Poplar, east London, commencing on 16 September 1895.

6. At the 1892 congress of the TUC the president declared that 'The door must be shut against the enormous immigration of destitute aliens ... they take work at any price – poverty stricken themselves, they bring poverty to others ... we must protect our own starving workpeople by refusing to be the asylum for the paupers of Europe'. 'Annual report of the TUC 1892', p29. This comment anticipated the decision of the congress to urge Parliament to legislate to prevent the 'landing of foreign pauper aliens on our shores', p69. Similar motions were carried at congress in 1894 and 1895.

7. Those delegates at the 1895 congress unhappy with the anti-immigration resolution from the previous year supported a move led by London tailoring unions to reject divisive policies – 'it is the capitalist system that sets the workers against each other' – and instead work towards the unionisation of all workers. Speaking in support,

James Macdonald of the Tailors' Union, who had stood in 1895 general election for the ILP, produced 'sensation and angry cries of protest' when he said: 'You talk of alien immigration bringing down wages, forsooth! Why, there are Englishmen, Scotchmen and Irishmen living in dirt and degradation fully equal to that of the foreigner. This is not the way to stop it. Let us begin at home. You miners, you operatives whether in cotton or boots, you co-operators, and the rest of you, I declare as a tailor that the vast majority of you are wearing sweated-made clothes ... It is the cursed out-system which is to blame. Let us have more Factory Acts, greater stringency in the matters of sanitation, more rigid and more widely extended inspection – that is what we want.' The attempt to amend the anti-immigration motion was lost by 266,000 to 246,000 votes, and Macdonald told the *Labour Leader* reporter that it would have gone the other way if the miners hadn't abstained because 'he had charged them with wearing sweated-made clothes'. 'TUC annual report 1895', pp45-6; *Labour Leader*, 14 September 1895, p6.

Edward, who was at the conference reporting for *Justice*, drew attention to some delegates known to be SDF members, including some from trade unions in the footwear industry, supporting the anti-immigration resolution: 'What are we to say to [those] supporting the exclusion of aliens when some of the SDF bootmen are not sound? Thank man and a growing sense that after all there is something in economics and the teaching of Karl Marx' that the motion passed only by a very small majority, significantly lower than in 1894. *Justice*, 14 September 1895, p5.

8. The National Sailors' and Firemen's Trade Union conference agreed a resolution on September 18 to 'urge upon the President of the Board of Trade to immediately compel all vessels registered in the UK to strictly conform to the Merchant Shipping Act, which provides that seventy two cubic feet of space should be allotted to each seaman on board ship in which they live'. It went on to 'earnestly urge upon the government the necessity of putting into force by Act of Parliament the unanimous recommendation of the Royal Commission on Labour to increase such space to not less than 120 cubic feet'. *Daily Gazette for Middlesbrough*, 20 September 1895, p3. Joseph Havelock Wilson (1858-1929), the union's founder, general secretary and then president, described the appalling living conditions of sailors on board many ships in his evidence to the Royal Commission in 1891. Wilson pointed out the cruel fact that while the union was demanding 120 cubic feet of living space, incarcerated prisoners were entitled to 380 cubic feet. Royal Commission on

Labour: Minutes of Evidence, Group B, Vol. 1. Docks, Wharves and Shipping, HMSO, 1892, C – 6708 -V, 9351-9352.

The Sailors' Union enjoyed some success recruiting foreign seamen working on British registered vessels, and by 1891 Wilson was able to claim 20,000 foreign members registered in branches across Europe. These initiatives led in 1896 to the establishment of the International Federation of Ship, Dock and River Workers, whose objective was to 'develop European solidarity to a point at which common strike action would be feasible'. Arthur Marsh and Victoria Ryan, *The Seamen*, Malthouse Press: Oxford, 1989, p53. Wilson, who was elected to Parliament for the Middlesbrough constituency in 1892, combined his views on the need to organise foreign workers with support for 'reasonable restriction' of continental labour into the UK. 'TUC annual report 1894', p.60.

9. Following the general election, Parliament sat from 12 August until 5 September, when it was officially prorogued until 18 November. This was subsequently extended on two occasions and Parliament did not meet again until 11 February 1896.

10. Joseph Chamberlain promoted a series of social policies, including proposals for old age pensions presented to the Royal Commission on the Aged Poor in 1893. In the months preceding the general election, Chamberlain attempted to convince Lord Salisbury and the Duke of Devonshire of these policies, without any success. See Peter Marsh, *The Discipline of Popular Government: Lord Salisbury's Domestic Statecraft, 1881-1902*, Harvester: Hassocks, 1978, pp235-7. In September 1895 Devonshire, who was now Lord President of the Council in Salisbury's Cabinet, killed off any prospect of introducing any scheme for old age pensions when he said that 'anything that might be proposed in that direction must be at first extremely tentative and gradual in character ... for a long time to come the greater proportion of even the most industrious aged poor must be dependent for their support on the same source from which they had hitherto received it, namely the Poor Law'. *Morning Post*, 19 September 1895, p2. For Chamberlain and old age pensions see Letter 4, note 39 and his article in *National Review*, February 1892, Vol. 18, No. 108, pp721-38.

11. Arthur Balfour's election address included reference to social questions with the words: 'In respect of all these questions something – and in respect to some of them, much – may, I believe, be done', *Westminster Gazette*, 9 August 1895, p2. It has not been possible to trace the exact words attributed to Balfour by the authors.

12. The controversy over the importation of foreign prison-made goods

into the British market emerged early in 1894, when a Manchester newspaper exposed what it believed to be a case of unfair practice, cotton goods produced by German prisoners and fraudulently stamped with a British manufacturer's mark. Subsequent investigations revealed other foreign prison-made goods, notably mats and brushes made in Belgium, Holland, and France, allegedly penetrating the British market, undercutting domestic production and destroying jobs. Questions were raised in Parliament, the Liberal government carried out investigations and the TUC passed a resolution at its 1894 conference instructing the parliamentary committee to promote and support legislation to prevent the importation of such goods.

In May and June 1895 a parliamentary committee investigated the issue and concluded that as quantities being imported were not damaging to British trade, no action should be taken. 'Departmental committee on the importation of foreign prison-made goods', HMSO, 1895, C. 7902. In spite of this, it became a general election issue in constituencies where it was believed local industries were adversely affected. In the East End of London a Conservative candidate reported that measures to deal with foreign prison-made goods and alien immigration were 'highly popular'. *Times*, 8 August 1895, p11. Chamberlain linked the two issues together in discussions with the Birmingham Trades Council, suggesting to its delegates that labour representatives in Parliament were indifferent on the issues. *Times*, 4 March 1895, p10. Always an astute populist politician, Chamberlain played the immigration and foreign prison-made goods cards when he knew they would go down well at election rallies. See, for instance, the reported speech in Walsall during the election campaign. *Walsall Advertiser*, 20 July 1895, p2.

13. Louis-Jules Trochu, president of the French Government of National Defence during the Franco-Prussian war, whose plan for defending Paris failed.

14. The Unionist government (led by Lord Salisbury) introduced a ban on foreign prison-made goods in 1897.

15. Bimetallists wanted Britain to come off the gold standard and instead adopt gold and silver as the guarantors of its currency, believing this would help the economy grow and enhance the nation's trading position. Linking the period of economic depression since the 1870s to the inelastic and insufficient supply of gold – too little money chasing too many goods – bimetallists argued that the addition of silver as a standard would raise the money supply and so encourage economic growth. A joint standard would also remove the competitive advan-

tage of countries such as India and Japan using the silver standard. The Bimetallist League was founded in 1881 in Manchester.

16. Bimetallism was a live issue in Lancashire because the cotton manufacturers and trade unions believed its adoption would make it easier to sell cotton goods in the large Indian market, as well as removing the competitive advantage enjoyed by the emerging Indian cotton industry. For this see E.H.H. Green, 'Rentiers versus producers? The political economy of the Bimetallic Controversy, c.1880-1898', *English Historical Review*, July 1988, Vol. 103, No. 408, pp596-7. In May 1895 the Gold Standard Defence Association was formed by bankers and merchants in the City of London to support the maintenance of the existing monetary system and oppose bimetallism.

17. Arthur Balfour, who sat for the Manchester East constituency, was sympathetic to bimetallism, which he made clear as a member of the Royal Commission on Currency in 1887-8. E.H.H. Green, *Conservative Political Ideas in the Twentieth Century*, Oxford University Press: Oxford, 2002, p24. As late as April 1895 Balfour was expressing support for the policy at the Bimetallist League annual meeting, where he declared the adoption of gold and silver as standards would enhance economic prosperity and ensure equitable international trade. *Standard*, 4 April 1895, p3. By August, when asked in Parliament for his views on a proposed international conference to consider reform measures, including the adoption of bimetallism, for a stable international currency, Balfour replied that he had no right to pledge his colleagues in government on the issue. Nor had he any grounds for thinking that an agreement would be achieved at any such conference. *Morning Post*, 23 August 1895, p4.

18. Balfour had published on philosophical matters since the late 1870s, and in early 1895 brought out *Foundations of Belief*, which was well received, the *Times* declaring it 'one of the chief contributions to philosophy made for many years in England'. *Times*, 8 February 1895, p12.

19. The Secretary of State for War was Henry Petty-Fitzmaurice, the 5th Marquess of Lansdowne (1845-1927), who had previously been Viceroy of India. For Lansdowne's reform of the War Office and the army, see Simon Kerry, *Lansdowne: The Last Great Whig*, Unicorn: London, 2017, pp106-23.

20. For Acland, see Letter 1, note 12.

21. For controversies on the London School Board, see Letter 1, note 10.

22. Acland's efforts to improve the condition of schools and education brought him into conflict with those offering denominational education in voluntary schools. After 1892 government funding became closely linked to a rigorous inspection regime requiring schools to

demonstrate efficiency in education and structural matters. Schools in the voluntary sector objected to these regulations, believing them to be onerous for those outside the board system. Some in the denominational sector suspected Acland, a secularist, of trying to eliminate church schools. The Church Parliamentary Committee – commonly known as 'the Church Party' – was established in November 1893 by backbench MPs to defend denominational education and the influence of the church in rural areas, which they believed to be under threat from the Liberal government's plan to introduce parish councils.

23. Following the general election, Lord Salisbury's government made clear they would introduce legislation to guarantee that denominational schools would not be at a financial disadvantage in relation to board schools. In November, senior church figures met Salisbury and the Duke of Devonshire, Lord President of the Council and ultimately responsible for education matters in the Cabinet, to state their case, which was sympathetically received. An outline of the church's arguments, briefly summarised by the authors, was published in the *Times* on 16 November 1895, p6.

24. Sir Charles Wentworth Dilke (1843-1911) was a Radical Liberal MP for Chelsea from 1868 until 1886. He was president of the Local Government Board between 1882 and 1885.

25. Dilke was involved in a divorce suit (1885-6) as co-respondent, having been accused of seducing the wife of Donald Crawford, a Scottish barrister and prospective parliamentary candidate in 1882, and then having a two-year affair with her. The court granted the divorce but dismissed Dilke from the suit with no case to answer. Hoping to expose what he believed to be lies made against him by Mrs Crawford, Dilke reopened the case in court, but was unable to prove his arguments, with the result that his reputation was further damaged. For the divorce case, see David Nicholls, *The Lost Prime Minister: A Life of Sir Charles Dilke*, Hambledon Press: London, 1995, pp177-211.

26. Dilke married Emily Francis Pattison (1840-1904), the widow of Mark Pattison, Rector of Lincoln College, Oxford, in October 1885. Lady Dilke, as she was henceforth known, was an acclaimed art critic and historian, campaigner for female suffrage, and supporter of women's trade unionism, especially for those working in the sweated trades. See Sean Hutton and Barbara Nield, 'Dilke, Emily (Emilia), Francis, Strong, Lady, (1840-1904)', in Joyce M. Bellamy and John Saville (eds), *Dictionary of Labour Biography, Vol III*, Macmillan: London, 1976, pp63-7.

27. After six years out of Parliament, Dilke was returned for the Forest of Dean constituency, which he represented until his death in 1911. Dilke 'achieved great local popularity, especially with the miners of what was a detached but significant coalfield. He vigorously pursued their interests and those of labour generally ... and was an important link with the Labour members and trade unionists'. Roy Jenkins, 'Dilke, Sir Charles Wentworth, second Baronet, (1843-1911)', *Oxford Dictionary of National Biography*, Oxford University Press: Oxford.

28. Dilke's interrogations of the Home Secretary, Sir Matthew White Ridley (1842-1904), whose family came from Northumberland (not Yorkshire), on fines and deductions from wages was undoubtedly informed by Lady Dilke's knowledge of employment where such practices were common. See Lady Dilke's article 'The industrial position of women', *Fortnightly Review*, October 1893, Vol. 54, No. 322, pp499-508.

29. For Timothy Healy, see Letter 6, note 36 and Frank Callanan, *T.M. Healy*, Cork University Press: Cork, 1996.

30. Sir Richard Webster (1842-1915), Attorney General in Lord Salisbury's government, was forced to apologise to Henry Dalziel (1868-1935), Liberal MP for Kirkcaldy Burghs, for a remark overheard during a parliamentary debate. On 28 August 1895, the House of Commons was considering the West Highland Railway Bill, opposed by Dalziel. In the debate, Sir Michael Hicks Beach, Chancellor of the Exchequer, suggested to Dalziel that his opposition was in the interest of rival companies, prompting Webster to mutter 'Probably he's paid for it'. A row ensued and Webster was forced to withdraw the remark unreservedly and apologise. *The Sketch*, 4 September 1895, p43.

31. A government fund established in the late eighteenth century to support those engaged in literary work.

32. George Brooks (1853-?), son of a Lincolnshire agricultural labourer, had been a congregational minister, shopkeeper, journalist and Liberal parliamentary candidate in 1886. In 1887 he was declared bankrupt and soon after switched political allegiance, declaring for the Conservatives.

33. Between September 1891 and January 1892, Brooks wrote a series of articles for the *York Herald* on 'Labour, capital and socialism', which he used as the core for his book *Industry and Property*, issued in the spring of 1893. Published from his home in Halesworth, Suffolk, with the aid of supporting subscribers including Arthur Balfour, *Industry and Property* mounted a defence of private property and offered a critique of trade unionism and socialism. The *Times* welcomed the book and described Brooks as a 'sturdy and vigorous champion of

individualism, an opponent and keen critic of socialism in all its forms'. *Times*, 14 April 1893, p13. Brooks was particularly hostile to new unionism, which he was encouraged to see defeated during the Hull dock strike of 1893, about which he wrote a pamphlet distributed by the Shipping Federation, the employers' trade organisation.

Brooks issued a second volume of *Industry and Property* in the autumn of 1894 and in the following year a condensed version of the two volumes was published by Sampson Low. In 1895 Brooks contributed a critique of socialist Robert Blatchford's ideas in a volume titled *God's England or the Devil's – A reply to Merrie England*.

34. Brooks was awarded £200 from the Royal Bounty Fund in the first week of September 1895 on the recommendation of Arthur Balfour 'in recognition for his literary ability and of the value of his writings in support of the principles of good government and in opposition to socialism'. *Times*, 7 September 1895, p5.

35. A number of pro-Conservative newspapers expressed unease about Balfour's award of £200 to Brooks, but it was left to Henry Labouchère's weekly *Truth* to pursue the matter to the end. (For Labouchère see Letter 3, note 38.) Labouchère, who had known Brooks since the 1880s when the latter was a Radical and contributor of a number of articles to *Truth*, was aware of his recent reputation as a 'self-advertising author, who has for the last year or two made himself an unmitigated nuisance by pestering wealthy men to subscribe to his works'. *Truth*, 12 September 1895, p614. Labouchère went further and accused Brooks of systematically writing more than a thousand letters to wealthy individuals requesting money to relieve financial difficulties. He went on: 'I feel justified in hailing Brooks as the prince of begging-letter writers ... where the mere journeymen in the craft beg for shillings or half-crowns, Brooks goes for £10, £25, or £50 – and what is more, gets it. *Truth*, 26 September 1895, p742. More than a year later Brooks took a libel action against Labouchère that ended on the third day with the jury informing the judge that they had heard enough of the case, returning a verdict in favour of the defendant. The jury added a postscript that 'Mr Labouchère had conferred a great public benefit in exposing the plaintiff.' *Daily News*, 18 December 1896, p4.

36. The Board of Trade began collecting comprehensive information on wages in 1886, a responsibility designated to the newly established Labour Department of the Board in 1893. Sir Robert Giffen (1837-1910) was controller general of the department and all reports, including the 'General report on the wages of the manual labour classes in the UK', C-6889, referred to by the authors, were issued

in his name. The authors' scepticism about the validity of the statistics produced by Giffen was also expressed by others: 'His [Giffen's] great purpose for many years has been to prove that nearly everyone was well off and was growing better off every year, only they don't know it.' *Reynolds's Newspaper*, 29 September 1895, p4; 'By judicious arrangement of carefully selected figures he arrives at the conclusion that the average wage of the British workman is not far short of 24s. 7d. per week. To arrive at his average this manipulator of figures has to practically ignore the unemployed and great irregularity of work in most trades.' *Justice*, 28 September 1895, p1.

37. The campaign for admission of women as students to Trinity College, Dublin began in 1892 with the presentation of a petition of 10,000 signatures submitted to the university's governing board. Delay and obfuscation meant the issue dragged on until July 1895, when the board issued a statement, ridiculed here by Eleanor and Edward, which rejected the demand of admission on the grounds that: 'Parents who place their sons in Trinity College, Dublin, do so in the persuasion that their morals will be subject of some supervision ... It has been suggested that female students should be required to be attended by proper chaperones; but it could not be left to the discretion of gate-porters to determine whether of two women passing the gate, one was of sufficient age to be a suitable guardian to the other. If a female had once passed the gate, it would be practically impossible to watch that building or what chambers she might enter, or how long she might remain there ... Even if no worse evil occurred than that parents found the son whom they sent here entangled in an imprudent marriage, they would not consider that evil small ... On the whole the board consider the introduction of female students into our classes would be attended with risks, which we are in no way called to incur and which they do not choose to run'. Susan M. Parkes (ed.), *A Danger to Men? A History of Women in Trinity College, Dublin, 1904-2004*, Lilliput Press: Dublin, 2004, Appendix B, p304.

38. Edward Dowden (1843-1913), professor of English at Trinity College, Dublin. Dowden was an eminent Shakespeare scholar whose influential *Shakespeare: A Critical Study of his Mind and Art* (1876) would almost certainly have been known to the authors.

39. The correspondence was published in William Graham Brooke (ed.), *Statement of the Proceedings from 1892 to 1895 in Connection with the Movement for Admission of Women to Trinity College, Dublin*, Ponsonby and Warwick: Dublin, 1895. Brooke (1834-1907), a graduate of Trinity, barrister and advocate for women's education,

played a leading role in the campaign for admission. Christopher F. McCormack, 'William Graham Brooke: advocate of girls' superior schooling in nineteenth-century Ireland', *History of Education*, November 2015, Vol. 44, No. 6, pp.749-64.

Index